Summary Execution

The Seattle Assassinations of Silme Domingo and Gene Viernes

BY MICHAEL WITHEY

WILDBLUE
PRESS

WildBluePress.com

SUMMARY EXECUTION published by:
WILDBLUE PRESS

P.O. Box 102440
Denver, Colorado 80250

WILDBLUE PRESS is registered at the U.S. Patent and Trademark Offices.

ISBN 978-1-947290-37-2 Trade Paperback
ISBN 978-1-947290-36-5 eBook

Interior Formatting/Book Cover Design by Elijah Toten
www.totencreative.com

"To Terri Mast and Cindy Domingo:
You are deep in my heart."

Bob:

Thanks for your commitment
to music, love and peace —

Keep the Faith —

Mike

Summary Execution

The Seattle Assassinations of Silme Domingo and Gene Viernes

TABLE OF CONTENTS

INTRODUCTION: 9

CHAPTER ONE: 20

CHAPTER TWO: 31

CHAPTER THREE: 39

CHAPTER FOUR: 50

CHAPTER FIVE: 61

CHAPTER SIX: 66

CHAPTER SEVEN: 70

CHAPTER EIGHT: 76

CHAPTER NINE: 80

CHAPTER TEN: 84

CHAPTER ELEVEN: 97

CHAPTER TWELVE: 101

CHAPTER THIRTEEN: 110

CHAPTER FOURTEEN: 128

CHAPTER FIFTEEN: 139

CHAPTER SIXTEEN: 145

CHAPTER SEVENTEEN: 150

CHAPTER EIGHTEEN: 154

CHAPTER NINETEEN: 158

CHAPTER TWENTY: 168

CHAPTER TWENTY-ONE: 174

CHAPTER TWENTY-TWO: 180

CHAPTER TWENTY-THREE: *190*

CHAPTER TWENTY-FOUR: *195*

CHAPTER TWENTY-FIVE: *200*

CHAPTER TWENTY-SIX: *206*

CHAPTER TWENTY-SEVEN: *210*

CHAPTER TWENTY-EIGHT: *213*

CHAPTER TWENTY-NINE: *219*

CHAPTER THIRTY: *227*

CHAPTER THIRTY-ONE: *234*

CHAPTER THIRTY-TWO: *242*

CHAPTER THIRTY-THREE: *254*

CHAPTER THIRTY-FOUR: *262*

CHAPTER THIRTY-FIVE: *272*

CHAPTER THIRTY-SIX: *289*

CHAPTER THIRTY-SEVEN: *311*

AFTERWORD *313*

TO THE READERS *319*

PICTURES AND DOCUMENTS *323*

APPENDIX A: CHARACTERS *331*

APPENDIX B: KEY ACRONYMS *343*

NOTES *346*

INTRODUCTION:

THE MURDERS

June 1, 1981

Local 37 Union Hall, Seattle

On the eastern edge of the Pioneer Square district in Seattle stood an historic but nondescript two-story terra-cotta building, crowned by a large, weatherworn sign that read "Cannery Workers ILWU Local 37" in blue and white paint peeling from the soft but incessant Seattle rain.

The union hall's entrance opened to a corridor that led to the dispatch hall. This was where seasonal laborers – predominantly Filipino – received assignments each summer for back-breaking jobs on the slime lines of the seafood canneries that hugged the shores of Alaska.

To get to the dispatch hall, the corridor first paralleled two offices on its left; the first office led into the second, an interior space used by the president of Local 37, Constantine "Tony" Baruso. Over Baruso's desk was a prominent picture of himself shaking hands with the president of the Philippines, Ferdinand Marcos.

The outer office was the domain of Local 37's Secretary-Treasurer Silme Domingo and Dispatcher Gene Viernes. Both men had been recently elected as union officers, but they did not share Baruso's politics. In fact, that afternoon they were waiting for their friend and fellow activist, David Della, to arrive for a meeting about their anti-Marcos efforts.

Dave was running late. While they waited, both men worked diligently in the stale air of the windowless office. Silme sat hunched over his desk, piles of yellowed papers at his right elbow. Gene stood at the filing cabinet, searching for information on a Local 37 member, Ben Guloy, who had called to find out if he could qualify for the next dispatch of cannery workers.

It was a question many of the union members had been asking recently. At the union's first dispatch of the season a few days before, to the Peter Pan Cannery in Dillingham, there had been trouble. On May 26, Gene had gathered the members in the dispatch hall and announced a controversial new procedure, which assigned jobs at the canneries based solely on union member seniority and past work history in the industry. This replaced the prior arrangement, where individual cannery foremen worked with Baruso to create lists of workers based on their personal preferences – as well as who paid them the most money under the table – to dispatch to each cannery. Both Gene and Silme explained to the members that they wanted to end the system where members felt they needed to bribe their own union in order to get work.

Gene's announcement was interrupted by a union member who was also the head of the local Filipino Tulisan gang. Tony Dictado rose from his metal chair so fast it collapsed backwards onto the concrete floor with a thwack. "My boys need to get dispatched now," he'd said in no uncertain terms. He demanded that Gene change the list to include Tulisan gang members who worked in the canneries and also ran gambling operations in the bunkhouses. When Gene refused, explaining that there were no exceptions to the new procedures, Dictado exploded, swearing in Ilocano before storming out.

Dictado was used to getting his way. So was Baruso. In addition to the bribes he received in exchange for priority in dispatch, it was common knowledge that Baruso was getting a percentage of the gambling proceeds from the foremen. But the two new officers were idealists, elected on a platform to reform the union and bring about a fair dispatch and stronger negotiations with the industry. Before their election, they had founded a Rank and File Committee (RFC) of union activists, and the independent Alaska Cannery Workers Association (ACWA). Both groups had bravely and aggressively confronted the Alaska seafood industry about the blatant race discrimination that existed in the canneries. Without Baruso or Local 37's support, they had been vigorously filing race discrimination lawsuits and challenging powerful industries in court.

Those were big accomplishments for two men who were not yet thirty years old, and their successes were largely a credit to how well they worked together.

Silme Domingo was born in Seattle in 1952 to a large Filipino family. His father, Nemesio Sr., was the vice president of Local 37. Silme often told me he admired how hard his father worked in the canneries, for his family, and for the union, but they often disagreed on how to oppose the dictatorial Marcos regime, which had ruled the Philippines with an iron hand since declaring martial law in 1972. Silme and his brother, Nemesio Jr., liked confrontation. Nemesio Sr. did not. He and Silme's mother, Ade, had expressed concern about Silme and Gene's recent efforts to present and push through a resolution at the International Longshore and Warehouse Union (ILWU) Convention, demanding an investigation into the plight of workers in the Philippines. "Don't make waves" was always Ade's advice. At twenty-nine, in his youthful exuberance, he didn't always follow her advice.

Gene Viernes was also twenty-nine years old that June, but beyond that, he and Silme seemed as different as night and day. Born in Wapato, a small town in eastern Washington, to a Filipino father and Caucasian mother, and family of ten, Gene grew up doing farm work and seasonal labor, including summer seasons in the Alaska canneries. He was the first in his family to go to college, attending Central Washington State College on a wrestling scholarship.

Gene was a born organizer who had great rapport with work crews. He had an avid interest in both the history of the "Alaskeros," the migrant Filipino workforce who traveled to the Arctic each year to work long hours in the canneries, and the history of the Philippines itself. Just a few weeks before, he'd returned from his trip to his father's homeland, where he'd met both his family and major organizations of the opposition to Phillipine dictator Ferdinand Marcos.

Gene and Silme worked well together: Silme was the sophisticated strategist who wore fancy clothes and drove a large purple Monte Carlo. Gene was a country boy who almost always wore blue denim overalls and a stained white beret. When I picture them, I always remember a typical day when the anti-Marcos activists were planting a community garden in the International District. Silme stood on a boulder and gave orders while Gene steered the wheelbarrow around the grounds and got his hands dirty.

Despite their differences, the two were close friends and comrades in the Union of Democratic Filipinos or KDP, an anti-Marcos organization they were leaders of. As Bob Santos, the unofficial mayor of Seattle's International District (ID), once said, "They were quite a pair. Inseparable."

At 4:20 p.m. on that sunny Seattle day, Ben Guloy entered the union hall with Jimmy Ramil, another member of the Tulisan gang. They stopped in the office doorway and Ramil pulled a .45-caliber MAC-10 , with a suppressor attached, out of a brown paper bag, pointed it at Gene, and fired.

Gene dove for the floor too late and landed with a dull thud, probably already dead. Blood seeped from two wounds in his chest, oozing across the tiles and dyeing his white shirt scarlet.

Ramil then swung his firearm to his right, firing at Silme. The force of the bullets spun Silme halfway around in his swivel chair and punched four gaping holes in his chest.

Not waiting to check the bodies, Ramil tucked his weapon back into the bag and, together with Guloy, left through the front door of the union hall, turning south and escaping down the adjoining alley. On the steps they passed a third Filipino, Teodorico Domingues, also known as Boy Pilay, who had been standing lookout at the entrance. When they were gone, Pilay limped across the street to a black Trans-Am with a large golden eagle on its hood. He slipped into the front passenger seat and the car sped off, a death wagon bursting through the bright day.

The driver beside him was none other than Tony Dictado.

Back in the Local 37 office, Silme gasped for air. He could see Gene bleeding out onto the scuffed white tiles of the office's floor. He gripped the edges of the desk and managed to stagger onto his feet. Clutching his chest, he moved from the office to the corridor, losing hot blood with every step. The door of the union hall rushed up to meet him, and he lunged through it, dragging his body down the steps before collapsing onto the sidewalk and calling for help.

Seattle firefighter James Huckins was working at Fire Station 10 on the corner of Main Street and 2nd Avenue, a block from Local 37, when a young girl ran in. She shouted that there was a man lying face down on Main Street. He looked injured and was crying for help. James immediately radioed for the aid car, grabbed a portable medic cart, and rushed out of the fire station toward the union hall.

Fellow first-responder Frank Urpman, upstairs at Fire Station 10, heard shouts for help outside. When he looked out the second-story window, he saw Silme lying on the sidewalk, blood staining the concrete beneath him. Frank ran downstairs and out into the street, reaching Silme at almost the same time James did.

"Were you robbed?" Frank said, his voice calm.

"N-no ... shot," Silme gasped, face twitching in pain as James and Frank ripped open packets of gauze and applied them to the gaping gunshot wounds.

"Do you know who shot you?" James asked.

Silme groaned, eyelids fluttering. "Yes ... I do. They ... might still be in the building."

"Who are they?"

"Ramil and Guloy," Silme said, his voice pained but otherwise clear.

Frank took out a piece of paper and a pen, wrote the names down, and showed them to Silme.

"It's Ramil, with an *L*," Silme corrected him. Frank crossed out the last letters, and wrote "Ramil" instead of "Rammo."

Silme was pale. His blood had fully soaked through his shirt, and he was breathing heavily. James continued to ask Silme questions to keep him alert – what day it was, where he was, and the names of the hitmen again. Finally, the aid car arrived, and Frank and Jim loaded Silme into the ambulance.

"Am I going to die?" Silme said, his voice a whisper.

Frank cradled Silme's head in his hands and spoke gently but honestly. "It looks bad." The ambulance roared off to Harborview Medical Center, sirens blaring.

Across the street from the union hall, a middle-aged man in a grey suit and dark glasses emerged from a telephone booth, looked at the scene in front of the union, and slipped into his car. As he pulled away from the curb, heading south on 2nd Avenue, he lifted a CB radio to his lips and started to speak.

BEACON HILL, SEATTLE

Terri Mast first met Silme in 1977 at a meeting of the Anti-Martial Law Coalition, a national organization that opposed the repressive regime of Ferdinand Marcos. She,

Silme, and Gene were also deeply involved in the Union of Democratic Filipinos, or KDP, a US-based democratic socialist organization that supported leftist opposition parties in the Philippines and advocated for Filipino rights in the US.

Patient, organized, and level-headed, Terri met her love match in the passionate Silme, who soon became her common-law husband. They shared major responsibilities for implementing reforms within Local 37, organizing in the Filipino community, and attending rallies and demonstrations as part of the anti-Marcos movement in Seattle. They also parented two young daughters, three-year-old Ligaya, and Kalayaan, a baby a few weeks shy of her first birthday. The girls were the joys of their lives.

Terri was at home in their Beacon Hill apartment, watching Ligaya play with trucks, when her friends and fellow KDP activists Elaine Ko, John Foz, and Shari Woo showed up unexpectedly.

"Terri, get your overnight stuff; we have to go to the hospital. Gene and Silme have been shot ..." Elaine's voice broke. Terri could see unshed tears in her eyes.

It took her words too long to form. "How ... Are they ...?"

"Gene is ... Gene didn't make it. Silme is going to go into surgery now. Shari will watch the girls."

Terri fell back onto the sofa when she attempted to stand, whispering, "No ... no ..." She felt shell-shocked. They all were.

Shari sat down beside her as tears poured down Terri's cheeks. "Silme was just talking last night about what would happen to us if something were to happen to him. What's ... what's his condition?"

"He was shot in the stomach," Shari admitted, "so not good. They need you and his folks down at Harborview as soon as possible." She forced herself to look into Terri's eyes. "Dave Della had a meeting with Gene this afternoon and showed up late … When he got there, he found Gene dead on the floor of his office. By then, Silme was already on his way to the hospital. Dave called Glenn Suson at the headquarters, and Glenn called us."

Elaine held out her hand. "Come on. We have to go. For Silme. We have to go."

Terri wiped the tears from her cheeks. "You're right." She nodded once and rose to her feet, Shari helping her as she walked out the door.

Shari watched them go down the steps. The moment she closed the door, she took Ligaya and Kalayaan into her arms and gently cradled them, worrying.

OAKLAND, CALIFORNIA

Cindy Domingo was at her apartment in Oakland when she received a visit from Dale Borgeson, a national leader of the KDP who also lived in Oakland. Motioning to Cindy's roommates that he needed to talk to Cindy alone, Dale spoke slowly as Cindy looked out the window at a peach-colored sky.

"I have some … some terrible news."

"What is it? What happened?"

"Your brother … Silme … he was …" He paused. To Cindy, those seconds of strained silence lasted for eternities, and when it ended and Dale told her what happened, she felt decades older than she had been.

The peach sky turned dark grey, suddenly ominous.

Cindy had earned a Master's Degree in Philippine History from Goddard College in Boston, Massachusetts, and worked at the KDP National Secretariat headquarters in Oakland in its National Education Department. The National Secretariat was the organizational center for the KDP's anti-Marcos movement, responsible for publishing its newspaper, *Ang Katipunan*, conducting educationals and scheduling membership and chapter activities. Cindy had recently been approved for a transfer back to Seattle to be closer to her family.

"It can't be," Cindy said, her voice louder than she'd meant for it to be.

"I'm so sorry," Dale repeated. "Cindy, can you fly up to Seattle with me tonight? We can go to Harborview where everyone is on vigil."

"Silme …" She noticed that sometime in the past few moments she'd sat at her kitchen table. Now she stood. "Okay, let's go to the airport. Has someone … has someone called my parents? I need to talk to them."

"Elaine is taking Terri to Harborview, and your folks are on their way there right now."

HARBORVIEW MEDICAL CENTER, SEATTLE

Ade Domingo, the matriarch of the Domingo family, clung to Terri in a long hug when the two women met in the Harborview ER lobby. While Ade had taught and encouraged her children to take a stand for people who were less fortunate than they were, she always worried about their work. This was her worst nightmare.

"Silme's in surgery," Ade told her daughter-in-law. "He is fighting for his life, shot in the stomach four times … Oh my son, my son…." She stopped, her voice catching on a sob.

"Can we see him? Is he conscious?"

"The surgeon said we need to wait until he is out of surgery. The staff will let us know." Ade clutched the rosary with enough force to turn her knuckles white.

Faced with a long wait, Terri's community organizing instincts kicked in. "We need to get everyone we know to the blood bank on Madison," she said, turning to the friends and family who already filled the small room. "He will need all the blood he can get with stomach wounds. After that, they can come here for a vigil."

She looked around the room. Nemesio Sr. sat on a couch beside his oldest son, Silme's brother Nemesio Jr., and his son's wife Curn. Nemesio Jr. had worked closely with his brother, and had founded the ACWA with Gene and Silme to investigate and file lawsuits against the industry for race discrimination.

Their sister Evangeline, or Vangie, lived with her family in Arizona. The youngest Domingo sibling, Lynn, sobbed quietly on one of the waiting room chairs. Kids were sitting nervously on the couches. Friends and family filled the foyer to offer their hope and condolences.

"Did someone call Gene's family in Wapato?" Terri asked. Gene had grown up surrounded by the farms and migrant workers of eastern Washington, about three hours from Seattle, and his family was still there.

"Yeah," Emily Van Bronkhorst, a longtime family friend and Rank and File Committee stalwart, said. "His brothers are heading over here now with Gene's friend Andy Pascua. Gene's sister Barbara is going to stay with the family for now. She will come over for the memorial."

Dave Della, the KDP activist who had found Gene's body, entered the waiting room with his hands shoved deep into his pockets. He addressed the room. "Hi, everyone. I know things are tough, but I wanted to let you know that the police believe Silme named the people who shot him. I talked to them after ... after I left the union hall." He was visibly shaken, eyes hollow and expressionless, his face ashen. He realized that if he had been on time for their meeting, Gene and Silme might be alive. Or he would have shot as well.

The murmurs went through the room.

"They didn't give me the names." Dave shook his head, and the room grew silent again.

"Where's Baruso?" Terri asked no one in particular.

Several people looked around. "I have no idea," Ade said. "Maybe he was at Boeing and doesn't know yet." In addition to his work at Local 37, Baruso worked as a production line manager at the Boeing aircraft factory in South Seattle.

Before anyone could respond, a nurse appeared at the ER doorway, putting thoughts of Tony Baruso out of everyone's minds. Silme's family leaned forward as she looked around apologetically. "Silme's still in surgery and will be for a few more hours. We will let you know when it's over. In the meantime, get as many folks as you can to the blood bank."

The whole room broke out in noisy conversation.

"Thank you," Ade told the nurse, looking around. "Is there a smaller room where we can get further updates? This waiting room reminds me of a political convention." The people near her laughed, a hollow and humorless sound. The nurse nodded and showed the immediate family, along with Elaine and Emily, to a side room.

Terri sank into a chair in the quiet space. "Dave will turn out folks to the blood bank. The word is out on the street about the shootings, and we need them there now, not here." Her voice and hands were shaking, but she stayed in control. "Has anyone notified Mike Withey?"

Elaine nodded. "Kozu went to *El Centro* to track him down. They'll head straight to the union to find out what they can and make sure none of Silme's KDP papers are taken."

Terri massaged her eyelids with her fingertips. "Yeah, he has all of the KDP plans, and also the names and contact information on all of our political comrades. Don't want that to get in the wrong hands."

CHAPTER ONE:

THE VIGIL

June 1, 1981
Seattle

When Kozu found me, I was about to address a group that had gathered at *El Centro de la Raza* to assess the large May Day demonstration and militant march we'd organized a month earlier. We had brought over ten thousand people into the streets of Seattle to protest the new Reagan administration's welfare cutbacks and their ongoing union bashing.

As a private attorney with a small solo practice, I was proud of the work I did and the clients I had, even if it didn't bring in much money. It had been a heady time as I helped found the Seattle Law Collective with my then brother-in-law, Dan Smith. Together we'd represented protestors, union members, and minorities in a series of controversial cases. We'd moved back to Seattle in 1978 after spending a year in Puerto Rico, fighting the good fight for the independence movement there as staff attorneys for the National Lawyer's Guild's Puerto Rico Legal Project there. My radical politics and those of the clients I represented had gotten me into plenty of trouble with some of the local judges. But my personal life had also suffered, and I was incapable of maintaining any real relationships, including with my wife Ellen. We divorced in 1978. Still, we parented two wonderful children, John, then aged 11 and Lisa, 8.

I wasn't thinking about all of that though as I prepared to deliver my summation of the march. I was in my element. "Hi everyone, I'd like to kick off this meeting by…"

The door at the back of the room flung open, and I saw Mike Kozu, a KDP activist I knew through his participation in demonstrations, burst into the room. His black hair was in disarray, shooting away from his pale face in every direction. The moment we made eye contact, he winced, face flushed in a way that made my stomach ache.

He ignored the crowd and rushed to where I stood. "Can we talk outside?"

I pardoned myself from the meeting and followed him into the hallway. I could tell from the strange way he shifted from foot to foot that something terrible had happened.

"Gene was shot and killed. Silme … was shot, but he survived and is in surgery." His words came all at once. They made no sense.

"Wha… how…" I met and became political comrades with both Gene and Silme in the early 1970s through our mutual involvement in the No Separate Peace movement in Seattle. Together, we'd supported the efforts of the United Construction Workers Association, led by Tyree Scott, to desegregate the construction trades. Silme had then brought me in to represent and advise Local 37 in legal matters, including how to institute the reformed dispatch plan.

I knew Silme and Gene as two men who shared my passions, my ideology, and my hopes and dreams. They were my brothers in arms, so to speak. I considered Silme my best friend and political mentor, though I was a few years older than him.

I clutched Mike's arm, though I couldn't feel the texture of the fabric beneath my fingertips. I couldn't feel anything at all.

"They were shot at Local 37," Mike continued, "and police are all over the hall. We need you to go down there to find out what you can about the police investigation." It sounded like he was speaking from the far end of a tunnel, even though he was quite close. "And we need you to retrieve Silme's briefcase. It has papers and identifying information on KDP activists that we don't want the Red Squad to get."

Kozu's reference of the Seattle Police Department intelligence unit, which had spied on "radicals" like us for years, jolted me back to the present. Silme needed me. He wouldn't want the police to compromise the security of KDP members, not all of whom publicly identified their affiliation.

"Sure," I said. "Of course. I'll take my car. Do you ... do you want to ride with me?" Mike nodded, and we hurried out of the building, not another word spoken between us.

The union hall was a beehive of activity. Police had roped off the crime scene, barring entry. But as I walked up, I saw a plain-clothed detective place a familiar, slender briefcase into a police van. I approached him.

"Officer, I am Mike Withey, the attorney for the Cannery Workers Local. I'm here to offer you assistance in whatever way I can, but can you tell me why you are taking Silme's briefcase? His wife Terri will want it."

"Can I see your ID and bar card?" Detective Henry Gruber asked, seemingly annoyed at the interruption.

I handed over the card and license. Detective Gruber glanced at it and handed it back. "This is a crime scene, counselor. You won't be allowed inside. We are removing and logging all items of evidence. Mr. Domingo's family and the union will be notified of the items we take, and I am sure you can get anything back that is not of evidentiary value." Detective Gruber turned back to the van, slamming the back doors shut, Silme's briefcase securely inside.

I frowned. "You have a briefcase that belongs to Silme Domingo and the union. It's hard to see how that could be of any evidentiary value."

"Well, that's not for you to decide, is it, counselor?" Gruber ambled away from me with a wave of his hand. Then he turned. "In fact, it's not for me to decide either. I just take anything that might tell us something about the person who was shot, like who his associates and enemies were. It's all for proving the case. We all want that, right?"

Before I had a chance to answer, a second detective, later introduced to me as Det. John Boatman, approached us. I intercepted him. "Detective, I'm the attorney for this union. What can you tell me?"

Detective Boatman hesitated and flashed a look to Gruber that I was unable to interpret. Gruber shrugged and went back to work, and Boatman spoke up. "You might be of some assistance, counselor. Mr. Domingo named the two people who shot him."

"I can't ... How in the world ..." My mind raced. This was huge; in fact, it changed everything.

Boatman nodded. "It took tremendous courage." He clearly admired my friend.

I was impressed. "Who did it?"

Detective Boatman flipped through a small black notebook. "Uh, Frank Ur... Urpman," he said, struggling to read his own scratchy scrawl, "was the fireman who wrote down two names: Ramil, Jimmy Ramil, and Guloy, Ben Guloy. Do you know them, or where we can find them?" Detective Boatman met my gaze squarely.

I shook my head. I didn't recognize the names, but Silme clearly did. "If they're union members, I can find out."

"How?" the detective pressed.

"The friends and families are up at Harborview holding a vigil for Silme. I can go there and report back to you, if that would help. But if they're cannery workers, the union might have their addresses in the records right here. Have you found those?"

Boatman leaned forward. "Not yet. Where are the records?"

"If you let me in, I can show you the union cards," I said. Detective Boatman considered for a moment before motioning to the sergeant guarding the front door of the union hall. He beckoned for me to follow.

I couldn't contain my reaction when I passed the dried spots of blood on the sidewalk and the trail that led up the stairs and into the hallway. I held my breath and hesitated for a second at the threshold before I forced myself to look inside. Dark red blood – Gene's blood – pooled on the floor. I was descending further and further into a nightmare.

It took me a moment to realize there were other men in the room besides Detective Boatman. Detectives were still working on the crime scene investigation, locating and identifying bullet fragments, finding empty casings, measuring distances and estimating angles.

Boatman seemed unfazed.

"Gene had Ben Guloy's membership card next to him on the floor. The desk here had a sheet of paper with Ramil's name on it," Boatman said, gesturing to where Silme had been shot. "So we know they're members. Can you find more information about both of them? We respect the union's privacy, but this is vital." Boatman looked back over his shoulder at me when I didn't respond. "Counselor?"

I shook my head, feeling the weight of what I saw deflate my usual confidence. Should I share private information on union members with the police? I didn't hesitate long. Apprehending the shooters was way more important.

"Sure. Let me see." I knelt beside my friend's blood and looked through the boxes he'd held just before he died. I pulled out a couple of cards out and handed it to the detective standing at his shoulder.

"Here they are. They're both union members. Ben Guloy has worked at canneries recently. And Jimmy Ramil was dispatched to Peter Pan a while ago, but not recently. There's an address here, but it may be old: 820 East Park Street in Stockton, California."

"Thanks." Boatman nodded once as he scribbled notes on his pad. He'd likely seen many murder crime scenes like this before, probably numbing him to the point that he no longer saw forlorn friends and families, only dead victims and hardened perpetrators. "We're on it. Head up to Harborview and find out what you can. Let me know," he said, handing me his card.

"Will do. I'll come downtown to the police station when I find out some information. You should also contact Tony Baruso, the Local 37 president. If he's at work, he may not be at the hospital yet. I may have his number in my office." Detective Boatman tilted his head as he considered this. "Let's go get Baruso's number first, but then you should head over to Harborview and see what folks there know."

I met Detective Boatman's gaze squarely, wondering if I had found an ally. "Thanks."

When I got to the hospital, I could hardly get inside the waiting room. The large space was fully occupied by the family, friends, and supporters of Gene and Silme. At least eighty people sat, cried, prayed, talked, and mostly hoped beyond hope.

Terri and Ade were deep in a conversation when I approached. Both women had swollen eyes, though neither shed a tear as I offered my condolences.

"We need a private area to talk," I told them quietly. "I have some information from the police." Ade glanced at Terri, who pulled me into the smaller family room. Both women looked at me with a confidence I was not sure I deserved. I couldn't bring Gene back from the dead. I couldn't ensure that Silme would live.

"Do you know Jimmy Ramil or Ben Guloy?" I asked.

Terri had sat down, but she jumped out of her chair. "They're union members, and Tulisan gang members too, or at least Jimmy Ramil is." I did not miss the adrenaline and anxiety that seeped into Terri's pitch. "Is that who Silme named? I was at a cannery with Jimmy my first year. He's a thug. Silme warned me about him. 'Watch that guy, he is cold blooded,' he said ... You know, I saw Ramil in the union office about a month ago. He asked if I remembered him. Chilling. Silme used to help Ben with money every once and a while. Do you think they'll be arrested?"

"That's my understanding. We need to cooperate with the police. I gave them Ramil and Guloy's addresses from union records." I shifted to the bad news. "They took Silme's briefcase. They said they would give it back when the investigation is over, but fat chance they won't have already read and copied everything. That's the least of our worries. What's the latest with Silme?"

"He's still in surgery. Hopefully he'll be conscious after and we can talk to him." Her voice trailed off. I could sense her angst, a tangible third presence standing between us. "Everyone's been donating blood. They told us to stop sending people. They are inundated." She smiled weakly.

I nodded, somewhat relieved. Hope was the easiest emotion to cling to in that moment. The situation could have been worse. "Then I suggest we try to gather more information on Ben and Jimmy. Anything that might help the police in their investigation."

Terri seemed to regain some of her color. "Let's see who's here who might know." She ducked out of the private room and waved for Emily von Bronkhorst and Elaine Ko to join us.

Emily listened as I told her what I knew, and her eyes panned over the crowd of people beyond the doorway. "John Foz and Glenn Suson may know these guys, and they're here now. Also, Angel Doniego knows all about the Tulisan gang. They tried to recruit him when he got out of prison."

Within minutes, a small group of seven union members – Terri, Emily, Angel, Glenn, John Foz, Dave Della, and Silme's sister Lynn – gathered in the private room. I began taking notes on what people knew about Jimmy Ramil and Ben Guloy. Angel provided the most useful information.

"Ramil is a *soldato* for Tony Dictado's Tulisan gang," he started. He went on to explain the Tulisans ran the two gambling dens in the International District, providing bodyguards and dealers for the owners. Guloy had been recently seen at the 609 Club hanging out with known Tulisan gang members, including Boyse, Eddie, Suk-Suk, and Mondo.

Glenn, who had lived with Gene at the KDP headquarters, chimed in. "Dictado runs the Tulisans, so he has to be involved. But don't forget that they shot them in the union hall. Didn't the Tulisan gang intimidate union members who were reluctant to pay Baruso's bribes? This hit was in broad daylight in Baruso's union. It was a message for sure. And it's hard to think they would have done it without Baruso's knowledge, or even permission."

"That makes sense." Emily turned to me. "You should also tell the police about the dispatch to Dillingham and the meeting Baruso and Dictado had at the union hall last Saturday during our Shop Steward training session."

"Tell me more." I was taking rapid notes.

Emily told me about the blowup at the first dispatch, when Gene refused to send Dictado's boys. She told us that the new Dillingham foreman, Robert San Pablo, had presented his dispatch list to Gene, the way foremen had always done before, but Gene told him that some of the people on it didn't meet the new criteria and would have to wait. That's when Dictado swore at Gene in Ilocano, not at all pleased that some of his gang members got left behind.

"That gives Dictado a motive," I interrupted.

Emily continued, "Then a couple of days ago, I heard Baruso ask an old timer, Mac Callueng, to fetch Dictado. They went into Baruso's office. I couldn't hear what they were talking about, but I should have known ..."

After a short silence, Terri stepped forward. "No time for remorse about what we could have done, Emily. None of us saw this coming."

"I need to get Angel's descriptions of Ramil and Guloy to the detectives," I said. They likely had a lot more information on the Tulisan gang, but these were great leads. I kept thinking how if Silme had died in his office chair, this would have been an unsolved murder. What courage!

Terri flung out her arm in a sudden burst. "Where in the world is Baruso? He must have been told, and yet he still hasn't come down to Harborview to be with his union officers. I am with Glenn on this: how could Baruso not have known?"

"I will call that sonofa," Ade said defiantly. "How is it that he doesn't even bother to come and console me and the family?"

"Thanks, Ade," I said. "But don't tell him we know it was Ramil and Guloy. We need to confront him in person," I said urgently. "I want to see his expression."

Ade nodded and went to the payphone bank. A few minutes later, she returned.

"He said he was working at Boeing and didn't hear until his wife called him. He went home, claimed he didn't know people were gathered here. He's coming down now." She paused. "He kept asking if Silme was talking. Nothing about Gene."

"Good job, Ade." Terri gave her mother-in-law a warm hug, as one of the other union members approached. "This SPD guy named Gruber is here with some pictures he wants to show Silme if he wakes up."

I was startled. "Gruber was the detective who took Silme's briefcase," I told the family. "I don't completely trust him, but we can't interfere with a police investigation." I wondered why they would need a photo ID when Silme had already named the shooters.

"He's over by the door to the ER." Terri cocked her head in that direction, and when I looked over, Detective Gruber was staring right back.

I hesitated. "I don't want to get up in Gruber's grill again. He didn't take kindly to me trying to retrieve Silme's briefcase." It seemed more important for me to get Boatman the information we had about Ramil and Guloy. "We should avoid him for now."

When Silme woke up, that would be different. All it could do was hurt the case if Silme, drugged and delirious, identified someone else. It could create reasonable doubt and screw up the prosecution.

Terri asked me to stay until Baruso arrived. I could go down to talk to Boatman after that.

"Will do." I wanted to reach out to Terri and give her a hug – for my sake as much as hers – but since she was all business, it was best I kept it that way too.

Half an hour passed quietly as we all sat in silence or prayer, thinking of Silme. Then Tony Baruso strolled into the waiting room, and the atmosphere in the room shifted. Sorrow turned to simmering but silent anger, even as Tony Baruso professed his shock to the families. He extended a firm handshake to me before finally taking a seat on one of the crowded blue hospital benches.

Terri spoke first. "So what do you know about this, Tony?"

Baruso shook his head, massaging his temples as if he hadn't had much sleep. "Not a goddamn thing. It's bad that my officers were shot at the union hall. What did the police tell you?"

"They are making arrests." I looked in his eyes for a reaction. There was a slight wince.

"Who are they arresting?" he said, hesitating.

"Who do you think shot them?" Ade asked.

"No idea. I thought you might know something."

I decided to press him. "The police informed us that Silme named his shooters. Did you hear about that?"

"I told you I don't know a goddamn thing!" His face grew red, and he was nearly shouting.

Ade took Baruso's hand and looked into his eyes. "My son named Jimmy Ramil and Ben Guloy. You know them, right?"

"I don't know those guys. Who are they?" Baruso stammered, locked in the brash guilelessness of Ade's gaze and touch.

Nemesio Sr. shouted, "Of course you know them! They are union members. They deal in the gambling halls you like to go to." His voice was shaking with rage and revulsion. "How can you claim you don't know them?"

Tony Baruso shrugged, pulling his hand free of Ade's and standing up. He went to get a cup of coffee before retreating to another corner, whispering his condolences to others as he walked. I heard him encourage the crowd to cooperate with the police investigation.

"There is nothing we can do, and we shouldn't get in their way," he said, looking menacingly at me as he spoke.

CHAPTER TWO:

THE SEATTLE POLICE INVESTIGATE

June 2, 1981
Seattle

I called SPD headquarters to leave a message for Boatman while I was still at the hospital. I was put through to Captain Slessman, who asked me to describe in detail what I had learned before I came to the station. He listened carefully and asked me to elaborate on the relationships between union members and its leadership, especially Baruso. I provided the description of both suspects that Angel Doniego and others had given me.

"Ramil is five-foot-two, maybe a little taller, thin build, light complexion, curly black hair, and dark eyes." I explained that he had been blacklisted by the union because of his involvement in an assault at a cannery in Egegik, Alaska, in 1980 – an incident which also involved Tony Dictado. "Ramil is from Stockton but is living in Seattle on South Garden Street near 48th. Guloy is twenty-seven years old, also five-two, but he's got a stockier build than Ramil and a round face. He lives on South Lafayette Avenue."

I confirmed that we could make witnesses in the union and Filipino community available to the police for additional background information. Slessman thanked me and said he would brief the detectives, but also suggested I come down to the station, even though it was after midnight. I left immediately, and when I arrived, Detective Boatman and his partner, Detective Mike Tando, were still there.

The detectives asked me a series of probing questions that felt like a fishing expedition. They asked who Gene and Silme's political associates were and whether they had met with anyone recently who might shed light on any antagonisms or disputes. I provided the contact information for Terri, Angel, Glenn, David, and Emily so they could give statements.

I asked whether the police had prior criminal background information on the Tulisan gang and received affirmative responses, though not a lot of substantive information. I also asked again to see Silme's briefcase, but Boatman insisted that the briefcase would be reviewed and shared with me when time allowed. I told Tando and Boatman about Baruso's strange and evasive conduct, and our sense that the murders could not have occurred in Baruso's union hall without his prior approval.

Boatman took notes without comment, but Tando seemed unimpressed. "We need hard evidence, not suppositions," he told me.

"But you do have enough to arrest the two murderers, at least?" I pressed.

"Don't tell a soul yet, but the arrest teams are in the south end right now, staking out Ramil's house. We think we have a lead on Guloy too. We'll go to the judge to have arrest and search warrants issued. It's just a matter of time." Boatman was confirming the addresses I had given them from the police records and some informants they had in the ID.

By the time the meeting was over, it was 2 a.m., and I decided to get a few hours' sleep before I headed back to Harborview. Before I left, I raised one final issue. "Hey, detectives, I seem to have gotten off on the wrong foot with Detective Gruber at the crime scene. Sorry about that. But he's up at Harborview with a photo display of suspects to show Silme when he comes to. If he comes to ..." I fumbled, and cleared the persistent frog in my throat. "But since Silme knew the two men and was able to name them, I'm not sure why you need a photo montage. His condition is terrible, he will be drugged and uncommunicative so the reliability of a montage is shot. Just think what it will do to your case if Silme can't ID a particular picture."

Detective Tando nodded. "I hear you, Mike. I'll talk to Gruber. But remember, let us handle the police work."

I went home, but couldn't sleep more than a couple of hours. I returned to the waiting room in the early morning. The vigil had actually grown in size since I left, and I found many familiar faces sleeping on couches and floors. Cindy and Dale had arrived from California, and I greeted them warmly. I had not spent very much time with Cindy but always admired Silme's younger sister.

"What's the latest?" I asked.

Cindy spoke with tears still fresh in her eyes. "He's been out of surgery for a few minutes, and Terri and Mom are in there now seeing if they can talk to him. We're hopeful, but it's not good." She shook her head and covered her face with her hands. "We just can't lose him."

My stomach went hollow. Her grief reminded me of the hours I'd spent in a hospital ER many years earlier, not knowing if my dad was going to survive his surgery for a brain tumor. He passed without me being able to say goodbye, sending me into years of emotional deep freeze.

It was only six in the morning, but I yearned for a shot of something cheap. Tanqueray gin was my personal poison. I'd always needed something to cope with the isolation of my kind of work, now more than ever. I tried to remember the promises I'd made to myself and to Ellen and, less directly, to my kids, but everything burned and blurred together in the haze of this grief.

"I'll go to SPD, then report back here later this morning."

But before I could leave, Terri and Ade emerged from the ICU looking pale and shell-shocked. Terri practically collapsed into the nearest plastic waiting room chair, and we all rushed to her side. I crouched at her knees as she told us, "The surgeon says that Silme's condition has deteriorated and is critical. He may need additional surgeries if the bleeding doesn't stop." Her chest shuddered as she exhaled.

"We saw him, but he's obviously in pain." She began to cry and, as if abruptly aware of the act, sniffled and stopped. "He confirmed that Ben and Jimmy shot him."

"That's good! The police have to charge them now," I said.

Terri nodded, but her mind seemed someplace else.

"What is it?" I pressed.

"It's just …" She paused. "There was something else. He kept pointing to his leg – squeezing my hand and pointing to his leg." She explained that Silme wanted a piece of paper and pencil, but when Ade gave it to him all he could draw was a circle.

"He couldn't speak. He's got tubes in his mouth, and he's too weak, but I know that he was trying to tell us something important. I feel like a fool for not being able to understand … He's done so much already …" She was so distraught, I didn't want to press her.

"Don't worry, we'll figure it out," I said. "Angel or Glenn might know."

Terri once again pulled herself together and turned to me. "That cop was hanging around the room, but he didn't show Silme any pictures, not after Silme nodded to us when we asked him to reaffirm that Ramil and Guloy were involved."

I nodded, but remained silent.

Terri sighed. "So what did you learn?"

"A lot," I said, and filled her in. "The good news is they're getting warrants issued for Ramil and Guloy. We may have an arrest later today." I tried to reassure her. "Boatman and Tando are really working this case and want me to keep feeding them information. I was just about to go back just to find out what happened at Ramil's house."

Terri seemed relieved. "Come back here after you go to SPD, okay?"

"Of course. I will be here whenever you need me. I am so sorry," I said again.

She thanked me, adding, "Bruce will be here later tonight, so let's meet to come up with a plan for Gene's memorial. We can't let these gangsters ..."

I agreed to the meeting. Bruce Occena was the well-respected leader of the KDP and our close comrade in the struggle against the Marcos regime. He lived in Oakland, but had come as soon as he heard about the shooting.

I ended up spending a few more hours with Silme's family and friends, and it was after eleven when I headed, somewhat reluctantly, back down to police headquarters.

I found Detective Boatman in his small office, and he informed me the police investigation was in full swing. He seemed very forthcoming, perhaps because I had been helpful so far.

I learned they'd already interviewed one witness, a teenager named Patricia Wilson, at her high school. She had just gotten off a city bus when the shooting occurred. She saw some Filipino men hanging around outside the union hall who she described to the detectives, but Boatman told me she was scared witless. Several others had called and left anonymous tips that high-level officers at Local 37 were taking money under the table for job placements in Alaska. This was confirmed by Dick Hubbard from the State's Attorney General Office, who told the detectives that his offices had received numerous complaints in recent years that the union president was taking payoffs for jobs in the canneries.

Boatman let me know that his detectives had taken up surveillance outside the Guloy house, and that Detective Tando was briefing Deputy Prosecuting Attorney Lee Yates on the progress of the case. Yates prepared an affidavit of probable cause charging Jimmy Ramil and Ben Guloy with one count each of the first-degree murder of Gene Viernes and first-degree assault of Silme Domingo.

I lingered in Detective Boatman's office, reading the plaques and commendations that filled the walls, until we heard that King County Superior Court Judge Jack Scholfield had signed the warrants, which were rushed down to the detectives at Guloy's house. Not too long after, Tando called to say that Guloy had been placed in custody, and various items were seized from his home as evidence.

"Guloy told us that he stayed at the apartment of a Boy Pilay, on the corner of Horton and Beacon, all night," Boatman said with a chuckle, and I got the sense that he was not particularly convinced by the tale. "He claims he spent the entire afternoon yesterday at the Chinese Park in Chinatown with Jimmy Ramil, Boy Pilay, and other Filipinos. Kid's called his lawyer now though. Some guy called Tony Meyers, who says we can't go anywhere near Guloy for an interview. Right now he's in the slammer, locked up on $250,000 bail."

Within an hour, Ramil was also arrested without incident, when the police found him hiding behind the curtains in his apartment. They recovered Ramil's .357 Röhm Magnum from a closet shelf, along with several boxes of ammunition. A men's black long-sleeved shirt, with a light print design, was found, newly washed, on the clothesline above the washing machine. It too was placed into evidence. As with Guloy, Ramil was placed on $250,000 bail: an amount that guaranteed they would remain in jail, hopefully through the trial.

With adrenaline keeping me awake and sharp, I kept asking questions. Who was Pilay? Why in the world would Guloy mention him? Was he involved? Boatman and I spent what seemed like hours chatting, pouring over possibilities, but the answers were not forthcoming.

Detective Tando, who had been at the prosecuting attorney's office, came back.

"You're *still* here?" he asked me, a small smile tugging at one corner of his broad mouth. Like me, he looked exhausted, with deep bags beneath his eyes the color of bruises.

"Sorry for taking up so much of your time. I think we're all wrapped up," I said contritely.

Detective Boatman nodded and rose to stand when I did. "We are on the case and will let you know of any developments."

He held out his hand, and I shook it firmly. "The family really appreciates your efforts. Please give our thanks to those working with you on this case. We are way ahead of where we would be if Silme—"

I was cut short by the loud voice of a young police sergeant in the bullpen just outside Detective Boatman's office. "Make that two counts of murder, folks!"

The world spun around me. I reached out to catch myself on the wall of the office, unhinging a vintage photo of downtown Seattle. It and I both crashed to the hard floor together, glass shattering beneath my palm. Both detectives rushed forward to help me stand, but I waved them off, taking a few moments to tuck my head between my knees and breathe evenly. Each inhalation was like sandpaper in my lungs.

"Silme's dead," I said to no one in particular.

I left SPD headquarters with red-rimmed eyes. My car crept slowly over the crest of First Hill toward Harborview, where the smell of plastic and antiseptic greeted me. I assumed that everyone would already know that Silme died, but found the friends and families still gathered in various corners of the waiting room, hoping and praying for good news. I would later understand the coroner was completing the autopsy.

Gritting my teeth, I approached Terri and Ade, who were still discussing Silme's frantic hand gestures.

In the end, though, I didn't have to break the news to them. Dr. Oreskovich, the surgeon, strode into the room before I reached them, and both women went silent. He asked to speak to the family alone.

Terri, Ade, Cindy, Lynn, Nemesio Sr., and Nemesio Jr. followed him into the small family room. They later told me Dr. Oreskovich had looked tenderly into Ade's eyes and said, "Your son fought valiantly for life, but in the end, he just lost too much blood. There was nothing more we could do."

Terri left the family weeping in the small space, and bravely went out to the waiting room alone to tell the crowds of still-hopeful friends. Supporters surrounded her, expressing their condolences, but no kind words or warm gestures would bring Silme back.

Terri stared grimly at those around her and said, "Bruce is coming in later tonight. Let's all meet at the KDP headquarters at nine o'clock and figure out what we're going to do now. In the meantime, get some rest." One by one, I watched as people hugged one another and filed quietly out of the waiting room. Sounds of poorly concealed crying filled the night. I too went home into what felt like that dark night. But not gently.

CHAPTER THREE:

FAMILY AND FRIENDS CARRY ON

June 2, 1981
Kdp Headquarters

Later that evening, I joined Terri, Bruce, and other KDP members and supporters in the dusty living room of the KDP headquarters on Beacon Hill. I'd been there many times before for KDP meetings and activities. None carried greater consequences than this one.

We formed a loose circle in the room, some sitting in broken chairs, others on the tops of paper-strewn tables, or on the floor. When there were no more surfaces, we leaned against bookshelves and metal file cabinets. Old copies of the *Ang Katipunan* were piled on the floor, and I watched Cindy listlessly pick through the dog-eared stacks. The savory scent of Ezell's fried chicken filled the room, but few ate.

After solemn, wordless greetings and hugs, Bruce signaled the meeting should start. As the leader of the KDP – which saw its role as participating fully in Filipino community politics, as well as staking out positions on international issues – Bruce had been very influential in the work that Gene and Silme, and the rest of the Rank and File Committee, were doing in Local 37.

"We will have time to mourn the loss of our comrades later, but right now we have to focus on the tasks at hand. We have a difficult choice, and it needs to be made quickly.

Do we leave this union to the gangsters and the seafood industry, or do we go back there tomorrow and try to pick up the pieces? There is unfinished work—"

"Bruce, it's too soon for this," Terri interrupted, her face still streaked with tears. "We've shed our blood and lost our leaders. How are we going to regroup safely? Who in the world is going to want to dispatch anyone after what happened? How is this union possibly worth such a huge sacrifice?"

Folks shifted uncomfortably in their seats. A long silence, everyone deep in thought. It was Dale Borgeson, a veteran KDP activist who had broken the news of the shooting to Cindy, who spoke next. Dale had settled in the US after being deported from the Philippines, and along with Cathy Tactaquin, he'd taken responsibility for the KDP's day-to-day operations nationally. He had known Silme and Gene well, considering them *kasamas*, Tagalog for comrades. Now he spoke slowly and deliberately.

"Silme knew that our roots are deep in this union. The reform movement has taken a huge hit with the loss of our friends, but we have strength, organization, and numbers on our side. They have only fear and intimidation. We can't be chased away by these thugs. Let's show everyone that this will not stand. What about taking to the streets? We pick up from where they left off." Though his hand shook as he gestured about the room, his voice did not waver.

Silence.

Then Bruce: "It's not that Local 37 itself is worth the blood we shed yesterday. But we have spent years of hard work getting to this point, and to give up now would signal defeat – not just in reforming this union, but in building ties to the labor movements in the Philippines and here in the US. Our work can and must go on, but with the new context of a justice effort to hold accountable everyone responsible for these murders."

"Otherwise they would have died in vain. I can't stand that," Emily added, desperation seeping into her tone. It was a feeling we all shared.

"Silme's dying wish was to get out of that union hall and name the hitmen," Elaine Ko said. "We need to follow his example."

Bruce leaned back on the desk behind him and said in a strong voice, "This is a painful challenge to us. But we have the political will and organization to make this a costly mistake for those involved." He met the eyes of several people in the room. "These hoodlums Ramil and Guloy didn't act alone."

Murmurs of agreement filled the room, mine among them, and eventually we all turned to Terri. She was the one who'd lost the most. We needed her with us. The tension was palpable.

"It's not going to be easy going back in there tomorrow," she said quietly, eyes focused on her hands.

Emily moved to her friend's side and laid her hand on Terri's shoulder. "You won't be alone."

Silence filled the room and seemed to last several eternities – or was it only the span of a heartbeat?

"So it's agreed then!" Bruce said. "We fight on!"

I watched as Terri looked up and around at her friends, those supporters and activists crowded around her – as they would forever be. She nodded. "Silme and Gene would have wanted me to fight. We fight: for them, for us, and for the union."

The mood of the room switched from hesitation and sorrow to determination and battle tactics, and Bruce resumed. "I can see three possible initiatives forward for us. First, we put out the word that we are going back in – but we're not going alone. Dale is right; we need to take to the streets in a huge march for justice. We can come up with a slogan to unite us all, like *Turn Anguish to Anger* or *Anger to Action* or ----------something like that. We need a banner that captures our determination not to bow to intimidation. That will be followed by memorial services for both Gene and Silme. We will fill the halls with their memory. The KDP can organize those with support from the various political movements and community organizations here in Seattle."

Discussion about possible march routes and outreach plans filled the meeting room, but after several minutes, Bruce drew our attention back again.

"Second, we need to form a committee to focus on our commitment to justice. Let's stay on the police and prosecutor to get to the bottom of these murders. We'll draft an Appeal for Justice asking everyone with any information about the murders to come forward. And lastly—"

"The dispatch," Terri said heavily, before Bruce could. "We're at the start of the canning season, and someone in the union has to approve the lists. We can't just let the foremen decide."

Bruce nodded. "That's the third initiative, and it's a crucial one. Given what happened, I propose that no one person can fill the dispatcher position alone. We could propose a dispatch team to implement Gene's new system by committee. There's strength and safety in numbers." He turned to look around the room. "Who's in?"

Dave Della, John Foz, and Glenn Suson immediately volunteered to work on the dispatch team. I was so impressed with their courage.

Dave spoke up next. "If we're going to dispatch workers safely, we need to bulk up security at the union hall, and make it visible. To start with, the police need to guard it." He paused and thought. "We could also build a stand-alone dispatch office with bulletproof windows and a foolproof lock." Assent filled the room.

"We need to have an all-member union meeting right away to make sure the members understand we are back in force and won't let the gangsters run us out," Terri added.

A sense of steely determination had begun to supplant some of the grief and fear that had engulfed us all day.

"What do you think, Terri?" Bruce looked to Silme's widow.

Terri sighed out of the corner of her mouth and ran her long, thin fingers back through her hair. "To be honest, I'm scared shitless. I have two daughters to raise, and their father is gone. This is not going to be easy." She hesitated. "If we respond, whoever killed Gene and Silme are not going to take it sitting down. Baruso's hand is in this, I just know it. And he has friends in high places. And low ones too…"

"True. But if we push back right away with a march to the union hall, a new dispatch team, and we mobilize the community to fight for justice, we have a good chance of putting Baruso and his gang friends on the defensive." Dale looked at Terri sympathetically.

Terri softened. "That would sure help. A committee for justice could organize our efforts and keep pressure on those responsible."

Elaine chimed in. "And provide childcare and food for meetings. We all will help with the kids, Terri. You won't face this alone."

The decision was now final. There was no turning back. Dale turned and addressed me. "What's the latest with the police?"

"Ramil and Guloy have already been arrested," I said, remembering for the first time that the day had borne some good news.

"Are you serious?" Cindy looked up from where she'd been folded in on herself, grief wrinkling her smooth, flawless face. Even in my own mourning, I recognized how strong Silme's sister was.

A wave of renewed excitement flooded the room, but Bruce held up both hands. "This is a step in the right direction, but we know they weren't acting alone."

I agreed. "We need to employ our own security measures. The police are doing what they can, but we can't rely upon them."

"Okay, Mike, we need you to form a legal team to keep on the police and prosecutors to make arrests, find witnesses, and win convictions." Bruce pivoted. "Jim and John can be counted on, for sure, but bring in others to round out the team. Make it look a little respectable, not just the usual bunch of lefties." At Bruce's not-so-subtle jab, laughter fluttered throughout the room – the first laughter any of us had heard that day.

Bruce had referred to John Caughlan and Jim Douglas. John, at seventy-one, was the elder statesman of our efforts, a longtime National Lawyer's Guild activist who had been blacklisted in the 1950s for refusing to answer whether he was a member of the Communist Party. He had a long career representing the Black Panthers and other radical groups. Jim was a contemporary of mine, an active member of the Guild and deeply involved in solidarity work with groups in Central America. Locally, his law firm represented workers in employment cases and Social Security disability claims.

I immediately knew I also wanted to bring in Liz Schott, a smart, outwardly friendly and inwardly serious senior staff attorney for Legal Services who could moonlight for us with her employer's permission. Together, they might bring the respectability Bruce wanted.

I stepped into the center of the room and spoke carefully. There was something that had been bothering me all day. "So far, the police are seeing this as a simple dispute over dispatch, hot-headed Filipinos shooting it out in the local union hall. As if getting shitty jobs and making a few bucks gambling in Alaska is worth killing someone for." I looked around the room and watched the doubt and, in some cases, outright anger flit from face to face. This reaction gave me the courage I needed to continue. "Folks, I'm not so sure. It doesn't explain Baruso's involvement. He isn't going to kill someone just for gambling proceeds or for bribes."

"I agree," Dale said, dusting his brown hair from his forehead as he slumped back against the wall. Crackling yellow paint flaked off onto the floor around his boots. "Gene and Silme were threatening powerful interests with their work. Wasn't Gene worried about being followed before he died?"

Gene's brother, Steve Viernes, spoke up. "He sure was. Definitely during that trip to the Philippines, but also when he came back here. Gene loaned me his truck and told me to watch out for anyone following me. That doesn't sound like Seattle Tulisans to me. It sounds more like Marcos' spies." Murmurs of concern and regret resonated through the room.

Bruce leaned back in his chair and stared up at the ceiling. "Yeah, or the FBI. Mike, we need a theory of exactly how these murders took place, who else was involved, and who stood in the shadows. Your team needs to start right away. Look at Gene's trip to the Philippines and the ILWU Convention in detail. We can provide you with background information on both. Those had to rub the pro-Marcos forces the wrong way. Work with the police and prosecutors, and help them understand the entire context. We won't expect them to adopt our theories without evidence, but they need to know we are not going to rest with convictions of just the two who pulled the trigger."

"I keep thinking about something," Terri said, lips twisting as if she'd just tasted a lemon. "What was Silme trying to tell us before … before he died? He was pointing his index finger at his leg." She touched her own thigh. "What did that mean?"

"What question was he trying to answer?" Dale asked.

"I told him we knew about Ramil and Guloy, and asked whether there was someone else involved," Terri said.

Glenn looked interested. "Was he saying that another gangster at the scene was shot in the leg? Maybe a stray bullet hit him? Maybe we should have the police check the hospitals for a wounded Tulisan gangbanger."

"On it," I volunteered, taking more notes.

"Or what about someone who had been shot in the leg in the past?" John Foz offered.

Glenn's eyes widened. "Boy Pilay? Guloy used him as an alibi. Angel says he's a Tulisan. And *Pilay* means limp or cripple in Tagalog, and he walks with a limp."

That realization hit me like a jab to the gut. It made total sense.

Bruce nearly shouted, "Someone call Angel. Maybe Silme saw Boy Pilay and he was involved somehow."

Glenn went to the phone and dialed Angel Doniego. Before Angel started coming to KDP meetings, he'd had a history of dealing and scamming on the streets. He spent hard time in a federal penitentiary, and had friends in the Tulisan gang. He'd left his life of crime and we saw him as a friend, though not formally a member.

Glenn tracked down Angel and told him about Silme's motion toward his leg. "Any idea what that means?" He paused to listen, then said, "Wait, wait, repeat that. I'll put you on loudspeaker."

On the tinny-sounding speaker, we all listened as Angel told us, "Pilay was shot in the leg a while back, and he walks with a limp." Whispers rose up over the sound of Angel speaking, and Glenn shushed the crowd in time to hear Angel say, "Pilay is also close to Baruso."

Glenn nodded. "Thanks, Angel. We're going to take this to the police, so keep your head down. Those Tulisans will be looking for you when they find out you're naming names."

The meeting took a break, and I used the opportunity to call Detective Boatman. Once again, he was still at the police station. I returned to the group as the meeting reconvened.

"I told the detective about Boy Pilay. He said he'd take statements from folks at the hospital who saw Silme motion to his leg, but he seemed dubious about the connection." Murmurs of dissent rippled through the crowd, but I raised my hand. "But check this out. When Guloy was arrested, he told police that he had spent the night at Boy Pilay's house. The stupid shit. That just implicates them both."

Pandemonium filled the room. "One other thing the police said." I had to shout now in order to be heard. "It's really important, folks! They have bulletproof vests for everyone involved in this work. Free of charge, to be returned when this is over. Detective Boatman strongly urges us to wear them. He also thinks we should all purchase firearms, get concealed weapons permits, and take target practice."

"Are you kidding?" Elaine cried as the sounds of triumph died as abruptly as they had begun. "I have never fired a weapon in my life."

I understood her concerns. Leftist activists like us weren't typically the type to bear arms. "Boatman is really concerned that the Tulisan gang will seek vengeance from the arrests and retaliate."

Bruce raised both hands. "It's not ideal, but we need to take this advice seriously. We'll all get the vests and firearms, and execute a security plan so that nobody is isolated. From now on, travel only in pairs and call in to KDP HQ every four hours."

People were resigned, and we broke the larger group into sub-groups, with members working on plans for the march, the memorials, forming a committee for justice, and the new dispatch team. An hour later, well past midnight, we regrouped to make sure everyone was on the same page.

Bruce held up both hands, and I was again reminded why he had earned our trust and admiration. He spoke with the confidence of a natural leader. "Okay, tonight we formed The Committee for Justice for Domingo and Viernes, co-chaired by Elaine Ko and Nemesio Jr. They will issue an Appeal for Justice. Let's make sure Uncle Bob is prominently involved."

Bob Santos served as the executive director of the International District Improvement Association (Inter*Im) and was universally liked. He helped mentor and provided meeting space for a generation of young Asian, black, and Chicano activists in Seattle, which earned him the nickname Uncle Bob, and he was often a pivotal liaison between community activists, private businesses, and government agencies.

"Bob can be counted on. And Nemesio is a natural," Elaine added, throwing Nemesio Jr. a nod from across the room. He smiled weakly. I could see how exhausted he was. We all were.

Bruce nodded. "We will ask everyone important in this city, from the mayor on down, to sign our Appeal for Justice. But the first person we should ask, and the first name on the Appeal, should be Tony Baruso."

"So clever!" Emily grinned. "I like it."

We discussed the logistics of the march, which needed to happen soon—ideally within two days. We would invite the leaders of every progressive community in the city. The new Union Executive Committee would meet even sooner, the next day. The entire Rank and File Committee would attend and demand that the union hire security and contractors to build a dispatch office with bulletproof glass enclosures. Then, and only then, would the new three-person dispatch team start its work. In the meantime, they would prepare a resolution for the membership, stating that only the new team of John, Glenn, and David had the right to dispatch.

The chatter eventually turned light, and Bruce closed the meeting with these words: "Folks, we have been hit hard. There is no denying that. But our years of activism and training have prepared us for this challenge. We need to build the broadest united and popular fronts to obtain justice. There is no task we can't accomplish."

Shouts of support and determination filled the room.

"For now, the core leadership collective will include myself, Dale, Terri, Elaine, Nemesio Jr., Cindy, and Mike. We will meet every evening to assess our progress. Security is essential. Remember: no one travels alone. Dave or John will get all of us bulletproof vests from the police. Wear them. Everyone packs a firearm after going to the firing range. Everyone reports any encounters that raise concerns. Call into HQ every four hours to confirm you're okay. Let's break up now and regroup tomorrow night. Same time, same place. Your personal lives are on hold until further notice."

Little did Bruce know that the "further notice" he promised wouldn't come for years.

CHAPTER FOUR:

THE CJDV ON THE MARCH

June 3-6, 1981
Seattle

Over the next few days, the initiatives that we plotted out the night Silme died were executed with precision. The Local 37 team – Terri, Dave, John, Glenn, and Emily – led a large march through the ID to the union hall. Our banner read "Turn Anguish to Anger." Thousands turned out to mourn, but also to demonstrate their commitment to get to the bottom of the murders. All along the route, community elders came out of their stores and apartments to wave support or join us as we marched through the streets. Apparently the residents of the ID were tired of the gangs and the intimidation too.

Ramil and Guloy were still in jail, unable to make bail. I hoped they could hear the chants of the marchers as we wound our way to the union hall just a few blocks from the county jail. Pictures of the march and banner made front-page headlines in the local newspapers. The television stations in Seattle, especially King-5 TV, carried it at the top of the news. Other unions, church groups, and many community organizations endorsed our justice efforts and lent their support. All sectors of the vibrant and now-activated Seattle political community came together to support the families and friends of Silme and Gene.

Separate memorials for the slain union brothers drew thousands of mourners and well-wishers. Gene's service was held on June 4 in a church in the ID, and his friends and family filled the aisles and pews. A second memorial was held later in Wapato, his hometown, and hundreds attended out of respect for the Viernes family.

The memorial for Silme, held at the Seattle Labor Temple on June 6, was attended by more than one thousand supporters, including many labor leaders and activists.

We heard powerful messages from Nemesio Jr. and David, on behalf of the KDP and Rank and File Committee.

The KDP issued a memorial statement that read, in part:

Far from deterring us from the struggle against injustice and exploitation, the deaths of our comrades has made us more determined than ever to move forward. Gene and Silme's lives were cut short but the injustices they fought and the cause they embraced lives on. It remains for us to pick up the heavy responsibilities they shouldered and carry on.

At the close of Silme's memorial, mourners stood as one and sang "The Internationale" and "Solidarity Forever", popular anthems of the US labor movement, in a full-throated tribute to our fallen heroes. There were few dry eyes amongst the throngs assembled as the union movement, leaders and RFC alike, demonstrated that we stood behind our fallen. We vowed that "there shall be no power greater anywhere beneath the sun." We truly felt that "we have been naught, we shall be all!"

The Committee for Justice for Domingo and Viernes, commonly called the CJDV, also held its first series of meetings that week and drafted an Appeal for Justice, which asked everyone to come forward with any information about the murders they might have and to support the prosecution of Ramil, Guloy, and anyone else who was responsible for the murders. The CJDV wanted to get hundreds of signatures and then present it to King County Prosecuting Attorney Norm Maleng. The Appeal was also designed to try to lessen the intimidation factor the murders caused by demonstrating our collective strength and support from community leaders.

As we planned, the very first signature on the Appeal was from none other than Tony Baruso.

Other endorsers included the families of our slain brothers; several city councilmembers; US Congressman Mike Lowry; Reverend William Cate, head of the Seattle Greater Council of Churches; the ILWU Local 37 Executive Board; and community leaders throughout the city. In addition, hundreds of people volunteered to work on the committee. At one point, the leadership team alone numbered over twenty strong.

Under the direction of Nemesio Jr. and Elaine Ko, the Outreach Committee was tasked with getting people to sign the Appeal for Justice and attend CJDV meetings. The Communications Committee, headed by Cindy, published a newsletter called *Update* to inform supporters and the media about any new developments.

Seattle's vibrant counter-culture movement embraced our cause and dove right in. One activist, Christopher Hershey, wrote a stirring song about Gene and Silme that he called "Martyr's Song." It became the unofficial anthem of the CJDV, and every meeting started or ended with it. It became a common emotional touchstone for all of us.

No one ever said that it would be easy.
No one ever said we'd all make it through.
Somehow I never thought we'd be going on without you,
Going on without you…
For if its justice that we're demanding,
Don't you know it won't come just in one day?
Don't you know we have got to keep on fighting?
They would want it that way,
Want it to be that way.

The legal team of myself, John Caughlan, Jim Douglas, and Liz Schott set out to find witnesses to support the prosecution and help police develop a theory about the higher levels of the murder conspiracy. From the very beginning, even before we knew how far the investigation would go, we also discussed the possibility of eventually initiating a civil suit.

To us, a civil suit could complement the criminal prosecutions in several ways. First, it would give us subpoena power to obtain documents, take depositions under oath, and conduct our own investigation. Second, it would give us the ability to shape events and control our own legal strategy without turning over the pursuit of justice to the authorities. Finally, putting the perpetrators on trial and hopefully getting a civil judgment against them would provide an important victory in the public perception.

At the same time, I continued to provide legal support for the Local 37 team, led by Terri and Dave, which we intentionally kept separate from the CJDV.

On June 3, the day after Silme died, Terri called a meeting of Local 37's Executive Committee to address the gaping holes in leadership left by the loss of Gene and Silme. The seventeen-member committee was the overall governing body and held the right to set policies, determine the dispatch procedure, approve resolutions to benefit the members, and guide the negotiating stance in collective bargaining with the seafood industry. Eleven of the members were new, elected in 1980 by members of the Rank and File Committee who were fighting for union reforms. I attended the meeting as the union's attorney.

In the sweltering heat of the second-floor union offices, Tony Baruso immediately and predictably objected to the new dispatch procedures that Terri outlined, brusquely reminding the committee that under the union constitution, the president also had the authority to dispatch.

During the heated discussion that followed, a window facing Main Street opened by itself with a loud thwack. Keyed up, I let out a whoop, and the room fell silent. Nemesio Sr. broke the tension by explaining, "Don't worry, that was just Silme opening the window for more air."

That moment cut the tension, and deflated Baruso. We all knew that Silme had gotten up at almost every board meeting to open that very same window. Eventually, Baruso relented to the certain passage of the resolution, and the new three-person dispatch team was on the job.

The all-members Local 37 meeting that followed was unprecedented. The union membership was over one thousand strong, and they came from all over the West Coast. Before the dispatch, they were dispersed geographically, and after dispatch, they were in the canneries. But now, in June, many of them were gathered in Seattle, waiting to be dispatched. And they had a lot of questions about how this tragedy would affect their lives and livelihoods.

On June 5, the day between Gene and Silme's memorials, at least 150 union members gathered in the large dispatch hall. Boy Pilay was there with Boyse Campo, another known Tulisan. The Seattle Police Department sent five armed officers to deter any disruption.

Pilay and Campo leaned against a far wall as Tony Baruso called the meeting to order.

"We are here to inform you about the murders of our union officers, Gene and Silme, and to tell you how we are going to get you all to Alaska in the coming weeks. We are saddened by these senseless murders, and anyone out there who thinks they can intimidate us better think again." Tony Baruso was looking down at his notes and did not seem to notice that Boy Pilay, who had headed toward the restroom, had stopped abruptly.

Baruso continued, "There are those who are claiming that Gene and Silme were anti-Marcos. I can tell you that President Marcos had nothing to do with these murders."

Terri and I looked at each other, surprised. At that point, nobody we knew had ever claimed Marcos was involved.

Baruso was still talking. "We have made changes to make this union stronger and better, and we are going to continue to reform this union."

A thunderous *bang* punctuated the already tense scene as Terri slammed her hand down on the table in front of her and shouted, "No!"

Silence filled the room for a moment, and then it broke into tumult. I saw both Boyse and Pilay reach inside their coats, and I waited for them to pull out firearms. But their hands stayed inside their jackets and Terri continued, glaring at Baruso.

"I am not to let you stand up here and claim credit for Silme's and Gene's years of hard work." Terri said. "You fought us every step of the way, and we are *not* going to take it anymore."

The room erupted in thundersous clapping. As she spoke, I thought that this was a woman I would follow anywhere. Terri walked to the podium and snatched the microphone from Baruso. She turned to the audience.

"Some think these murders had to do with the dispatch. Well, we aren't going to be intimidated. Anyone wanting to go to Alaska has to be dispatched by the new team, no one else. We are going to follow the union constitution, and the three preferences stated in this flyer the members of the Rank and File Committee are handing out to you now."

She went on to explain the same thing that Gene had a week before. First dispatch priority went to those workers who had been employed in a particular cannery the prior year; second priority went to those who had worked for a particular employer the prior year, even if at a different cannery; and the third priority went to everyone else.

Terri allowed the members to read the explanation of the dispatch procedures, then filled in what wasn't printed. "Nobody has to bribe anyone to get to Alaska anymore." She looked directly at Baruso as she spoke. "If anyone is asked to pay a bribe, bring it to the attention of the team or our lawyer, Mike Withey, and we will report it to the police. The next dispatch to Egegik is next Monday. If you think you have one of the three preferences to work there, show up early. We will process your application, and the new team will conduct the dispatch quickly and efficiently."

The room filled with shouts of approval.

Terri wiped tears from her eyes and looked out over the anxious crowd. "Whoever committed this crime got one thing wrong. They thought by killing Gene and Silme they would be done with the reform movement. But Gene and Silme never saw this as a struggle for just the two of them. They built an active and vibrant movement, our Rank and File Committee, and we stand here ready, willing, and able to make sure this union survives and is run right. They killed our brothers, but they can't stop us. Any questions?"

Wild applause again broke out in the hall. Supporters rushed to Terri's side to offer her support.

As the meeting broke up, I watched Tony Baruso and Boy Pilay, concerned they would do something foul. Baruso, red-faced and angry, approached Pilay. I saw him signal to the men's room. Pilay went in first, followed by Baruso. Inspired by Terri's courage, I walked right after them. Baruso and Pilay were at the urinals, side by side, whispering in Ilocano.

"What are you two up to?" I said, allowing my suspicion to color my tone.

"Just taking a piss, Mike, what do you think?" Baruso snapped, and the two finished their business and left the hall. But I was sure something else transpired between them in the men's room, and I reported it to police detectives later that day.

It didn't take long before my suspicions proved right. The very next day, while we were busy at Silme's memorial service, Tony Baruso ignored the resolution of the Executive Committee and personally dispatched Boy Pilay to the Peter Pan cannery in Dillingham.

The Rank and File Committee was outraged. Terri called the plant manager at the Dillingham cannery, who told her that he'd needed to replace a worker who had been fired for pulling a knife on the foreman, Robert San Pablo. A few hours later, the fired worker himself, Perceval Draculan, called the union hall and asked that we file a grievance against Peter Pan for his wrongful termination. He said he never pulled a knife on San Pablo. We agreed it seemed like a convenient excuse for Baruso to dispatch Pilay, and Terri and I privately wondered if San Pablo was involved in this deception.

We convened an emergency Executive Committee meeting for the following week and proposed to authorize the union to file a formal grievance as set forth in the Collective Bargaining Agreement to protect workers against wrongful termination.

The meeting was contentious. Terri asked the committee to authorize a trip for herself and me to Dillingham to process the grievance, which they did. We also confronted Baruso on the violation of the rules. He brusquely blew us off, claiming that Peter Pan's plant manager had called him directly and said they had too much salmon and not enough crew. He said he needed someone sent right away and couldn't wait for the next dispatch. Terri told him he was wrong to dispatch Pilay, because he wasn't first preference. Baruso turned away, but then unexpectedly countered by saying he would join Terri and me on the trip to Alaska to help with the grievance.

Baruso rarely traveled to Alaska during the canning season, and it seemed obvious that he was just concerned about what we might find in Dillingham. But as union president, Baruso had every right to go. The trip was set for early July. It felt like we had a date with the lion's den.

After the meeting, I asked around about San Pablo. I knew he'd been present at the May 26 Dillingham dispatch, but didn't know how strong his ties were to Dictado or Baruso. I learned that San Pablo was born in the Philippines, and he had been recommended for the post of foreman by Tony Baruso earlier that year, shortly after moving to Seattle. I also learned that the foreman at the Dillingham cannery the year before had made close to $3,000 in gambling commissions – nearly ten percent of every pot. It wasn't a leap to assume that San Pablo was anxious to make a deal with the Tulisans to get in on that game.

When I went home that evening, I told my two roommates, Rick and Drew, also CJDV activists, about our plans. They both said I was crazy to go to Alaska with Baruso and urged me to cancel the trip.

I tried to sleep, but the stress of the past few days left me agitated and restless. Sometime around two in the morning, I woke up in a cold sweat. I had been dreaming I was in a small, unfamiliar office, sitting at a desk, when two dark figures burst into the office with weapons drawn. They fired at me at point blank range. I felt the slugs tear into my stomach and then my mind went blank.

I felt my heart stop, and my mind sank into utter darkness.

After what seemed an eternity, I woke up shaking uncontrollably. Too shaken to go back to sleep, I got a glass of water and sat in a chair, deep in thought. That was what it might have been like for Gene and Silme. So sudden, so unexpected.

So final.

I was overwhelmed by the feeling that my friends could not die in vain.

I took out a pen and legal pad and started to sketch out what I knew. I drew one large circle, then three large intersecting circles. I wrote *Ramil* and *Guloy* in the middle of one circle and then *Baruso* in another. The third circle was blank. Then I drew an arrow connecting Baruso to Ramil and Guloy. The third circle stayed blank. I put a question mark inside it and fell deep into thought.

Too many questions rushed at me like a runaway train: on track but out of control.

Ramil and Guloy were acting for Baruso, but who was Baruso acting for? Himself alone? Or was there someone else? Who?

What were Baruso's motives? Did Baruso feel threatened by Gene and Silme, or the Rank and File Committee? Probably, but surely he knew Silme was not planning on running against him for union president anytime soon. Could he really be the mastermind for these murders? Petty graft and taking bribes was one thing, but murdering two fellow union officers in broad daylight was way beyond that.

Was he pressured by Dictado? If so, why did he summon Dictado to the union hall two days before the murders, and not the other way around? Why would the Tulisan gang kill Gene and Silme when the next dispatch would have sent most of the Tulisan boys to Dillingham anyway? Sure, they were blood thirsty and Gene had crossed Dictado, but it made no sense. Baruso was higher on the food chain than Dictado, and the hit took place in Baruso's union hall, not in some dark alley.

The fact that the murders could not be adequately explained as a vengeful act by either Dictado or Baruso led me to a hunch. Were they acting for someone else?

Did someone very powerful feel threatened enough to have Silme and Gene liquidated? Who was capable of that?

I remembered Baruso's unprompted assertion: *I can tell you that President Marcos had nothing to do with these murders.*

Where did that come from?

I looked at the blank circle. Was it possible? Was there something about Gene's trip to his father's country or the ILWU Convention resolution that made them targets of the Marcos regime?

Bruce had told me that Gene carried money to deliver to the anti-Marcos movement. Was that dangerous? But how would the Marcos intelligence agencies have found out? Gene traveled under an alias, but he'd met with two powerful organizations that were creating plenty of problems for Marcos: the NPA guerillas in the countryside and the KMU independent labor movement in Manila. I was sure these groups were heavily monitored and infiltrated by Marcos agents. Meeting with an American labor leader was a big deal. Someone was sure to talk about it. So I had to consider it likely that Marcos intelligence operatives found out about Gene, his trip, and his intentions.

Terri and Emily had told me even before the murders that pro-Marcos members of the ILWU in Hawaii were upset about Gene and Silme's resolution in support of workers in the Philippines. It seemed possible that Marcos had found out about that defeat for his regime. Had Marcos, or his notorious Chief of Staff General Ver, made sure that they never again left US soil?

Had Marcos instructed Baruso to hire gang members with their own motives to do away with two influential activists?

I hesitated. The idea seemed extreme. Maybe I just wanted it to be Marcos. Maybe I just wanted to believe that Gene and Silme's anti-Marcos work cost them their lives, and they weren't random victims of an out-of-control street gang. Sure, I was politically biased against the Filipino dictator, but damn it all, something about this murder just didn't make sense.

I wrote the words *Marcos regime* into the third circle. I left the question mark. Then I fell back to sleep, completely exhausted.

CHAPTER FIVE:

THE FBI INTERVENES

June 7, 1981
Seattle

I was cleaning out my office early in the morning after Silme's memorial when Terri called with a new dilemma.

"What's going on with the FBI? A bunch of our Rank and File members were questioned this morning by FBI agents asking about Gene and Silme's political associations. They haven't gotten to me yet, but a lot of our folks are pretty upset."

I was taken aback. "I have no idea. The SPD is investigating the murders, not the FBI. I'll see what I can find out. Who was questioned? I need the name of the FBI agent."

"Start with Emma and Vilma," Terri told me. Emma Catague and Velma Veloria were two active members of the RFC.

From them, I learned that the FBI agent heading the investigation was Special Agent Lee Zavala, and that his boss was longtime Seattle Station Chief George Fisher, a holdover from the days of J. Edgar Hoover, whose operations against the Left in the US were infamous.

Hoover's Cointelpro program had been brought to light in 1971 when a Citizens' Committee to Investigate the FBI removed secret files from an FBI office in Media, Pennsylvania, and released them to the press. The files revealed that the FBI had used dirty tricks, black bag jobs, illegal wiretaps, and surreptitious entries into private homes and offices as part of a decades-long campaign against anyone who was seen as radical, revolutionary, or leftist. The anti-war and black liberation movements were the main targets. FBI agents resigned from the Bureau and blew the whistle on illegal covert operations. That same year, the *New York Times'* publication of the Pentagon Papers, the top-secret history of the Vietnam War, exposed years of official, systematic lies about the war.

I called Terri and started to tell her what I had learned, but she interrupted. "Mike, we need to get on top of this. The FBI is asking a lot of nosy questions about who Gene and Silme were associating with before the murders. It sounds politically motivated. We need to put the word out that no one should talk to the FBI until we understand the purpose of this investigation. You need to come down to the union hall right now, and we can gather folks here." Terri hung up.

While Terri gathered Rank and File members, I called Special Agent Zavala. He explained that Virginia Squires at the Equal Employment Opportunity Commission (EEOC) in Seattle had heard about the murders and called the FBI, concerned that the Domingo brothers' race discrimination suits against the seafood industry may have cost them their lives.

"We are looking into a potential Hobbs Act violation here, counselor," Zavala explained. "The Act protects union officials from retaliation, including acts of violence, in the performance of their duties as union officers."

"I am well aware of the Hobbs Act," I bristled, "but your agents are spreading a dragnet of fear throughout the union membership. People want to cooperate in a legitimate investigation into the murders, but asking about political associations is way out of line, and you know it. The FBI probably has dossiers on Gene and Silme already, and for sure the KDP. Go read those if you want to know about their activities."

"Oh, I doubt the FBI has files ..."

I stopped him. "Save it. Get me the names of the union members you want to interview, and I will meet with folks and let you know what we're willing to provide. We're already working with the SPD and the King County prosecuting attorney on the murder investigation. This Hobbs Act thing seems like a sideshow."

Special Agent Zavala, clearly agitated, pushed back. "There are two separate investigations now. We will work with SPD, but we have plenty of authority to investigate a violation of federal law. Your fears are misguided, counselor."

After a few more terse words thrown back and forth, I hung up and went to meet Terri and the Rank and File members. Tony Baruso was working at Boeing that day, which was too bad. Terri and I both wanted to make sure he knew the FBI was involved. It would increase the pressure that he was undoubtedly feeling.

Terri kicked off the meeting and summarized what had happened so far, then I stood and explained to those gathered that we had to cooperate with this investigation. We needed to get to the bottom of the murders. But we also needed to assure ourselves that the union members' own political associations would not be asked about.

"You can tell them about Gene and Silme's associations, especially the anti-Marcos work, but we won't let them get too nosy about your own."

Terri backed me up. "Please don't answer any questions along those lines. We will organize lawyers to be present with you when you give statements. Just stick to the basics of what you know, if anything, about the murders."

I told the group I would draft a letter to the US Attorney, Gene Anderson, and to the head of the FBI in Seattle to tell them what we would agree to offer. We would agree that the FBI had every right to interview union members, but only with an attorney present. We would also ask for copies of the interview reports that the FBI agents generated. We reiterated that there could be no questions about the political associations of the members themselves, but we would answer any questions about Silme or Gene's political work that might have gotten them killed.

I reminded the union members that they had a constitutional right to not answer questions about their politics. If the FBI tried to violate that, we would shut down the interview.

I ended by saying, "We believe that the FBI has been after the KDP for years, and I have no confidence that this investigation is going anywhere. I won't let this become a witch hunt into your political beliefs."

My statement produced a wave of relieved thanks and light applause. After the meeting concluded, Terri and I checked in with Bruce.

"I have way more faith in the Seattle Police Department than the FBI," Bruce said, teeth clenched. "SPD has been trying to roll up the Tulisan gang for years, and this is their golden opportunity."

"Yeah, we need to shake that tree hard and see what falls out of the upper branches," I said, pacing. This new twist had me riled up.

"Good way to put it." Bruce nodded. "Listen, the FBI has been tailing the KDP since it was founded, and their files must fill cabinets by now. I don't trust them as far as I can throw them. But Mike, you should repair any broken fences with Zavala. He may prove useful if they come up with evidence SPD hasn't uncovered yet."

Bruce was right, of course, so I called Zavala and told him we would cooperate. I also gave him the heads up about the letter I was sending to Gene Anderson and George Fisher, and agreed to drop a copy off at his office. "Please don't have your minions contact any union member in the meantime. Get me a list. I'll produce them for questioning if we are convinced this investigation is legit. Sound good?"

Special Agent Zavala didn't sound pleased. "I don't care about people's politics. I just want to solve these murders."

As I placed the phone back onto the receiver, I caught Terri's worried stare. "They have no choice," I tried to reassure her. "They have to agree, or be exposed as conducting a political fishing expedition. We would trash them in the press."

Terri shook her head slowly. "I'm not so sure."

In my heart I knew she was right. The clouds on the horizon were dark and gathering fast.

CHAPTER SIX:

A THEORY EMERGES

June 10, 1981
Seattle

At the CJDV leadership meeting that evening, I summarized what I'd been told by the SPD detectives investigating the murders. After talking with Angel, Boatman was convinced that Ramil was the trigger man. Angel's theory was that Guloy's participation was probably an initiation rite to become a full-fledged gang member.

Based on ballistics, Ramil fired six rounds with a .45-caliber weapon – not the weapon recovered from his house – of unknown make or model. Boatman said it was probably equipped with a suppressor. "The only other person in the union hall that afternoon was the janitor, Johnny Siador," I told them, "and he said he heard nothing."

"Of course he said that," Terri blurted out. "Siador is old and probably scared shitless the Tulisan gang will come after him next. We can't bank on his statement."

I nodded. "It's a good point, but the police say that none of the witnesses outside heard gunfire either. Finding the murder weapon would be huge, but no one should hold their breath. It's probably in the mud of Elliott Bay or the glaciers of Mt. Rainier by now."

Bruce probed, "What about Pilay?"

"Tando and Boatman aren't convinced Boy Pilay was there. Silme's pointing at his leg is too speculative for them, at least without something to corroborate it." I shook my head.

"That's bullshit." Terri's temper was flaring with her grief.

We continued to speculate until we could articulate a succinct theory to take to the cops. We believed Ramil and Guloy were the hit team. They ran out the front door after the shooting. Silme followed, bleeding, and saw Pilay, but when the firemen arrived, he first wanted to make sure they wrote down the names of the hitmen. Then he was told to save his breath. He was intubated in the ambulance, then went right into surgery. He didn't have another chance to tell anyone anything until he was out of surgery, when he saw Terri and Ade. He tried to name Pilay but couldn't talk.

"And the police still think the motive is a shooting over dispatch?" Bruce asked.

I nodded.

"I just don't buy that," Terri said, her eyes steely. "It explains one of Tony Dictado's motives, but it doesn't explain Baruso's involvement."

We reviewed the dispatch schedule again, and confirmed that according to the new rules, most of those gang members left behind in the first round would have been dispatched in the second. So why take the risk of killing two people over ten or fifteen percent of the gambling profits from a limited staff of cannery workers when only two weeks later a fully employed cannery would have plenty of gamblers?

"They have the whole goddamn summer to make money," Terri finished. "It's not like we were going to try to stop Filipinos from gambling in their bunkhouses up there."

I mentioned that if we told the prosecution about the next dispatch, they would have to turn that over to defense counsel, who could use it to poke a hole in the prosecution's theory on motive. "Let's hold off mentioning it for now unless we're asked directly. The prosecuting attorney's office put one of their best trial lawyers on this case, Joanne

Maida. She has a great track record of getting convictions in homicide cases. Tough as nails and straight as an arrow."

Dale nodded. "We can support the prosecution of Ramil and Guloy on the dispute over dispatch theory, but only so far. We need to ask who had the most to gain from these murders, and it wasn't just them."

I leaned forward, eager for this conversation to happen. My yellow legal pad, the one with my interlocking circle drawings, was in my briefcase.

Picking up the thread, Bruce spoke next. "That's the right question. Baruso had something to gain by getting rid of the thorns in his side, but he wasn't going to lose his power." Bruce's suspicions were leading him higher up the chain too. He outlined a train of thought similar to my own: Gene's trip may have drawn the attention of Marcos' intelligence forces, and the ILWU resolution promised even greater problems for the government. Gene and Silme were likely to lead the ILWU delegation to an investigation of the labor movement in the Philippines. That wouldn't happen now.

Bruce looked at me and I nodded to affirm that I understood where he was coming from and had reached the same conclusion. "Mike, we need your team to study Gene and Silme's work in the months before the murders, and who was threatened beyond the Tulisan gang. At a minimum, Baruso's involvement means there's more here than meets the eye."

"Let's not leave out the seafood industry from our list of suspects," Terri interjected. "There's still a lot of bad blood over the discrimination cases, and Baruso is constantly trying to please them."

"I agree, although the same could be said about Baruso's connections to the Philippine consulate here," I countered. "When I went to a meeting at the consulate with Baruso a few months ago, the local consul general – what's his name, Querubim? – was bad mouthing the KDP. He had no idea I was close to you all. But Baruso did, so he tried to laugh it off, saying that Querubim's comments didn't apply to our union officers, just those around them. Querubim looked at him like he was crazy."

"And it's not like we were going to take over the canneries and steal their profits, for crying out loud," Terri said. "We have okay contracts, the workers are reliable, salmon is being canned in record numbers, and their profits are rolling in. Why would they have someone killed? They didn't shed any tears, and they probably celebrated when they heard about the murders. But I don't see them pulling this off."

There were too many possibilities for us to make sense of them all in that moment. Bruce reluctantly brought the meeting to a close. "This has been a good discussion. We need to develop and refine our theories, but we need to test them against the facts as they come in."

We filed out into the night, headed out to our cars. I was feeling relieved that Bruce and Dale at least had similar hunches about the third circle in my diagram. *At least I'm not the only paranoid one*, I thought.

Cindy caught up to me as I reached my beat-up Honda Civic. "Hey, Mike, do you mind if I crash at your house tonight? I'm too tired to drive up to my mom's house in Ballard and don't have someone to come with me. We need to travel in twos, right? I'll sleep in one of your kids' beds."

I nodded and opened the passenger door for her. "Sure, but no funny stuff. I'm in no mood."

I laughed as Cindy rolled her eyes. "In your dreams, counselor."

Midnight bled into a new dawn without incident.

CHAPTER SEVEN:

BARUSO FEELS THE HEAT

June 1981
Seattle

As the longer days of spring marched slowly toward summer, it became clear to us that Tony Baruso was under a lot of pressure – and not just from Terri and the reform movement. Although he continued to come to the union office a few days a week, he always closed his office door and stuck to himself. Who knew what he was working on?

One morning, I was in the hall when I heard him slam down the phone and watched him run out of his office, yelling to no one in particular that he "wasn't going to take this any longer." Union members reported that Tony Dictado's black Trans-Am had been cruising the streets around the Local 37 union hall. It looked to us as if the Tulisan gang wanted protection from prosecution, and Tony Baruso wasn't in any position to provide them that.

If Baruso didn't seem particularly busy, the rest of us had plenty to do.

We'd received a final and totally unexpected gift from Silme. On June 3, an insurance binder arrived by mail at the union hall. On May 29, two days before he was shot, Silme – as the Secretary-Treasurer of Local 37 – had taken out term life insurance policies for $50,000 on each of the union officers.

Gene and Silme's families both dedicated the insurance proceeds to the pursuit of justice in the case, and I was offered $1,000 a month to work for CJDV full time. It was a huge pay cut, and with two kids to feed and provide child support for, money was tight. But this was too important not to do.

It wasn't a hard choice. I had dedicated my life and legal career to representing the little guy against powerful interests, and Gene and Silme's families needed me. Leaving them would be no easier than deciding not to breathe. I just hoped that one day my kids, who were eleven and eight at the time, would understand. John and Lisa had already put up with a lot from their divorced, distracted dad. Living with two other activists, I could barely house them properly, and we'd shared one too many Top Ramen dinners. But one day, I told myself, they'd understand. One day.

I referred out my other cases to my attorney friends, closed my law practice, and dedicated myself to the CJDV. I moved into a small office in the ID that the ACWA had used during the race discrimination cases.

I stayed in close contact with the SPD, which was busy interviewing witnesses, taking statements, and investigating the possible involvement of others, including Tony Dictado and Boy Pilay, in the murders. The crime scene investigation team assembled the ballistics evidence from shell casings and bullet fragments taken from the office walls and Silme's swivel chair, including an additional spent slug that John Foz found while working one day.

We received King County Medical Examiner Donald Reay's report on Gene's body, which he'd examined at the crime scene. His conclusion was that Gene must have seen the gun and dove for the floor before Ramil fired, in an effort to avoid the fusillade of bullets. He was struck in the back going down. The police also tracked the trail of blood left by Silme onto the sidewalk.

The CJDV held a public meeting on June 22 to launch the organization. It was attended by 120 activists and supporters, a multi-racial gathering with strong representation for the Filipino community, labor unions, community leaders, and veterans of the gay and lesbian rights struggles. As attendees signed in, CJDV activists asked them to volunteer for one or more of our committees, including fundraising, distributing the Appeal for Justice, and conducting community outreach to unions, women's groups, churches, the Asian community, the gay rights contingent, and the Left.

We started with "Martyr's Song," which always seemed to bring folks together in an emotional bond. Nemesio Jr. highlighted the importance of Gene and Silme's work toward union reform, and Dave Della helped place that struggle in the broader context of international workers' rights.

The CJDV had invited Fernando Beltran from the El Salvadorian labor movement to speak to the group about how the right-wing junta there had assassinated many labor leaders, and how peaceful protestors were killed for demanding democratic rights. Gene and Silme had seen a parallel between the treatment of labor in El Salvador and in the Philippines, and this was a part of their work that we thought was important to continue.

That community meeting was also the first time we publicly shared our theories of the murder conspiracy that went far beyond the two men currently sitting in jail. Nemesio Jr. and I had discussed my diagram of three interlocking circles, and shared it with the leadership team, including Dale and Bruce. We had debated whether to lay out our theories publicly, and decided in the end that we owed it to the CJDV supporters to not hold back our thinking, even if it wasn't much more than hunches.

Nemesio Jr. and Elaine Ko presented a revised set of interlocking circles, which now showed three levels of the conspiracy:

1. The Tulisan gang, including Dictado, Pilay, Ramil, and Guloy

2 Tony Baruso

3 The Marcos regime?

We acknowledged the evidence of direct involvement of the Marcos regime was highly circumstantial, but we laid out our arguments for why it should be considered. Baruso had to have a push to make him jump from petty crime to murder, and our hunch was that he was induced to act on behalf of the Marcos regime, if only to curry further favor from a powerful figure he admired. Plus, he was in a position to make this happen, using his friends in the Tulisan gang. Dictado's dispute with Gene formed a convenient cover story.

After the spirited meeting, our supporters fanned out through the community, handing out the Appeal for Justice, getting signatures, and encouraging people to come forward if they had information about the murders.

Our people were often more willing to open up to us than the police, and so the CJDV legal team steadily interviewed family members, friends, and union members about Gene and Silme's deaths, encouraging them to talk to the investigators if they had not done so already. Our efforts drew twelve key witnesses who later testified in the trial of Ramil and Guloy, despite their fear of retaliation from the Tulisans.

With Silme's dying declaration and the testimony from numerous witnesses about the interchange between Dictado and Gene a few days before the murders, we were optimistic the case was coming together. However, the prosecuting attorney, Joanne Maida, and her boss, Norm Maleng, were not nearly as convinced as we were. They still lacked a murder weapon or any other corroborating evidence of Ramil and Guloy's involvement, and they continued to press the families to encourage people to come forward. With both defendants still in jail and the police promising protection to anyone with information, we hoped that the threat of Tulisan intimidation had been reduced.

Our relationship with Maida was complicated by the fact that, as much as she valued our involvement in bringing witnesses forward, she did not buy into our theories about the middle and upper level involvement. For us, the key to getting to those levels was the prosecution of Tony Baruso. The teeth of a possible criminal conviction would make Baruso break and put pressure on those higher levels. Shaking the tree.

To try to make the case stronger, my good friend Michael Fox, a stalwart civil rights attorney who represented the ACWA race discrimination cases against the Alaska seafood industry, called the prosecuting attorney's office to inform them of the intense animosity Tony Baruso had shown Gene and Silme throughout the various depositions taken in those rancorous lawsuits. These discrimination lawsuits had struck a raw nerve, he reported, not only with the companies being sued, but with Baruso himself, who routinely took the industry's side against the reformers.

Mac Callueng, the union old timer, also confirmed what Emily had told us before. On the morning of May 30, Baruso asked Mac to find Dictado in the ID and have him come to the hall. So we now had confirmation that Baruso sought out Dictado, not vice versa.

The prosecutors were unmovable. They weren't ready to expand their case past Ramil and Guloy.

In the meantime, I knew that any public description of the murders that negated or reduced the role of the lower level motive – the conflict between the new union officers and the Tulisans over the dispatch – could backfire and undermine the prosecution. We needed to get convictions of the hitmen, no matter what, and so our public talking points always included the tension over gang members not being sent to Alaska to run the gambling operation.

Maida and Maleng kept us at arm's length, as was appropriate, and we didn't share all of our theories and evidence with them either. We didn't want to lose control over events.

At Bruce's insistence, our friends at Local 37 kept constant tabs on Baruso when he was in the union hall, including his mood, reactions to events, and movements in and out of the building. Baruso's emotional state gave us insight into how much pressure he was under from others in the conspiracy, and the prosecutors.

At the executive board meeting two weeks after the murders, Baruso described the fact that he'd heard gunshots outside the hall. Positioning himself as a potential victim of the same violent gang that felled Gene and Silme, he blustered that he wouldn't be intimidated by anyone. The rest of us suspected that the shots came from Dictado, who was pressuring Baruso to help get Ramil and Guloy out of jail. Baruso must have refused: either because he couldn't help or he wouldn't, we didn't know.

CHAPTER EIGHT:

A DANGEROUS TRIP

July 1-3, 1981
Dillingham, Alaska

"I just can't seem to get used to wearing this vest, Mike. It's so bulky. And packing a Glock isn't a day at the beach," Terri whispered to me as we climbed into the small island hopper that would take us from the airport in Red Salmon to the small, isolated Dillingham cannery. The only people in the plane were the pilot, Tony Baruso, Terri, and me.

I was actually fairly comfortable with my .45-caliber weapon, having spent a summer at a ROTC boot camp at Fort Lewis in 1967. I'd earned a sharpshooter rating and had excelled in my training enough to be named the Company Commander for ROTC at the Claremont Colleges in Southern California my senior year. I was even a Distinguished Military Graduate at Pomona College, despite the fact I never got higher than a D+ in any ROTC course and had turned decisively against the Vietnam War. The 1960s made some strange brews.

The flight was short, and as we crossed the tundra and waterways that connected the canneries to the mainland, I could see the evidence of many airplanes which, overweighted with tons of canned salmon, had lost altitude and crashed into the sea. It was a submerged trail of woe.

Terri seemed nervous. "Silme hated flying up here and looking at all these wrecked planes."

"I'm worried about a lot of things on this trip, but a plane crash isn't in the top ten," I told Terri.

She rolled her eyes. "How reassuring."

When we arrived at the cannery that morning we were greeted by the plant manager, Norm Van Vacter, and his assistant. The grievance hearing would be held at 11 a.m. in the plant office, and Robert San Pablo would be the sole witness against Perceval Draculan, the discharged worker.

While Baruso and Van Vacter chatted, San Pablo himself came to the door and motioned for Terri and me to speak with him outside.

"Glad you two came. I have something I need to talk to you about after the grievance. Where are you staying?"

Terri hesitated and looked to me. I stalled. "What do you need to talk to us about?"

"Just some information I have to share with you. I'll track you down in the bunkhouse after lunch." He walked away without another word, leaving Terri and me staring warily at his back.

We didn't have time to discuss it, as we set out to interview Draculan in a separate room.

The fired worker seemed straightforward, but there were inconsistencies about his story. "I own a knife, but it was under my bunk bed at the time. Everyone up here has one," he explained. "This is unfair, but thanks for appearing for me."

"Why would San Pablo make this up?" I asked.

"He's had it in for me ever since he became the foreman this year. I didn't like the way he ran the crew meetings, always bossing everyone around like he was a big shot. I have worked here longer than he has," Draculan explained.

"We will call you as a witness on your own behalf. Did anyone else see any altercation between you two?" I asked.

"There was no altercation," Draculan said, exasperated. "He is making this shit up to get rid of me."

"What if we got you sent to another cannery instead of staying here?" I asked.

"I would go for that in a second." He looked hopeful for the first time since we had begun speaking.

"How stupid would someone have to be to pull a knife on the foreman?" Terri whispered to me as we were leaving the room.

I hedged. "He may be a wacko, as far as we know." But in my head, I suspected she was right. The story about the knife seemed far-fetched. With no witnesses and a suspect foreman, it seemed more like a convenient excuse for Tony Baruso to get Boy Pilay out of town and to check up on the new foreman, who might know something more about what happened at the Dillingham dispatch.

Under the cover of preparing for the grievance, I asked Van Vactor how Boy Pilay came to replace Draculan on the job. He told me that on June 3, after San Pablo reported that Draculan had pulled a knife on him, he immediately called Tony Baruso to tell him he needed another crew member as soon as possible. Here, at least, his story matched Baruso's: the season was off to a strong start, and he needed crew sooner than the next official dispatch. But then he told us that Boy Pilay had just shown up at the cannery a few days later, saying he had been dispatched by the union. Van Vacter seemed concerned the union would also challenge Pilay's dispatch and demand Pilay be fired.

As Terri and I made our way down the ramp to the canning floor to visit the workers, who we heard were devastated that their leaders had been murdered, Boy Pilay emerged from the slime line. He walked up the ramp past us, making a grunting sound at us before he entered the plant office, where Tony Baruso was chatting with San Pablo and the plant manager. When we came back, Van Vactor told us that Baruso and Pilay had made a phone call to Tony Dictado in Seattle, but none of it was in English.

"Shit, what we have here is a reunion of the fucking murder conspiracy. What are we doing here?" I whispered to Terri and glanced around, genuinely fearful.

"*Now* you tell me we shouldn't have done this?" Terri said, color rising in her cheeks. "A little late for that, isn't it?

"Let's just process the grievance and get the hell out of Dodge before sundown." Terri didn't disagree.

During the grievance hearing, we negotiated a compromise which sent Draculan, without his knife, to the cannery at Egegik, in exchange for Local 37 dropping our grievance and Draculan agreeing not to pursue a wrongful termination lawsuit against Peter Pan. After the meeting ended, Terri and I suggested to Baruso that since there was still light in sky, we should take the next puddle hopper to the Bumble Bee cannery at South Naknek, where the union shop steward and our members were having success in confronting management over a number of grievances. The union had a strong presence in that cannery and wanted to make sure the members there knew they had our support.

Baruso, who seemed as anxious about the situation as we did, agreed immediately. San Pablo was nowhere in sight.

As we sat on the tarmac, I wondered why Baruso was so keen to get out of Dillingham. But as the plane lifted slowly out of the Dillingham fog and headed south across the tundra, my mind drifted back to the summer before, when Silme, Gene, and I had been on a similar flight, to a similar destination with a similar purpose: visiting work crews across Alaska. Whenever they entered the plant, the workers shut down the slime line and came walking up to them, greeting them warmly. They missed them.

I missed them.

CHAPTER NINE:

THE EXECUTION PIECE

July 13, 1981
Seattle

"Hey Mike, Detective Boatman calling for you," Glenn Suson shouted over the din of an animated discussion at KDP headquarters. It was another sunny summer day in Seattle. I went into the kitchen to take the call.

"What's the good word, detective?"

"I need confirmation on Tony Baruso's full, legal name."

"What for? Are you making an arrest finally?" I pressed.

"You'll know soon enough. Can you help us with his name?"

"Sure." I had prepared enough legal papers for the union to know the answer. "His full name is Constantine Victorio Baruso, Connie or Tony for short."

"Thanks, that's just the confirmation we needed. It checks out. Where will you be for the next few hours, in case we need to get back to you?" Boatman asked.

"Right here. What's up?" I tried to play cool, but my heart was pounding and I knew Detective Boatman would hear the excitement in my pitch.

He laughed lightly. "You'll be the first to know. Just don't let any cats out of the bag."

"You got it." Hanging up the phone, I turned back to the group, which included Bruce, Terri, Cindy, Dale, and Elaine. The CJDV leadership team had added a longtime KDP activist, Cathy Tactaquin, who had transferred to Seattle from the Bay Area to help with our community outreach efforts. Ramil and Guloy's trial date was set for mid-August, and the CJDV was in high gear.

Just a few hours later, Boatman called back to say Baruso had been arrested. He told me that they'd unexpectedly discovered the firearm used to kill Gene and Silme. It had been sitting in a police evidence locker for ten days after an old man found it in a dumpster in West Seattle, not far from Tony Dictado's house. When the police ran the registration, it came up as belonging to, of all people, Constantine Baruso. Ballistics tests showed that it was definitely the murder weapon.

The police had brought Baruso in for questioning and showed him the gun – a .45-caliber firearm usually used by drug dealers and pimps – and asked if he recognized it. Baruso looked nervous, and said he had never seen it before. When Boatman and Tando showed him the registration with his name on it, he changed his story and claimed that he'd bought a gun, but it was stolen before he even opened the box. He told the detectives that he had claimed this theft on his insurance policy, but when they'd called his insurance agent, Lucho Singh, the agent had no record of a claim.

That night at the CJDV community meeting, jubilation reigned.

"This is a huge break," I told the crowd of more than one hundred supporters. "The murder weapon links Baruso to the hitmen. We think that Baruso let Dictado use his gun to prove he stood behind the hit. Dictado held onto it after the murder, but maybe he got pissed that Baruso couldn't get Ramil and Guloy released or even pay their bail, so he dropped it in a dumpster near his house, expecting it to be found." I told them what I knew about the arrest and interrogation, including Baruso's claim that the gun had been stolen before he opened the box.

Dave Della jumped in. "No way is that story true! Baruso showed us that gun last January, around the time of the FCC elections." He was referring to the annual elections of the Filipino Community Council, which had pitted the pro-Marcos old guard and its allies against younger, reform-minded KDP activists. "He brought it to the union hall and called us into his office. He said, 'If those guys try anything …' And then he pulled this piece out and showed it to Gene, Silme, Glenn, and myself. He took it out of the box and was waiving it around. I remember Silme saying something like 'I don't want to be at the other end of that thing.'" Silence filled the room as the irony of this revelation sunk in.

Jim Douglas, always a lawyer, broke the silence. "Dave, you have to go give a statement to Boatman right away. That's huge."

"That isn't Baruso's only gun," Glenn added. "Remember how he pulled a gun at a union meeting about a year ago? I don't think it was the same one."

Lynn shook her head. "Shit, Baruso never went without a gun. He carried one in his briefcase and made no pretense about it."

My heart was racing. "Jim is right. We need you all to make statements."

"What does this arrest mean for our theory of the murders?" Cindy asked. It was the question on everyone's minds.

Dale answered. "It could create an issue for the prosecution of Ramil and Guloy. Why would Baruso give his gun to the hitmen if this was a dispute over the dispatch? Or even gambling in Alaska? He could dispatch anyone he wanted."

The group let that sink in for a minute.

Still at the podium, I told them, "I also learned some interesting information from the FBI today. I called him to see if he'd heard about Baruso's arrest." FBI Special Agent Lee Zavala had been briefed by the Seattle police about the murder weapon, but while we were talking, he told me about a witness he'd interviewed a few days ago who worked for one of the Seattle Seven, as the seven largest seafood companies were called.

"This guy heard about the FBI investigation and came out of the woodwork. Special Agent Zavala says he was reliable. He placed Baruso in a meeting with heads of some of the Seattle Seven days after the murders." I paused, taking a breath. "This is going to be difficult to stomach, but the witness claimed that Baruso was laughing about the size of the bullet holes in Silme's chest, and the industry leaders joined in."

The room erupted in shouts of anger.

"Sorry, folks, but that's what the FBI has. It shows that Baruso probably talked to one of the hitmen right after the murders, or else how would he be able to describe the wounds? He never saw Silme. But it doesn't necessarily implicate the seafood industry in having them killed. Baruso may also have been just talking shit."

Terri rose, and the room grew silent. "Folks, this is no surprise. We knew from day one that Baruso was involved. This just gets us closer. It's hard to believe he was stupid enough to have his gun used, but now we have to press hard to make sure he's charged, along with Dictado and Pilay."

Applause filled the community center, and the meeting broke down into subcommittee meetings and got to work.

CHAPTER TEN:

GENE AND SILME'S LAST MONTHS

July 14, 1981
Seattle

The day after the CJDV meeting, the legal team and the CJDV leadership sat down for a marathon meeting to review what we knew about Gene and Silme's work, and consider how it might threaten powerful interests. With Baruso behind bars, this was our chance to really test the theory that the Marcos regime had become alarmed by Gene and Silme, specifically, in the months before their murders.

We decided to focus on the two important events that had happened in the weeks just before their deaths: Gene's trip to the Philippines and the passage of the ILWU Resolution. We had Gene's journal of his travels and the official records from the ILWU Convention to assist us, and the legal team had interviewed Geline Avila and Rene Cruz, two important KDP leaders in the Bay Area, about the Philippine trip, and members of the Local 37 team about the convention in Hawaii. We were looking for credible evidence, not suppositions and conjectures.

Gene had wanted to travel to the Philippines for some time to better understand his family roots. His father's family came from Central Luzon, and he spoke often of his desire to meet his uncle Mariano and the rest of his family. The KDP encouraged him to travel and witness firsthand both the armed struggle of the New People's Army (NPA) against martial law in the Philippine countryside and the upsurge in militant labor activism headed by the *Kilusan Mayo Uno* (KMU) in the cities.

Geline, Rene, and Bruce had helped him plan his trip. Geline and Rene were veterans of Philippine politics and vocal opponents of the US Naval presence at Subic Bay on the western coast of the Philippines. Marcos had been a strong supporter of the war in Vietnam, and the Subic Naval Base and Clark Airfield had been major deployment and operational centers for waging that war. In return, the US overlooked Marcos and his New Society's dictatorial excesses and massive corruption, as long as he remained an ally in the war against communism.

Gene stayed at the national KDP headquarters in Fruitvale, California, near Oakland, for a few days in April while he got ready for his trip. While there, he was briefed on the political situation in the Philippines, his contacts when he arrived, and the meetings the KDP had organized for him with anti-Marcos leaders.

The mood of the country was restive. In January 1981, Marcos had declared an April plebiscite to "lift" his martial law, though it was only cosmetic: Marcos would retain all executive and military powers either way. Gene would be there for the balloting, but the opposition had announced that they would boycott the plebiscite.

Marcos had held a press conference claiming that communists were infiltrating the unions, specifically mentioning that the outlawed KMU was getting funding from abroad. He proudly claimed that the incoming Reagan administration had promised cooperation in going after the US-based anti-Marcos movement. These statements were widely covered by the Manila press.

Geline gave Gene an alias, John Fernandez, to use when he traveled to visit the NPA and the KMU, both outlawed by the Marcos regime. "John Fernandez" was a journalist writing stories about the Filipino diaspora and their employment in the fields and canneries in the US. It was a perfect cover story, because Gene was actually writing a history of the Alaskeros.

Gene's trip went well from a personal standpoint. His journal described his feelings about meeting his family, as well as his observations about heavily armed security, thronging masses, sweltering heat, and the lives of ordinary people.

He did not write about his trip to the zone controlled by the NPA in the Bicol region, about 230 miles south of Manila, both for security reasons and because he did not want to raise the suspicions of his hosts by taking notes. He went to observe, learn, and discuss how the NPA worked with the area peasants against the large landowners. He observed firsthand how the local workers, hurt by declining productivity and abused by the military, were unhappy and ready to fight.

The NPA, with an estimated six to eight thousand guerrillas just in that region, and twenty thousand across the country, had replaced Muslim separatists in Mindanao as Marcos' number one security headache. They were allied with communist-led labor federations in the urban areas, and their political arm, the National Democratic Front (NDF), had led the opposition boycott to Marcos' plebiscite. First Movement) in the cities. The NPA was growing in strength and was engaged in audacious attacks on the Philippine military in remote provinces.

Created on May 1, 1980, the KMU was the Left-led independent labor federation in the Philippines promoting militant unionism. It represented unions in dozens of industries and was aligned with progressive organizations in the country that advocated dismantling the two US military bases at Subic Bay and Clark Field. The federation had grown rapidly in size and included unions representing hundreds of thousands of Filipino workers in key export and industrial sectors.

A more moderate, "elite" opposition to the current political repression was led by the exiled Senator Benigno Aquino Jr. and the former secretary of foreign affairs Raul Manglapus. They disavowed armed struggle and preferred to pursue an electoral path to power if and when martial law was truly lifted. Recently, however, Marcos had accused even the moderates of fomenting violence. After the April 6th Liberation Movement took credit for an urban bombing spree in Manila in the fall of 1980, the Philippine military arrested a Seattle-based American citizen, Ben Lim, for the bombings, and tightened their watch over incoming tourists from the US.

Into the middle of this, Gene carried $2,900 in cash that Geline asked him to deliver to their allies. The money had been raised by the KDP through fundraising and member contributions. He would conceal it in a plain brown bag to give to a secretary in the office of the Task Force Detainees in Manila, part of the Association of Major Religious Superiors.

When Gene returned from visiting the NPA in Bicol, he met with the leadership of the KMU, led by Felixberto "Bert" Olalia, in Manila. Located in a simple, white, two-story building on a main thoroughfare, Gene reported that the KMU headquarters required heavy security.

Gene was planning to go straight from Manila to the ILWU Convention, and he wanted to bring a personal description of the KMU's leadership and the level of repression directed against it. Bert confirmed to Gene that more KMU labor leaders, including the leadership of the Jenney Drivers' union and the president of the Kaiser Drug Employee Association, had been arrested by the local Metronome police at Marcos' direction the previous September.

Gene told Bert he would return to Manila as the co-leader of an ILWU investigative team with the intention of documenting the repression of Filipino workers. He pledged to give support to KMU's right to strike and collectively bargain with employers.

The plebiscite vote, as expected, ratified the "lifting" of martial law, paving the way for a June 16 election, the first in nine years. However, Marcos threatened to arrest even the moderate politicians, like Aquino, should they return to Philippine soil.

Before leaving the Philippines on April 21, Gene wrote his final entry:

The beauty of the Filipino people is indescribable. On the surface, one must be prejudiced by western civilization standards. Today I am no longer ashamed, in fact I am proud. Proud of my father, proud to be a Filipino descendant. What made me change my outlook? It was a process of understanding. I read of my father's exploits as he met, head-on, the racism of a white dominated society. Jobs to be the found as a young immigrant. It was depression time. Of difficulty unprecedented in modern man's history. My father lived a poor hard life bringing with it the riches to be gotten in America. Jobs to be found only in kitchen or factory work. Education was futile. Because of exorbitant costs, land could not be bought by Filipinos. Filipinos could not inter-marry with whites. Filipinos could not walk down the street without being called brown little monkeys. Life in America was a fight for existence. And fight my father did. Despite the odds he survived. Such is the root of my pride.

Together, Silme and Gene wrote the ILWU resolution on the situation in the Philippines. With input from Bruce, they recounted the deplorable conditions facing working people in the Philippines, called attention to the repression of the labor movement in general and the KMU in particular, and called upon the ILWU leadership to dispatch a delegation to investigate Marcos' anti-labor decrees. They presented it at the annual ILWU Convention in Honolulu in April, just days after Gene returned from the Philippines. They knew it was destined to stir up controversy, given the strong feelings Filipinos in the ILWU workforce had toward Marcos and their homeland. The regime would have viewed with great alarm the resolution of a strong mainstream union like the ILWU, with many Filipino members, which supported the outlawed KMU and sent an investigative team to the Philippines with the full glare of publicity. It would greatly boost the KDP's stature and influence in the Filipino community and within the US-based anti-Marcos movement.

For their measure to succeed, Gene and Silme needed first to win the leadership caucus of the large ILWU Local 142 in Hawaii. Even in the business-controlled, anti-union political and social climate of the early 1980s, Local 142 boasted over twelve thousand active members, more than all of the other Locals combined. They made up the majority of the delegates at the convention. Under the accepted principle of democratic centralism, if the Locals' leadership approved of a particular resolution, their members must vote for it.

When they had 142's support, they then needed the resolution to pass the ILWU's Resolutions Committee, headed by pro-Marcos delegate Eddie Tangen.

Finally, they needed a majority of the credentialed delegates of the convention itself to vote in favor of it. At every step, they knew the pro-Marcos forces on the island, headed by Consul General Trinidad Alconcel, would maneuver to defeat it.

Gene, Silme, and the other Local 37 delegates – which included Emily, Terri, Silme, Nemesio Jr., longtime union member Abe Cruz, and Cindy – went to Hawaii early and checked into the old Reef Hotel, about a block away from where the ILWU Convention was being held. In the days leading up to the convention, Gene and Silme met with Local 142's leadership to describe their strategy for the resolution.

The KDP had carefully studied the political balance of forces in Hawaii, including the militant history of Local 142. They elected to keep the resolution factual, leaving out any anti-Marcos rhetoric that might seem flamboyant to some wavering delegates. They simply contrasted the conditions of the Philippine labor movement, represented by the KMU, with what the ILWU enjoyed in terms of the ability to organize, collectively bargain, and strike.

The teeth of the resolution was the agreement to send an ILWU investigative team to observe the conditions facing the Filipino workforce. The team would report how the regime had threatened the basic collective bargaining rights of the independent unions.

Given that Marcos had recently made a huge deal about the KMU's ties to foreign interests and its funding from abroad, and had arrested its leadership and banned the organization from existence, it seemed likely the regime would try to prevent the ILWU from coming to the islands. Marcos would not want to face the barrage of international media attention and criticism.

The Local 37 team worked closely with Local 142's president Carl Damaso to make revisions that might make the resolution more palatable to the delegates. Carl was initially not optimistic about their chances. There were pro-Marcos members in Local 142, led by Bart Alcaraz and Benny Quitives. But Eddie Tangen was the main problem, because, in Carl's words, "his politics suck and he has influence."

However, Carl himself thought the time was ripe for this resolution, and he was pretty sure his leadership in Local 142 would agree, as long as it was not an outright condemnation of the Marcos regime. Carl wanted a call to support the right to organize and strike—something all trade unionists could support.

To that end, Gene made sure the resolution's "Whereas" clauses focused on the deplorable conditions of the unions specifically. When they met with the entire Local 142 leadership, he used his own recent, personal observations to elaborate on the facts, while Silme added anecdotes about why the right to strike was so important, tying it to Local 142's own history in the islands. In the end, the leadership still made a few suggestions to water down the language, committing the ILWU to only consider and not actually send a delegation. The final resolution read:

The ILWU International Officers consider the Philippines as the destination for the next foreign delegation program as a means by which up-to-date information can be obtained on the state of the trade unions, working conditions, and civil liberties of Filipino workers.

The resolution carried the Local 142 caucus by a comfortable but not unanimous margin. The resolution was given number R-34 to be presented to the Resolutions Committee.

The next day, Eddie Tangen addressed the thirty delegates on the Resolutions Committee. While most of the proposed resolutions had been preapproved without discussion for presentation to the delegates, Tangen made a special case out of R-34, complaining, "It pits worker against worker, depending on whether you are pro-Marcos or anti-Marcos."

Gene reminded the committee that the resolution did not condemn Marcos or martial law. He said that it instead offered support to the beleaguered brothers and sisters in the Philippines who were at poverty-level wages, with no right to organize or strike, and who could be arrested by the regime for protesting those limitations. He argued that the ILWU had a long and proud history of supporting workers in other countries who struggled to attain the same basic rights, and reminded them that the KMU was in the process of organizing against Dole-owned plantations – the very same company that Local 142 had struck against in 1946.

Bart Alcaraz and Benny Quitives acted as Carl predicted. In apparent consultation with the Philippine consulate, they spoke out against R-34, claiming the facts and figures Gene and Silme used as the basis of the resolution were lies, intended to slander the Marcos regime and foment dissent on the ILWU Convention floor.

Silme protested, arguing that the merits of the resolution were not up for debate by the Resolution Committee. That would happen on the convention floor the next day. In a close vote, the resolution was approved to go to the convention floor, but Tangen warned that Gene would need to defend the facts on the floor.

The next day, on April 30, 1981, the convention took up R-34, and ILWU President Herman invited Gene to come to the front of the assemblage to explain it. Gene approached the podium, but according to the official transcript of the convention, Tony Baruso jumped in front of him and spoke first. He said he was speaking in favor of the resolution, but added, "This resolution never has and never will in any way attempt to condemn the Marcos regime as martial law." Baruso went on to describe his own experience as an officer of Local 37 and his experience in chairing delegations.

Baruso's support of the resolution was a surprise to his fellow delegates from Local 37, given his pro-Marcos sentiments. Terri's theory, which she shared with our CJDV legal team, was that Baruso realized the resolution was bound to pass, so he decided to posture himself in such a way that the ILWU leadership would appoint him, rather than Gene or Silme, to head the delegation.

When Baruso was done, Gene took the podium. He began by pointing out that there was no condemnation of the Marcos regime, stated or implied, but also said that "presently the main source of information in the United States carries a distinct bias towards the Marcos government and it carries the distinct bias presented by the United States State Department."

Gene went on to explain that he had been an ILUW member for fourteen years and had just returned from the

Philippines, where he'd sought out information about the conditions facing workers there. He described this trip to the other delegates.

While I was there, a trade union confederation, the Kilusan Mayo Uno Labor Center, made a call to plan a May Day celebration. The KMU is over 150,000 strong. Its chairperson, Bert Olalia, is also the chairperson of over a 350,000 strong coalition union called the United Federation of Filipino Workers. While at the May Day Planning Convention, I was able to have the privilege of meeting with Chairperson Bert Olalia. I was able to meet with Ernest Arrellano, Secretary General of the KMU. He'd only recently been released from prison after having been arrested in September for his part in organizing a demonstration against the right not to strike. These leaders expressed a need for international support for the trade union movement in the Philippines, they went further to give me a letter addressed to this body conveying a call to solidarity.

When Gene was done, applause filled the convention center, muffling the first part of Bart Alcaraz's rebuttal speech. When things settled down, Alcaraz said that although he supported the motion, because as a member of Local 142 he had no alternative, some parts of the resolution were misleading. He said the new Marcos government had built more bridges, was exporting more rice, and he claimed, contrary to all evidence, that the "richest people are from the barrios."

Benny Quitives then took the floor and tried to undercut the facts of the resolution, arguing that the stated rate of inflation was false. Terri's impression was that most ILWU delegates were astounded that both Alcaraz and Quitives had taken the floor to essentially condemn a resolution that Local 142's leadership had already approved. Their talking points clearly came from the local consulate, which we agreed was evidence that the Marcos regime was deeply concerned about Gene and Silme's work and travels.

Silme, ever the diplomat, seized on this sentiment to reassure people. Taking the podium next, he said,

I think what we are asking for is that we take a step toward beginning a process to inform workers on the conditions in the Philippines. And it is a controversial question. I think it is important that we acknowledge that we are talking about Chile and El Salvador and so forth. I think when it comes to the Philippines, it gets a little closer to home.

Making the Central America connection was critical. For years, the ILWU had stood against repressive regimes abroad that suppressed union movements. Dockworkers had refused to load or unload cargo for repressive countries such as El Salvador and Chile, whose right-wing governments had also suppressed trade union rights to organize and collectively bargain.

The Local 37 team waited anxiously while Silme returned from the podium and President Herman stood before the twelve hundred delegates and asked for a voice vote. "All in favor of R-34 say aye." A loud chorus of *Ayes* filed the cavernous room. "Opposed say nay." There were few but nevertheless boisterous *Nays*.

President Herman announced the result: the resolution passes.

As we looked back in light of the murders just a few weeks later, the CJDV team recognized that this act of international solidarity must have been of particular concern to Marcos, whose economy depended on trade with the US, which was dependent on the docks in Hawaii and the West Coast that the ILWU controlled. And bad press could adversely impact the upcoming battles in Congress over whether to renew the US-Philippine Bases Agreement. Equally important was the fact that the ILWU was the only US union to pass such a resolution. In fact, Cesar Chavez, of the United Farmworkers Union (UFWU), visited the Philippines a few years earlier and praised Marcos, to the consternation of some of his Filipino leadership in the UFWU. The resolution was a political coup.

We also suspected the regime was not happy with Baruso, its supposed ally, for allowing the *Mao-Maos* within his own Local to outmaneuver him to get the resolution passed. Even so, we acknowledged that our theory of the Marcos regime's involvement had plenty of holes. We had no evidence that Gene was observed in Manila, or that reports about him had made it up the chain of command to Malacanang Palace. Nor was there any hard evidence that Philippine officials made it known to Baruso that they wanted Gene and Silme gone.

We had talked this through for hours, and the CJDV team was exhausted. However, we had one more question to address: if we could prove Marcos was involved, how could we hold him accountable?

"I don't know about anyone else here, but I don't have a whole lot of experience trying to prove a foreign government murdered two US citizens. Summary executions aren't exactly a topic they have legal seminars about." I deflected the question as the rest of the team chuckled.

Jim jumped in. "What if we found someone who had experience investigating political assassinations? There was that nuclear worker, Karen Silkwood, who was run off the road and killed in Oklahoma a few years back."

"There is a book about that." I nodded. "I think it's called *Who Killed Karen Silkwood?* Plus, I was in DC and heard the explosion when Orlando Letelier and his assistant were killed in a car bombing back in '76. He was Salvador Allende's ambassador to the US, and the Chilean military junta was suspected. No charges were brought, but the families must have investigated."

"Jeez, Mike. You definitely know how to get yourself into trouble," Cindy quipped. I smiled at her.

Jim stood up and begin pacing. "You know Janet Duecey, right? She's a CJDV supporter, and my law partner used to be married to her. She was close friends with Charles Horman. He and another journalist disappeared during the Chilean coup by Pinochet in 1973. The military was suspected. There was a book called *Missing* and they even made a movie out of it."

We were on to something. "Let's educate ourselves," I said. "Jim, reach out to the Silkwood folks. I will do the same to the Letelier family, and can you try to contact Horman's widow through Janet? We need to tell them about our case and ask if they would be willing to share strategies, thoughts, and concerns as we move forward. In the meantime, let's all read the books about all three cases and see what we learn."

As people pulled out pads and scratch paper, comparing notes in the dank, crowded space, I felt a smile play at the corners of my mouth. We had the makings of a theory. We had resources. We were organized, ready, and committed, all of us in it together for the long haul.

CHAPTER ELEVEN:

PRESSING THE PROSECUTION

August 1981
Seattle

Norm Maleng and Joanne Maida greeted us with genuine affection when Terri, Ade, Cindy, Nemesio Jr., and I walked into the prosecuting attorney's office after Baruso's arrest. Plaques adorned the walls celebrating Maleng's long history in fighting crime and displaying his close connection to the community.

"We are so sorry for your loss," Maleng began, looking at Ade. "From everything we hear, your son and Gene were amazing young men. Rest assured, we are doing everything we can to bring those responsible to justice."

Terri responded, "Thank you. Your office has been great."

Maleng's office had initially won the support of the CJDV when they agreed to respect the family's wishes to not prosecute the case under the death penalty law recently passed by the state legislature.

Over the next hour, we summarized our evidence against Baruso, emphasizing his ownership of the murder weapon. I had statements from Dave Della and Glenn Suson about the day Baruso showed them the gun. When I told them about Silme saying *I don't want to be on the other end of that piece*, I noticed Maida recoil.

Ade described the conversation she had with Baruso at Harborview after the shooting, when Baruso denied knowing Ramil and Guloy. Terri talked about how Baruso dispatched Pilay to Dillingham against the rules, and our belief that this was to make sure San Pablo didn't talk.

Maida surprised us at that point, telling us that Robert San Pablo had contacted the police directly, at the urging of his Dillingham bosses, and agreed to testify against Ramil and Guloy. Detective Boatman had gone to Alaska to interview him about the events of the May 26 dispatch, and it had gone well. She said San Pablo was willing to testify that after Dictado yelled at Gene, he turned and said in Ilocano, "Mother, I will get you." Then San Pablo ran into Dictado, Ramil, and Pilay at a restaurant in the ID and Pilay told him privately that Dictado was going to kill Gene.

Terri and I looked at each other incredulously, thinking that maybe the trip to Alaska was worthwhile after all.

To me, the case against Baruso was strong. "My sense is that if you were to charge Dictado, Pilay, and Baruso, one of them would turn state's evidence and beg for a lighter sentence. There should be no deal for Baruso unless he implicates higher ups though. He needs to sit in prison for a long time."

"We'll see. But as for those higher ups, don't expect us to buy into your theories about Marcos being involved," Maida said dismissively. She must have read the recent CJDV newsletter article which described the three interlocking circles and drew connections between the Marcos regime and the martyred pair.

I shook Maleng's hand when he stood, ending our meeting. "Thanks so much for your assistance. The witnesses you have brought have been invaluable. Joanne will let you know our decision soon."

It had been a valuable meeting, but still, they didn't commit to charging Baruso. The delay was concerning.

Every day we went without a formal charge was torture for the families and friends.

At the CJDV community meeting that Friday night, Elaine Ko summed up the concern. "We have to be aware of the class bias that operates in a situation like this. The Tulisan gang members are scum, lowlifes the police want off the streets. But Baruso is a prominent member of the Filipino community. He has a good job at Boeing. He's the union president, and even ran for statewide office once, years ago. They think they need more evidence for someone like that."

"I can't believe that the murder weapon isn't enough," Dale said, outright revulsion crossing his narrow face. "Something's going on and I don't like it."

Nodding, Cindy said, "Look, right now we need to focus on filling the courtroom for the trial of Ramil and Guloy. Everyone in our network gets contacted, asked to come, and their hours of attendance noted. It's okay if they get turned away because the courtroom is overflowing – it will send a message to the gangs, Baruso, and the prosecutors that we mean business. Tell them to come back after lunch or the next day."

The meeting then broke up to discuss the mobilization plans. Filling the courtroom would take a lot of work, but we had the people behind us. Our strongest support, in addition to the prominent names on our Appeal for Justice, came from numerous local and international unions, including the ILWU, municipal and state workers, transit drivers, and the Services Employees International Union. The Church Council of Greater Seattle and its leader, Reverend William Cate, were staunch allies. The Japanese American Citizen's Action League, which had fought against the Japanese interment during World War II, was actively involved. Representatives from all of the local minority coalitions contributed their ideas and resources. The gay and lesbian community was represented by activists Kris Melroe and her partner Ellen Earth. It was an impressive coalition. As folks filed out, Cindy pulled me aside to ask if she could spend another night at my place rather than returning to her parents' house in Ballard. I liked Cindy as a person, and I admired her as an activist. Beyond that, I couldn't help but be drawn in by Cindy's pleasant smile and genuine affection. I agreed without question and we walked to the car together.

CHAPTER TWELVE:

THE COVER-UP WINS A ROUND

August 1981
Seattle

On the Monday after his arrest, Tony Baruso walked out of jail without any charges filed against him. Maleng told the press that the investigation was ongoing, and that in no sense was Tony Baruso off the hook.

We were devastated. The CJDV issued a strong press statement condemning the failure to charge Tony Baruso with the murders and asking the prosecutor's office to reconsider. It was to no avail. My calls to Maida for an explanation were met by what was to become a tired refrain: "It's an open investigation and we will bring to justice all who were involved."

Despite this huge setback, the prosecution of Ramil and Guloy was moving forward, aided by two major developments in the case.

The first was Robert San Pablo. In his interview with Detective Boatman, San Pablo provided an inside look at the hitmen's behavior before and after the murders, and gave eyewitness testimony that both Jimmy Ramil and Boy Pilay were directly involved. He also implicated Tony Baruso in a number of ways.

San Pablo told prosecutors that Boy Pilay told him Tony Baruso offered to pay the gang $5,000 for killing Gene and Silme. The legal team analyzed this statement carefully, and I discussed it with Joanne Maida as well. Although technically a hearsay statement that would not typically be admissible in court, we believed that one or more of the many exceptions to the hearsay rule should apply. Specifically, when someone says something that incriminates themselves, or a statement against their own personal interest, it is considered to be reliable and can be testified to. Boy Pilay telling San Pablo that he knew about the payment for the murders was self-incriminating.

We had a similar issue with getting into evidence the firemen's testimony about Silme's dying declaration naming the hitmen: it was hearsay. Silme had to be in reasonable fear of death in making it for it to be admitted to the jury.

Curiously, Pilay also told San Pablo that Baruso had not paid the money he promised. To us, that explained why Dictado was pressuring Baruso after Ramil and Guloy were arrested. Baruso balked because he was fearful of being implicated, and Dictado decided to "lose" the gun in the dumpster.

San Pablo's second bombshell was that as soon as Pilay arrived in Dillingham, he approached San Pablo and threatened to blow up his car and kill him if San Pablo told the police what he knew. This was clearly the reason Baruso dispatched Pilay there—to shut San Pablo up. This was a threat that would aid all of the members of the murder conspiracy, including Tony Baruso. Thus, it was likely that San Pablo would be allowed to testify about this statement too, despite the fact it was technically hearsay. It was the co-conspirator statement exception to the hearsay rule.

Finally, San Pablo provided a letter, written on Local 37 stationery, that Tony Baruso handed him when we were all at the Dillingham cannery in July. In it, Baruso asked him to send "something" to his home address because those *Mao-Maos* – Terri and I, presumably – were around. We assumed he was referring to his cut of the gambling proceeds, or maybe his payoff for giving San Pablo the foreman position.

That letter would help establish Tony Baruso's motive, at least as it related to the dispatches and gambling.

San Pablo's effectiveness, though, depended upon how credible he would appear to the jury. The defense would point out he was aware that Gene was about to be killed and did nothing to let the police know. But I had a high opinion of Maida's ability to properly prepare a key witness like San Pablo, including explaining that he thought Dictado's threats to kill Gene were all bluster. She seemed genuinely convinced he was telling the truth. Still, we needed the judge to allow San Pablo to testify about this statement made by Pilay too, because it was technically hearsay. Maida had to establish that the statement was made in furtherance of the murder conspiracy and/or to cover it up.

Our second key witness development came from Jaime Malabo. In early August, the CJDV's outreach into the community paid dividends. Lynn Domingo heard that a young Filipino had come to Local 37 on the afternoon of June 1 to find out about the dispatch for his mother and had witnessed something significant. In the weeks that followed, his mother had urged him to come forward to the police, as did Lynn, but the eighteen year old was completely intimidated. Finally, his best friends, Ross Landon and Ferdie Orbino, promised to protect him from the Tulisan gang, and he reluctantly agreed.

Without knowing the precise nature of his testimony beyond his mother's promises that it would help the prosecution, Lynn and Ferdie convinced Jaime to talk to the police.

He told them that on June 1, he drove down to the union hall late in the afternoon. Heading south on 2nd Extension, he passed the union hall on his right and saw Silme lying on the sidewalk. Not realizing that Silme was dying in front of him, Jaime turned right on Jackson, and at the entrance to the alley on his right, he saw Ramil and Guloy walking away from the direction of the union hall. He recognized both of them from the gambling halls.

Ramil was carrying a large brown paper bag. They hurriedly got into a car that Jaime recognized as Ramil's. Jaime considered honking and saying hello, but turned up the alley instead, toward the hall. He again saw Silme on the sidewalk as he reached the end of the alley next to the hall, and it was only then he realized something was amiss. He left immediately.

Maida told me that Jaime was squeaky clean as a witness. This testimony by a neutral and objective observer, if believed by the jury, seemed to seal the hitmen's fate. It was music to my ears.

The weeks between Tony Baruso's release and the criminal trial were busy. Although Baruso was not charged, the fact that his gun was the murder weapon was widespread knowledge in the Filipino community. The CJDV's *Update* newsletter discussed the implications of this development, pointing out that Tony Baruso was the first to sign the Appeal for Justice, yet was unable to explain how his own gun got into Ramil's hands.

The Local 37 team came up with a strategy to further isolate Baruso and increase the pressure on him: they wanted him removed from office.

One hot Sunday morning in August, the CJDV and Local 37 leadership teams gathered together at KDP headquarters. Listening to "Easy Like Sunday Morning" by Lionel Ritchie and eating brunch together, the mood was lighter than normal. The dusty living room with the faded wallpaper and revolutionary posters had become familiar, a safe and habitual haven. There was power of place there.

Straddling the back of an old wicker chair, Terri kicked the discussion off. "Folks, we need to get rid of Tony Baruso. I can't stand working at the hall with him around. He has no business being the head of this union, whether the prosecutor charges him or not. What can we do?"

Dave was the first to answer. "There must be something in the union constitution for conducting an internal investigation and trial for an officer who commits a crime, right?" He proposed working with the Rank and File Committee to put out a special edition of the *Alaskero News*, demanding Baruso resign and threatening a recall if he refused.

Emily spoke up. "A recall campaign would really be a great rallying cry for the members. It would focus us on continuing Gene and Silme's work, and allow us to talk directly to every member we dispatch or who comes back from Alaska about what our goals are."

Glenn offered to write the article. Terri stood up and moved to the window.

"It's going to be a lot of work," she said, her voice heavy. "There are old guard members who will want to keep Baruso." I saw nods around the room as she turned to face us. "But when we decided to fight for this union and go back into the hall the day after the murders, it meant getting rid of the gangsters and Tony Baruso. I think we can pull this off."

Terri's leadership and determination once again won the day. The group took the campaign to the larger Rank and File Committee, who concurred it was time for Baruso to go. They published a special edition of *Alaskero News* and distributed it to all union members in mid-August. It committed Local 37 to three things: 1) to continue to reform the union despite the murders; (2) to dedicate the union leadership to get to the bottom of the murders of our brothers; and (3) to rid the union of the reactionary and hoodlum elements which gave the industry the upper hand.

Glenn and Terri wrote articles pointing out that Baruso had run for an open position on the ILWU International executive board three weeks after the murders. He was defeated, but he somehow received 420 votes from Local 37 membership. The problem was that nobody remembered voting in the ILWU election. When ILWU International looked at the ballots, they determined that all 420 ballots sent to them were filled in with the same pen and same format. The article argued that due to election fraud and owning a gun that was a murder weapon, Baruso was seriously compromised. The union could not afford another scandal. It pointed out that under the union constitution, Article XIV, a trial should be held to determine whether Baruso should be recalled. Strategically conceding that Baruso was entitled to the "presumption of innocence," the article called for him to resign his post or face a recall election.

Baruso did not publicly respond, but neither did he resign. He was hunkered down and rarely appeared at the union hall that summer, and he must have felt the pressure from all sides.

The RFC drafted and printed the recall petition. A simple ballot was devised: "Should Tony Baruso be recalled as President of Local 37, ILWU?" It had boxes for *Yes* and *No*.

The RFC notified ILWU International of the recall election and asked for its expertise in conducting a fair election. This assistance was freely given, and the recall election was approved as proposed. The ballots were distributed immediately, but since most of the members were still in Alaska, the vote count was scheduled for mid-December. If recalled, a new election for Local 37 President would be held in January 1982.

Given the obstacles before him, we did not expect that Baruso could match us in organizing meetings and conversations with the work crews coming home from Alaska. I thought Terri's election as the next Local 37 President would be a shoo-in.

The combined initiatives of preparing for Ramil and Guloy's trial while also conducting the recall campaign were taxing. Meetings consumed most evenings and, as predicted by Bruce, our personal lives were on hold or nonexistent. The CJDV worked tirelessly to organize, regularly sending out *Update* newsletters to describe and disseminate information on the murder conspiracy and the prosecution's efforts – or lack thereof, in Baruso's case. We held regular community meetings that were attended at times by hundreds of supporters, as well as more intimate sessions with the prosecuting attorneys to assess the prospect of convictions. The legal team and I tried to remain up-to-date and one step ahead of the prosecution. Without convictions on Ramil and Guloy, our strategy of shaking the tree would fail.

The pressure was hardest on Terri and her girls. Terri was devastated by the loss of her partner and best friend. Yet there was no respite and no time to grieve. The increased demands of the work, the constant reminders of the threats, and the strains of being a mother of two fatherless daughters took an enormous toll on her. The CJDV organized childcare for Ligaya and Kalayaan, and Terri's parents did everything they could, but Terri knew that her daughters' early childhoods were devolving into a series of endless shuttles between this event and that, with sympathetic-but-different childcare workers taking care of them every night rather than their father. Emily was a constant help and companion to the family, but she, too, was up to her eyeballs in the swamp that nobody was draining of alligators.

And Terri wasn't the only one feeling the stress. We all worked seven days a week. The national KDP leaders – Bruce, Dale, and Cathy – got caught up in the constant demands of the work in Seattle. Bruce was particularly vulnerable because he also had tremendous responsibilities for leading the KDP nationally, as well as involvement in other projects for justice and democracy. He worked late and long hours and traveled between Seattle and the Bay Area on a weekly basis. I could see he was starting to get strung out. Nevertheless, in those difficult early months, he was always there to provide direction and leadership.

Even when we were at home, threats plagued us all. Anonymous, threatening phone calls came to the KDP headquarters, to Terri's house, to Ade and Nemesio Sr.'s house, and to me. A typical pattern emerged: the phone would ring, and when we would answer, there was just silence on the other end. Or we heard muffled voices saying "you better stop" or "this is the last warning."

Emily, Terri, and the girls began to hear knocking sounds in their apartment, and then later in the house they moved to on South Beacon Hill for greater security. There was a certain rhythm to the knocks, though they occurred at the most random times and places: inside a closet, behind a door, or in the upstairs bathroom. Some visitors heard them as well, and we began to believe it was Silme, trying to tell Terri something. To find his killers. To find justice.

My relationship with my young children also suffered. As a divorced dad, I was responsible for them every other weekend, one dinner a week, and three weeks in the summer. I rented a separate room for them in the house I shared, and considered myself completely dedicated to keeping them in my life, but in those difficult months, I was not always successful. I often had to turn to their mother Ellen, her brother Dan Smith, and Dan's wife Linda Turner – all of them godsends – to pick the kids up from school and take care of them when I was out late.

John and Lisa were troopers. They let me drag them around to CJDV meetings on the weekends, where they could be the big kids compared to Terri's girls and those of the other activists. They never complained, although I know I left them reasons to want to. I can't count how many dinners I put together by adding spinach and eggs to Top Ramen. They'd look at me like I was crazy but would pretend we were all eating a feast. John once asked me over a bowl of Grape Nuts whether this was what it was like to be poor. "No shame in being poor, son" was my response.

I was barely being a father. Still, they never gave up on me, and because of that, I felt like the luckiest father in the world.

Of all of us, Cindy Domingo seemed to keep it together the best. She persevered through her grief and the scope of the work she assumed, even as her parents and siblings struggled through oscillating bouts of depression. Her staying overnight at my house became an increasingly regular occurrence as the weeks passed, and our relationship grew intense. Late one night, after a particularly difficult meeting, we shared a glass of wine, then the whole bottle as we wondered how it had all gotten so crazy. After that, she wasn't sleeping in my kids' bed anymore.

We both used drugs and alcohol to cope through the long nights and even longer days. But each day, when dawn broke, we got up and trudged on. One foot after the other, we said. Except now we also had a relationship to manage, and I was terrible at it.

CHAPTER THIRTEEN:

THE TRIAL OF JIMMY RAMIL AND BEN GULOY

August-September 1981
Seattle

The trial of the *State of Washington v. Jimmy Buloson Ramil and Pompeyo Benito Guloy* began on August 14, 1981, in the courtroom of King County Superior Court Judge Lloyd Bever. Judge Bever was a former insurance defense attorney who had been the trial judge for hundreds of cases.

He made some key pre-trial rulings on evidence, the most significant of which was whether to allow the testimony of firefighters Frank Urpman and James Huckins as to Silme's "dying declaration" naming the hitmen. It was a tough and case-shaping argument. To establish a "dying declaration," the person providing the statement (i.e. Silme's statement to them that Ramil and Guloy committed the murders) must have been in genuine and immediate fear of death, yet alert and oriented enough to recall events accurately. To me, the key testimony was from fireman Frank Urpman. He testified that Silme had asked him, "Am I going to die?" Rather than reassure him, Urpman told him bluntly, "It looks bad." In the hearing on the motion, Joanne had carefully established that Silme was both alert and oriented, knew the day, who the president was, and that he was capable of naming his assailants. Defense counsel argued ably that Silme had been shot four times at close range, was bleeding profusely, was obviously in great pain and that his statements were simply not sufficiently reliable to constitute admissible hearsay.

Judge Bever considered these arguments carefully and retired from the bench before announcing his ruling. I was nervous and paced up and down the courtroom before he re-entered. When he returned, it was clear he was struggling with his ruling, perhaps aware that the entirity of the prosecution's case could well hinge on whether to admit this evidence. He seemed to rest his reasoning on the fact that the witnesses in court were veteran firefighters who were highly experienced and reliable witnesses and whose recollections about their interaction with Silme at the scene were clear, consistent, and accurate. In the end, he came down strongly. The testimony would be admitted; the motion to suppress the dying declaration was denied.

This huge hurdle cleared, I entered the air conditioned courtroom, chilly enough that I could have used a parka, and sat beside Cindy on one of hard-backed courtroom benches. The space was filled to capacity with CJDV supporters, and family members. Ben Guloy's mother was also present for most of the trial, as was Josie Ramil, Jimmy's wife.

Ramil was represented by criminal defense attorney Jim Grubb, and Tony Meyers represented Guloy. The jury was selected without significant incident, although most prospective jurors acknowledged they had heard of the murders from the extensive news coverage.

After a detailed opening statement, Maida started her prosecution with evidence from the crime scene investigation, principally the testimony of SPD Homicide Detective Harry T. Gruber, the man I'd first met when he took Silme's briefcase. Detective Gruber presented in painstaking detail his experience at the union hall, including the layout of the building and the location where Gene's body was found. He described the location of the bullet fragments, spent shells, slugs, wall markings, and drops of blood leading out onto the sidewalk. He noted that there was no blood on Silme's swivel chair. This suggested that, although mortally wounded, Silme had bolted from his chair to chase the hitmen, before his blood even had time to fall. The drawings, photographs, and testimony of Detective Gruber went into evidence without objection and seemed well received by the jury.

Criminologist Frank Lee from the Washington State Crime Lab followed with a lengthy discussion of the ballistics tests undertaken to establish that the MAC-10 .45-caliber firearm, registered to Constantine Baruso, was the murder weapon. He testified that there was only one firearm responsible for all of the bullet fragments and spent shells. He gave his expert opinion that a suppressor had been used, based upon the fact that each of the bullets found at the scene (and one found by the surgical team inside Silme) had two separate markings on either side of the bullet. One marking was caused by the bullet traveling down the barrel of the gun, and the other marking made after the bullet cleared the barrel and was rubbed by another structure; in this case, the suppressor.

This testimony was further supported by the opinions offered by King County Medical Examiner Dr. Donald Rhea, who described the entry and exit wounds suffered by Gene. He explained his opinion that Gene dove for the floor in a futile attempt to avoid the bullets heading his way. He testified that this explained why the entry wounds were in Gene's back and the exit wounds in his chest.

The police testimony was backed up by a number of witnesses who were present at the scene. Guy Reynolds was a city bus driver who was waiting at the bus stop on Main Street near the union hall. He saw a man on the sidewalk, holding his stomach, yelling for help. Reynolds called Medic 1 and testified that he heard the man say, "He shot me. He shot me."

The high school student, Patricia Wilson, testified that she got off Reynolds' bus and saw a man come down the steps from the hall to the sidewalk, holding his chest. She saw another Filipino man emerge from the hall and get into a black Trans-Am with white dice dangling from the rearview mirror and drive away. She heard the injured man cry out, "He shot me. He shot me," pointing at the man who got into the car.

Maida next called David Williamson from Port Orchard. He was one of Baruso's coworkers at Boeing, and he testified that he sold the MAC-10 to Baruso in December of 1980. Both Williamson and Roy White, the registered firearms dealer who completed the paperwork on the gun transfer, were reluctant witnesses and provided inconsistent statements. Williamson at one point claimed that Baruso told him the firearm was stolen, but this contradicted a prior statement he'd made.

Both Ade Domingo and Terri Mast testified to the exchange they had with Silme in the recovery room after Silme's surgery, including his acknowledgement that he'd named Ramil and Guloy. They both said he seemed intent on naming another hitman, one who had been shot in the leg. Terri, along with Emily Van Bronkhorst and John Foz, also testified about the union dispatch, gambling at canneries in Alaska, and the reform work Gene and Silme had pioneered. John described how he had found the last bullet slug on the office floor after becoming one of the dispatchers. Angel Doniego testified about the Tulisan gang and its criminal enterprise.

Robert San Pablo testified as to the statements Dictado made at the May 26 dispatch and the threats to Gene. He recounted in detail running into Dictado, Ramil, and Pilay the day after the dispatch when Pilay discussed the murders. He was not shaken on cross-examination other than having to explain why he didn't tell anyone of the murder plot. "I didn't think they would carry through with it" was his excuse.

In a surprise move, Joanne Maida called Tony Dictado as a hostile witness. He testified about the Tulisans, which he called a "group of friends," but would not say that either Ramil or Guloy were members of it. He did name Boy Pilay as a member, along with Boyse Campo and others. I presumed that Maida thought that although Dictado had tried to exculpate himself and the two defendants, the lasting impression on jurors would be the inconsistencies with much of the other testimony, including what Maida thought Ramil and Guloy might say.

Shortly after Dictado's testimony, Maida notified the court that her office would charge Dictado with two counts of first-degree aggravated murder of Silme Domingo and Gene Viernes. In the same statement, we learned that the police and prosecutor's office were trying to locate Boy Pilay to also testify, but were unable to locate him. Charging Dictado had a price: Pilay had absconded.

The next witness was crucial: Jaime Malabo was the only witness who could physically place the hitmen together near the union hall.

Jaime Malabo was the witness the CJDV supporters felt the most anxious about how his testimony would be received. Although he may have been well prepared by Joanne, I knew that his youth and great reluctance to come forward made his presence uncertain. I had no real conviction that he would even show up. Jaime had requested police protection before and during the trial, and the SPD was happy to oblige. Detective Boatman himself was assigned to escort Jaime to and from the courthouse. When Joanne called his name out in open court, I wiped my sweaty palms, gasped, and turned around to see him enter the courtroom.

The courtroom was dripping with tension when the boyish-looking Jaime nervously walked through the courtroom doors, took the witness stand, and looked down at his shoes. It was September 8, and his testimony lasted well into the following day. Jaime had seen the hitmen at a crucial time and place where others were unable to place them. Seeing Guloy carrying a brown grocery bag with Ramil right behind him confirmed Silme's dying declaration that they were involved. To our great relief, he had done well on the stand. But now came the cross.

Both defense counsel attacked Jaime's testimony on their cross-examination. Jim Grubb was able to establish that immediately after leaving the scene, Jaime drove to the West Seattle house of his friend Ross Landon, and that Ross and his friend Ferdie Orbino were protecting him from Tulisan reprisals. Jim implied that Orbino was a member of a rival gang, called the Ongoys, or Monkeys, who were at odds with the Tulisan gang, and that they had unduly influenced Jaime's testimony.

Jaime told the court that at first both of his friends advised him not to get involved at all. Only after they watched the case unfold in the press for weeks did Jaime come to the police and prosecutors, just ten days before the trial started.

When he was finished, the mood of the CJDV members was upbeat. Jaime's testimony had clearly made an impact on the jurors, and we expected convictions of both men.

When the defense presented their case, Jimmy Ramil and Ben Guloy each took the stand in their own defense. As we expected, they tried to create the alibi they both had been dealing Hi-Q, a high stakes gambling game, at the 609 Club in the ID on June 1. This was backed up, under oath, by a number of their gambling buddies and the club's owner, Charlie Penor. Guloy even claimed he had been a member of the KDP for six years, but it was clear no one in the courtroom took him seriously, including the jury.

But that wasn't the biggest surprise in the defense's testimony.

That occurred on Friday afternoon, September 11, at the very end of the trial, when Ramil's counsel Jim Grubb approached the bench. The judge dismissed the jury. In a discussion off the record but in open court, Jim informed the court he had been called by a man who stated he was an eyewitness to the murders, and after seeing the two men on trial in the courtroom earlier in the week, the caller realized that a miscarriage of justice was taking place.

I looked at Cindy, thunderstruck.

He claimed that neither of the defendants was the single person he saw going into and coming out of the Local 37 Union Hall on the afternoon of June 1. Grubb indicated that he had interviewed the witness, taken him to the scene of the murders, and found his recollection of events to be credible. He felt it was important that, as a neutral and independent eyewitness, he be allowed to testify.

Joanne Maida was apoplectic and objected to having an eleventh-hour mystery witness testify, especially since she'd had no opportunity to interview him. Judge Bever ruled that since Grubb hadn't known about the witness until very recently, the requirement to name him in pre-trial disclosures was satisfied. He gave Maida the weekend to interview the new witness and prepare to cross-examine him the following Monday when the trial resumed. We sweated out the weekend, unsure of what the next week would bring.

Maida interviewed the witness, LeVane Malvison Forsythe, by telephone. She found out later that he recorded the telephone call without her knowledge or consent. We never found out why: perhaps he was trying to draw Maida into some kind of prosecutorial misconduct and wanted a recording to prove it. However, recording without permission was illegal under Washington law at the time.

On September 15, Jim Grubb called Forsythe to testify. From the very beginning, everything about Forsythe seemed strange to me. He came to court in a rumpled grey suit with what looked to me like an Alaska Airlines plane ticket in his pocket. I thought, *This guy is heading out of town right after this.*

After establishing Forsythe was a project manager on large construction projects in Alaska and Washington, Grubb asked how it was that he happened to be at the corner of 2nd Extension South and Main Street on June 1. Forsythe testified that he parked his car at 4:15 p.m. at that location because he saw a phone booth and needed to call his architect, a man named Alex Bertulius of Seattle, before 4:30. He was trying to find Bertulius' office but had gotten lost.

Unable to reach him, Forsythe left the phone booth so that a "colored man" could make a call. While outside the phone booth, Forsythe saw a man walk into the union hall across the street, then come running out.

"He was in a hurry when he came out of the building, like, he tripped and almost fell," Forsythe said. He claimed the man was carrying something under his arm, which could have been the firearm depicted in a photo Grubb showed him. He stated the man got into a dark green Trans-Am or Firebird and drove off down 2nd Avenue. Grubb handed Forsythe a picture of the black Trans-Am registered to Dictado's wife, Carol Williams, which had been identified by other witnesses as being present at the scene.

"It's not this car, no." Forsythe explained that he got a good look at this individual both as he ran across the street and while he drove away. He had "Oriental eyes."

Grubb asked Jimmy Ramil to stand up and asked Forsythe, "Is this the man you saw?"

"No, absolutely not." Forsythe was resolute, and a burning anger filled my gut. What was happening? Cindy reached over and touched my leg, and I could see that same rage shining in the darkness of her eyes. She was just better at keeping it together.

Grubb asked Ben Guloy to stand. "Is that the man you saw?"

"No, absolutely not."

I looked for any sign that the jury was buying this fairy tale. Nemesio Jr., on Cindy's other side, took her hand.

Grubb asked Forsythe what drew his attention back to the union hall.

"This fella coming out, hollering for help."

"What did you do when you first saw the man come out and heard him hollering?"

"I asked him, you know, what's wrong?"

"What did he say?"

"He said he'd been shot. 'I'm shot.'" Forsythe said, "I asked him who shot him, you know, and he said he didn't know, but he knew who had it done."

A gasp came from the CJDV supporters, and I almost bolted out of my seat. Cindy's hand on my thigh, her nails grinding into my pants in a way that was nearly painful, kept me grounded.

Grubb continued, "Are you positive that he said he didn't know who had shot him?"

Forsythe nodded. "I'm positive of that, yes." Forsythe said the man gave him no names, but asked him to call an ambulance. He didn't want to move. Forsythe said he went back across the street to the phone booth, but the "colored" man was still on the phone and wouldn't give it up.

Next he said he went to his car and tried to get 911 on the CB, but was not able to get anyone. He said that happened in certain areas, so he got into his car and drove around the block, coming up the alley adjoining the hall. He parked and got out of his car, and at no time did he notice anybody in the alley. He could see a fellow bending over the man who had been hollering and heard them say that an ambulance was on the way. Forsythe testified that since help was on the way, and since he wasn't able to reach anyone on his CB radio, there was nothing he could do by sticking around. So he drove to the ferry terminal because he "really didn't want to get involved."

On the ferry back to Port Orchard where he lived with his wife, Rebecca, Forsythe wrote out a statement of what he had seen. This was admitted into evidence. Forsythe related that he talked to his wife and a neighbor, who was a retired naval officer, when he got home. His wife had heard about the shooting on the news and argued strongly for him not to get involved.

Forsythe testified that he and his wife followed the case in the news, and that during the trial, he had talked his wife into coming into the courthouse on August 27. There, he saw "two fellas coming in, handcuffed, out in the hall and I knew definitely it was neither one of these guys that was in that car, you know." He wrote down the names of the defense attorneys on the same paper as his statement and called Jim Grubb's office that same day. He offered to take a polygraph test to prove he was telling the truth, but Grubb's office told him that such an offer would not be admissible into evidence.

Tony Meyers, on behalf of Ben Guloy, asked a few clarifying questions before Joanne Maida started her cross-examination. She focused at first on the inconsistencies between Forsythe's statement he claimed he wrote on June 1 and his trial testimony. He wrote, for example, that he had gotten out of his car to grab a cup of coffee in a restaurant when he saw the guy hollering for help. She got him to describe the wounded gentleman as older, with a slight build, who "could have been Filipino," but Forsythe described him as "white," not black. Forsythe described a man with an accent "from the very little conversation we had." He explained that he used "slight" to indicate someone smaller than he was, and he weighed 200 pounds. When Maida pointed out that Silme was, in fact, 220 pounds at death, Forsythe explained that the man was bending over, hunched up in pain. Despite the gleam of sweat on Forsythe's forehead, and the quivering of his fleshy jowls, he refused to relent.

At the lunch hour, Cindy, Nemesio Jr., and I huddled in a corner of the law library, trying to make sense of what had just happened. "Jesus Christ, this one witness has tried to knock down every piece of the prosecution's case," I practically shouted.

Equally enraged, Cindy bit her lip. "Do you think the jury is buying this guy?"

I shrugged, though I wondered if either of them could see the sweat on my forehead. "Joanne better do something more dramatic on cross than nibble around the edges. She has to take him out."

Cindy and I went to the phone booth and called Terri. Cindy spoke: "We need an emergency CJDV meeting tonight. This trial just went south." The tension in her voice was palpable.

Back in the courtroom after the lunch break, Joanne Maida paced before the witness stand. In a moment that I'll never forget, she asked quietly, "Isn't it true, Mr. Forsythe, that you previously told another jury under oath that you were the secret witness…"

Jim Grubb rose from his seat, shouting, "Objection, Your Honor, as to the form of the question. I'll object to the subject matter, and ask the jury be excused." His face was beet red, and the jury was immediately excused.

During the colloquy that followed, Joanne explained that she wished to question Forsythe about his prior testimony that he was "the secret courier to Howard Hughes."

Cindy and I looked at each other with open mouths. Grubb pounced. "I believe that this witness, if asked, would indicate that he was questioned and that he took a polygraph at that time, that he passed a polygraph, and that he was subjected to a polygraph examination on three different occasions. I think that unless counsel is prepared to offer the transcript of the testimony and something that would substantiate what her allegations are," he paused, "the evidence should not be admitted."

Maida argued that this testimony would contradict Forsythe's statement that he had not wanted to get involved. She stated she had every reason "to attack the reason why Mr. Forsythe has come around at the end of this trial to give this type of testimony."

Judge Bever ruled quickly. "Inquiry may be made as to the testimonial background of this witness for appearances in court. Testimonial experience of a witness may be inquired into as going to the weight of the evidence offered by a witness. And to that extent, the Court will permit the line of questioning."

Grubb responded, "If counsel's going to be able to pursue that line of questioning, then I think I should be able to establish by the witness' testimony that, in fact, he took a polygraph and that, in fact, he passed the polygraph."

Judge Bever agreed. "Well, insofar as it relates to the subject matter of inquiry presently and not related to the instant case, if it's opened up, I suggest it'll be opened up all the way."

To which Maida replied, "All right. Then I'll take that risk."

Judge Bever told the bailiff, "You may bring in the jury."

As she began her questions again, Maida spoke with the confidence of a lioness on the hunt. "Mr. Forsythe, isn't it true that you previously told another jury, under oath, that you were the secret courier for Howard Hughes, who delivered the so-called Mormon will of Howard Hughes to Melvin Dummar in the Nevada desert?"

Forsythe said, "No, I didn't say that I was a secret courier."

"What did you say?"

"I said that I was the person that delivered the will, yes. I was the person who delivered it."

"And isn't it true that you told the same jury in 1978 an incredible tale ..." The defense attorneys cried out. The court sustained their chorus of objections, but Forsythe jumped in.

"No," he said, "I never went to any jury, I was never in a jury. I never was in the trial."

Maida questioned Forsythe about his claim to have worked with his father for Howard Hughes. Forsythe seemed comfortable answering the question. "Right, we did a lot of sets for Hughes, directly under his supervision at the Corrigan Ranch. My son now works for the same Hughes organization. I'm very friendly with Nadine Hensley, which is Hughes' secretary … As a matter of fact, last year she came up here and visited me. So I was given a document to deliver, I made the delivery. What happened to it after I made the delivery is not my concern."

Stopping midstride, Joanne turned to face him, her small frame filling the whole room. "Didn't you pop up as a surprise witness in the middle of that?"

Crimson swirled in Forsythe's cheeks, but he squinted with his narrow eyes. "No, I don't think I popped up. I think people were aware of me … There were a lot of people aware of me in the Hughes organization, including Bobby Maheu, which runs the Hughes organization in Nevada."

The mention of Robert Maheu sent chills down my spine. I had first come across the name through my personal interest in government reports about the Kennedy assassination, the Warren Commission Report, and later, the House Select Committee on Assassinations. I recognized Maheu as the ex-CIA agent who ran Hughes' operation in Nevada and who had been used by the Kennedy administration to contact the Mafia about possibly assassinating Fidel Castro. That Forsythe knew him, let alone claimed Maheu could vouch for him, was unbelievable.

I turned to Cindy and whispered, "Boy, do we need a meeting."

On redirect examination, Jim Grubb drew out that Forsythe gave a deposition, rather than during a trial before a jury, and had undergone and passed three separate polygraph tests, including one by Dr. Raskin, whom the US government itself used to administer polygraphs.

Then, acting as if nothing major had occurred, both Grubb and Meyers questioned Forsythe about additional details of what he had witnessed on the first of June. The witness was excused, and the trial recessed for the day.

At the hastily-called CJDV meeting that night, pandemonium reigned. Elaine Ko drew a chart with 'LeVane Malvison Forsythe?' scrawled at the top, followed by *Martian? Publicity Seeker? Professional Witness?*

Who was he? Where had he come from? And why was he with us right now? During our subsequent discussion, we focused on the many gaping holes in Forsythe's testimony, beginning with the fact he thought Silme was of "slight build" and spoke with an accent.

"That alone shows this guy wasn't properly prepared," Elaine said furiously.

Dale shook his head. "The fact Silme was born in the US and had no accent was a detail he would have no way of really knowing. Everything else he testified to was really damaging and carefully rehearsed. I don't think he is a lunatic – or Martian," he said, shooting Nemesio Jr. a quick look. "A professional witness is more like it. Either that or he's part of the higher-level cover-up by who-knows-who. Or maybe both."

Terri nodded, moving to the board, where she circled option number three. "He knocked down every major piece of evidence the prosecution had. Jim Grubb must have showed him what to say." She threw the marker down onto the desk.

"I'm just glad Joanne had the weekend to get book on this guy. I think her fiancé works for the feds. Maybe they had access to the NCIC database," I said, referring to the National Crime Information Center, the FBI's extensive database of criminal records. "That Mormon will was a huge deal."

The trial I referred to happened in 1978 as part of a battle for the enormous and far-flung corporate empire of the reclusive wealthy businessman Howard Hughes. A local Utah man, Melvin Dummar, had supposedly found Hughes wandering in the desert in the middle of the night and saved his life. In return, Hughes had re-written his will, leaving a small fortune to Dummar and a large sum, oddly, to the Mormon Church, of which Hughes had never been a member. The will was challenged in court, and declared a forgery.

What was mysterious to me was that Hughes, eccentric as he was, would have entrusted his new will to someone like Forsythe. Maybe Forsythe *had* worked for Hughes and Maheu?

"It seemed to me that Joanne had other information on him she wasn't using," I told the group. "It's just a hunch. The judge let her bring in the Mormon will, but was pretty limiting in what she could ask."

"We won't know the effect of this testimony until the verdict, I guess," Terri said, slumping down against the wall, exhausted like we all were. "But I think Joanne raised enough alarm bells about him to cause them to doubt."

I kept Terri's words in my mind as I listened to the closing arguments on September 21. I again sat next to Cindy, hoping some of her amazing inner strength would rub off on me.

The court informed the jury that to convict of the crime of aggravated murder, the defendants had to have acted with premeditation and that more than one victim was killed as a result of a single act of the defendants or as a result of a common scheme or plan.

Joanne Maida's argument was strong. "The murders here were not random killings that were committed in the heat of the moment. They were intended to be a power statement to the Chinatown District, and they have been a very powerful statement indeed.

"Under the law," Joanne continued, "it is not necessary to show which of the defendants actually pulled the trigger. Silme Domingo identified both Jimmy and Ben as the killers, and there is also the possibility that other people were involved. Accomplices in this scheme."

She described Boy Pilay and his statement to Robert San Pablo that Jimmy Ramil used a suppressor and that Tony Baruso paid $5,000 for the hit. She stated that Boy Pilay was sent to Alaska outside of the reformed dispatch procedures to remind San Pablo to keep quiet.

She reviewed the evidence that was presented, building to the meeting between Tony Baruso and Tony Dictado on May 30, and she even described the probable conversations between the two about the murders, despite strenuous defense objections that she engaged in speculation.

What surprised me was that Joanne chose to place the onus of who originated the murder conspiracy on Dictado rather than Baruso. She suggested that Tony Dictado implored Tony Baruso to provide his gun and money for the murders. She carefully ignored the testimony that the meeting was first proposed by Baruso.

This speculation was not something Maida had discussed with me, and not surprisingly, it struck me as totally backwards. But I also realized that the jury would more easily believe Tony Dictado hatched the murder plot. And this wasn't Baruso on trial.

Maida started to wrap up her statement.

In retrospect, perhaps Gene Viernes should have compromised himself. If he had, he might still be alive today. But from what we know of Gene Viernes, that would have been quite unlikely, having grown up in poverty and worked in the canneries at an early age. He had seen the discrimination and the working conditions and the poor union practices... and so he was killed because he refused to compromise himself...

She drew out the fact that Silme had not only named Ramil and Guloy, but had corrected the spelling of Jimmy's name when the firefighter Urpman wrote it down wrong.

"One must consider Silme Domingo's character, his reputation, his intelligence in assessing the reliability of his identification ... the first Filipino to obtain a Phi Beta Kappa status at the University of Washington." She concluded on a powerful note.

Silme Domingo fought back with what must have only been a tremendous effort to overcome. If his final words meant anything at all, they spoke the undeniable truth of the two men who were accomplices to his death. Nothing else in this case approaches the truth more than the last words uttered by Silme Domingo brought on by the clarity of his impending death. It is upon his strength, his integrity, his honest, that this case is built ... Those two names cut out all the verbiage, all the frailty of human memory, all the excuses, all the alibis. And on the truth of the words that spilled out of the mouth of Silme Domingo, the State rests its case.

I thought to myself, *what a great finish to a strong trial.* Neither Grubb nor Meyers was up to the task and their closing arguments paled in comparison. We went home to await a verdict. It came soon enough. On September 24, the jury indicated they had reached a verdict. Joanne called us and we put out the word to the community. It spread rapidly. Judge Bever's courtroom was tense as we waited for the jury to enter. We had again filled the courtroom. Ade and Nemesio Domingo Sr. sat stoically in front. The four months of building tension rubbed hard into me and I shook as I took my seat next to Cindy in the crowded courtroom.

When the jury foreman solemnly handed the verdict to the bailiff, my heart skipped a beat and I hung my head. The jurors had no expressions. Then the bailiff passed the paper to the judge, who looked at it, asked the defendants to rise, and spoke in a clear, strong voice. "The jury finds the defendant Jimmy Ramil ..." He hesitated. "Guilty of the crime of aggravated first-degree murder in the murder of Silme Domingo."

Huge relief. I squeezed Cindy's hand. The judge continued: Same for Gene Viernes. Same with Guloy for both.

Unanimous. Conclusive. Total victory.

But there were no cheers of victory from us. No celebrations or parties. Just the sober recognition that we had a long way to go. With the verdicts, both Ramil and Guloy would spend the rest of their lives in prison with no possibility of parole.

After the verdict was returned, Ade Domingo, surrounded by her family, rose to leave the courtroom. Ben Guloy's mother came up to her with tears in her eyes and said, "We have both lost our sons."

CHAPTER FOURTEEN:

THE PATH TO MARCOS

September 1981
Seattle

Even as the CJDV prepared for and monitored the trial of Jimmy Ramil and Ben Guloy, and then celebrated their convictions, the legal team continued to work to refine our theories on the middle and higher levels of the conspiracy. We also researched the legal basis of filing separate, civil lawsuits against those responsible for the murders.

Under the Civil War-era Civil Rights Act (42 USCA Sections 1983 and 1985) and the *Bivens* doctrine, a conspiracy to violate one's civil rights could result in a lawsuit being brought against the perpetrators. Our research showed a civil case could be brought against all of those who had conspired against a group of people based upon their national origin and/or their exercise of free speech. But first we needed evidence. In all of this, the support and advice we got from the legal team for Karen Silkwood was invaluable.

Silkwood had been a nuclear worker at the Kerr-McGee plant in Oklahoma. She had been seriously contaminated by radiation at work, and after raising a stink and offering to provide secret documents to a reporter from the *New York Times*, in 1974 she was mysteriously run off the road and killed.

The legal team representing her estate brought a lawsuit against the Kerr-McGee Corporation in 1979. After what was the longest trial in Oklahoma history, the jury awarded $505,000 in general and compensatory damages and $10 million in punitive damages to the Silkwood family. The Wyoming "buckskin cowboy" lawyer Gerry Spence was the chief trial attorney for the estate, but most of the investigative and pre-trial work was performed by Daniel Sheehan and his investigative team, headed by Father Bill Davis at the Christic Institute.

In phone discussions and personal meetings that were arranged with utmost secrecy and security, the Silkwood team provided us with much-needed investigative advice and resources.

Father Davis, specifically, proved to be an outstanding investigator. Formerly a Jesuit priest and an ardent adherent of liberation theology, he willingly took on the task of gathering more information about Gene Viernes' trip to the Philippines by personally retracing Gene's steps from Seattle to Oakland, then the Philippines, Hawaii, and back to Seattle.

We employed others as well, including Christopher Hershey, the CJDV activist who had written the "Martyr's Song," but who also had investigative experience. Hershey wrote a detailed report on Tony Baruso, including his personal background and employment history, highlighting his links to the Marcos regime, Ferdinand Marcos personally, and the Alaska seafood industry.

By far the most promising information came from a referral from an out-of-state attorney with experience in federal civil rights litigation. They warned us that the guy was a real spook – a former military intelligence officer who went by "Bill" – with anonymous sources in a number of US intelligence agencies. But they vouched for his reliability.

We first met Bill in the presence of his attorney in Jim Douglas' Seattle law office. Bill was tall, tan, and of military bearing. Before he would say anything else, he started debugging Jim's conference room, cautioning us not to say anything sensitive while he completed his work. When he was satisfied there was no one listening or recording, we had a preliminary discussion of the scope of his work. He established his bona fides as a former military intelligence officer with close ties to various US intelligence agencies.

"So what can you do for us, Bill?" I asked.

"That depends on what you want and how much you want to pay. I suggest that I start by making a few inquiries of some of my sources to see if anything useful turns up." His tone was measured and relaxed. "Then, if the inquiry looks fruitful to you, we can create a game plan and a budget for further investigation. Some of this I can accomplish on secure communications, but other interviews will have to be in person. Which means travel costs, including for me and my counsel."

I was relieved we didn't have to commit to a ton of money right off the bat. I asked him what agencies he thought he could approach first. He said the FBI and Naval Intelligence were the two most logical places. "The navy does a lot of dirty work for the CIA, and the Naval Investigative Service has to have an interest in the anti-Marcos movement opposed to the Subic Bay base."

"Great. Let's start there and see what we come up with."

We paid his attorney their initial retainer. I was somewhat skeptical, but also relieved that Bill seemed to have no political or ideological motivation. He was simply doing this for the money, which didn't bother us a bit. He was trained and seemed well connected. We couldn't expect ideological purity from a spook. He said he would start right away, contacting his sources to find out what he could about the murders, including what role, if any, the Marcos regime played, and whether any US intelligence agencies were involved. He would have a preliminary report with a "go" or "no go" recommendation within a few weeks.

We purposefully did not tell Bill some key details about Gene's travels or his associations, including that he had carried money to the anti-Marcos groups and the amount ($2,900). Our intent was to see if his sources had access to information about Gene and Silme that was not publicly known, but that we had or could verify on our own.

It was perhaps no coincidence that we received Bill's preliminary investigative report on September 18, 1981, only a week after Forsythe perjured himself in the Ramil and Guloy trial and shortly before the murder convictions were rendered. Forsythe's attempt to throw the trial and the FBI's abrupt intrusion into the murder investigation had made us more suspicious that sinister forces were involved in covering up this murder. Bill's report confirmed our worst suspicions.

Bill had made initial contact with six independent sources of information within the FBI, Naval Investigative Service, and other US intelligence agencies. The names of the agencies were not specifically mentioned in the written report, but were disclosed to us verbally. The sources themselves were only identified by letters. Five of the six sources were able to provide detailed and incriminating information from the files of their respective agencies. One source warned Bill not to get involved in the case.

According to Bill's sources, Gene and Silme were part of a "communist element" within the US. Their files were red flagged and classified for national security purposes. One source indicated that Marcos' intelligence agency and one or more US intelligence agencies had expressed interest in Gene's activities in the Philippines and the US in the early part of 1981. The US State Department had recently made inquiries into the murders, although it was not clear how.

Another key source, V-1, initially provided detailed information about the murders that corroborated what Bill received from the others. Then, on August 23, V-1 contacted Bill. He warned him that the sixth source – the one who did not want Bill to follow this case – was personally involved in the investigation of Gene and could not be trusted. We understood that this sixth source was in the FBI. As a result, Bill elected not to re-contact that source lest he be compromised.

Bill set up a series of in-person follow-up meetings with his sources as well as one new contact. One source told him that US intelligence had information that Gene had delivered a large sum in cash and/or negotiables, estimated to be $290,000, to the armed opposition in the Philippines. The new source indicated that the documents he expected to be able to find on Gene, including his re-entry paperwork to the US after his trip, could not be located.

On September 9, V-1 reported that the documents about Gene that he had seen previously had also been purged from the files of that agency. He stated that the involvement of US intelligence in investigating Silme and Gene was being covered up, and that the "cat's out of the bag" about Bill's interest in the murders and cover-up. He opined that the US government had surveillance on Gene and Silme and was aware the two activists had been in danger.

In the report, V-1 stated that "a deep pocket paid for this one" and that "it was the Philippines." V-1 also indicated there had potentially been a meeting in mid-May 1981 between a local consular official, a lieutenant colonel from the armed forces of the Philippines, and Tony Baruso – likely related to the murders.

On September 14, another source, C, told Bill that Gene and Silme were the subjects of routine surveillance by US intelligence agencies in Seattle and Northern California. We understood this included the FBI in Seattle, and the FBI and Naval Intelligence in the Bay Area; in particular, the NIS operating out of Alameda Naval Air Station. The source stated he had seen one report which noted that Gene had carried a "large amount of money from the US to anti-

Marcos organizations in the Philippines during the month of March 1981."

V-1 and C both reported the same information, even though they had access to different documents in different files at different agencies. We believed this confirmation by two sources underscored its reliability.

C also stated that the US agency files about Gene included Philippine intelligence documents. He saw a report on Gene's activities while in the Philippines from a US intelligence group operating there. We assumed this was the CIA or the NIS. There were file cabinets full of documents on the KDP. Another source stated he saw two folders that had been purged, and that the cabinets and files on the KDP were banded **National Security** with very limited access.

C also mentioned a US Congressional Subcommittee that was considering holding hearings on the US-Marcos relationship. When a group like that starts a probe like that, he said, the files tended to disappear. Bill advised us, as his sources had him, to immediately bring Freedom of Information Act (FOIA) requests to all relevant agencies, to all of their offices, on behalf not only of Gene and Silme, but also the KDP and its entire leadership.

Bill told us that Tony Baruso had called the State Department three times within twenty-four hours of the murders, and these calls each lasted between three and nine minutes. One of his sources had seen photographs in the FBI files of the inside of Silme and Terri's apartment on Beacon Hill, and the KDP headquarters on College Ave. He strongly urged us to do everything we could to figure out who could have taken those pictures, and to reassess our security measures, lest that person or informant still be operational.

It was so much more than we were prepared to hear. When the CJDV leadership team met to assess the significance of this report in late September, we were dumbfounded. Our discussion that night ranged far and wide, and our conclusions were reached only after a lot of thought and collective input. Finally, we wrote out eight key findings from Bill's report.

1. Silme Domingo and Gene Viernes were leaders of the KDP, a "communist/socialist" organization which was a "burden" on the US-Marcos relationship. Their murders were paid for by a "deep pocket" (the Philippines).

2. Marcos intelligence believed that Gene carried $290,000 to aid the opposition to Marcos.

3. Reports in US intelligence files kept on the KDP were sent to Marcos' intelligence apparatus.

4. Leni Marin – a KDP member and Filipino-American who sought exile in the US to escape the Marcos regime and now lived in Seattle – was under specific "intense surveillance."

5. FBI Special Agent George Fisher in Seattle was involved.

6. Tony Baruso had a high-level, top secret, US national security clearance.

7. Marcos' and General Ver's intelligence "octopus," the National Intelligence and Security Agency (NISA), was the relevant operational intelligence command center with access to US intelligence files.

8. The murders were committed in "pseudo-amateur style" to mask the true motives and plotters.

There it was in a nutshell. Unbelievable. We then compared the report to what we knew and/or suspected.

Geline Avila informed us that there was a KDP member in the Bay Area named Monty Martinez who she strongly suspected was an informant for the navy. He took a lot of pictures at KDP events, was always interested in finding out who was traveling to the Philippines, who was in leadership of various chapters, etc. If her suspicions were correct, we reasoned, the navy informant might have found out about

Gene's trip to the Philippines and reported it to his control agent in the navy.

When we learned that someone in US intelligence informed their counterpart Philippine intelligence officers that Gene gave $290,000 to the opposition, we were astounded. We didn't think it was an accident that someone had misplaced a decimal point, and we reasoned that information would have sent the vaunted Marcos intelligence apparatus into a stepped-up operational mode, including conducting surveillance on Gene and the Philippines, Hawaii, and Seattle.

Marcos had made a number of press statements that the KMU received foreign money. He also publicly accused anti-Marcos forces of being couriers for foreign money to support the opposition. Had the regime believed the money with Gene came from the People's Republic of China? Did they think Gene was funding the New People's Army (NPA) in the countryside or the Communist Party of the Philippines (CPP)?

I couldn't wrap my head around this theory. Despite the rhetoric, surely the Marcos regime knew the KDP had broken ties with the CPP and NPA, and was critical of Maoism and China's world view? Plus, the KDP couldn't raise $290,000 — or anything near that. Marcos must have known that.

When it came to Leni Marin, Bill's report seemed ominous. We had never mentioned Leni's name to Bill, let alone her significance to the KDP and her work for the CJDV. She was not present in any meeting with him.

Leni lived with Mila De Guzman, the Filipina-American whose family Gene stayed with while he was in Manila. Knowing Leni was being closely watched was ominous, given her close and ongoing political alliance with Gene and Silme. Such monitoring evidenced a far-reaching intelligence operation which defined the supposed "threat" to the Marcos regime posed by the KDP very broadly—not limited only to the senior leadership.

On the other hand, knowing that Special Agent Zavala's boss George Fisher was involved was not a surprise at all. It confirmed our suspicions that the local FBI would thwart any serious investigation: or worse, help in covering up the murders. Knowing Fisher was involved helped confirm our suspicion that Forsythe was an undercover agent or FBI informant, but it also raised additional questions: was he a professional witness who tried to exonerate the hitmen? We believed Fisher was a holdover from the Hoover days of the FBI and may well have been part of its counter-intelligence program against the Left. Or did he know beforehand that the murder would occur and was dispatched to watch it come down? Either way, it was a cover-up, but the former theory was far more sinister.

As to who could have taken the photographs of Silme and Terri's apartment and the KDP headquarters, we discussed and ruled out some names, and our suspicions focused on Paul Liam, a navy veteran who had tried to befriend many KDP members and who frequented the Anti-Martial Law Alliance (AMLA) activities. Like the suspicious navy man in the Bay Area, he had been constantly taking pictures of activists at various meetings and rallies and had certainly been inside both Silme's apartment and the KDP headquarters. Paul had ingratiated himself with Ade Domingo and a few KDP activists, paying special attention to them, bringing them food, taking their pictures and sending them copies, running errands, and the like.

The information in the State Department files about Tony Baruso was explosive. Why would he need a national security clearance, let alone a high-level one? Perhaps it was routine for every Boeing employee, but we agreed it bore further investigation. If Baruso really was tied to the US intelligence apparatus, this confirmed our theory he was involved as the go-between for Marcos' military intelligence to the hitmen.

The fact that the FBI and NIS had extensive files on the KDP, including knowledge of Gene's trip to and activities in the Philippines, confirmed KDP's leader Bruce Occena's worst fears. We had to assume the government had access to detailed information about all of our personal habits, travel plans, political beliefs, and contacts.

Not everyone saw Gene and Silme's murders as pseudo-amateur, an observation which required some discussion. "That does not describe Ramil and Guloy," John Caughlan argued. "They were hired executioners. It wasn't a slipshod plan. They had a trigger man, a decoy, a lookout, and a getaway driver. All but Ramil came with some deniability. Six shots with the execution piece and it's done. Nobody lives. If Silme didn't ..." He stopped. We all looked down.

We had been through the details of Silme's death so many times, but we weren't growing callous. Sometimes it was just too hard.

I was next to speak. "I think this is saying that they were not killed in a car bomb like Letelier. They were not gunned down by a sniper, in broad daylight, like JFK or Dr. King. This was made to look like hot-headed Filipinos fighting over gambling, not a hit by a foreign government." Many people nodded, but there was no reason we needed unity. All possibilities were open for discussion.

Setting the report down, we stared at one another. I could see the agitation play out on my friends' faces. This really did change everything

"Those sons of bitches," I seethed. "We can't let this stand."

Our political experience had steeled us to believe that the US might well be involved on some level. Now, knowing we were right shattered any remaining illusions that the murders resulted from a mere dispute over dispatch, that the FBI was really investigating a Hobbs Act violation, that the prosecuting authorities would go after the higher levels of the murder conspiracy, and that the Marcos regime and its American allies would eventually be held accountable.

We got to work. Jim and John were tasked with drafting detailed FOIA requests to all of the federal agencies for any files related to the KDP and its leadership. Those started going out a week later.

There were powerful forces aligned against us and many unknown agents standing in the shadows, intent on blocking our way. Doors would slam shut, documents would disappear, and witnesses would vanish. This we knew. But with that knowledge, we were armed and steeled for the fight. We needed to outsmart the cover-up and it wasn't going to be easy.

CHAPTER FIFTEEN:

NEW PRIORITIES

December 1981
Seattle

As we looked ahead to 1982, the CJDV published an *Update* which set the stage. Looking at Ramil and Guloy's life sentences, Cindy wrote: *The sentence is just although it will not bring my brother back. This is just the beginning of our search for justice. We have a long way to go but we are determined to see this effort to the end no matter how long it takes.*

The Rank and File's plans to rid the union of Baruso went exactly as planned. As the work crews from Alaska came back from the summer season, reform-minded activists sought them out to talk about why Baruso needed to go and how a reformed union, under Terri's leadership, would best protect members against both the industry and the gangster elements.

There was no point in trying to convince them that the Marcos regime was involved in the murders. It was enough that they agreed to vote Baruso out of office, paving the way for Terri and her supporters to win and govern going forward.

The ILWU had brought charges against Baruso and Abe Cruz, the Local 37 member who had traveled to the ILWU Convention in Hawaii, for election fraud tied to the forged ballots in the international union election. A five-person adjudicative body appointed by the top leadership of the ILWU in San Francisco (which we called the International) conducted an investigation and trial, and found Baruso and Cruz guilty. The International did not automatically strip Baruso of his current office, but it certainly helped convince union members that Baruso should be recalled.

Despite efforts from some who were close to the old guard to disrupt the balloting or intimidate members, a record number of votes were cast – each filled in, sealed, and secured in a locked vault in the union office until the December vote count. As the ballots were being slowly counted in the Local 37 Union Hall under the careful supervision of the International representative, it became clear that Baruso's hold on the union and its members was about to meet its end. Terri announced the decision and those present celebrated by singing "Solidarity Forever." The Union makes us strong! The reform movement was again victorious. Baruso was recalled by an overwhelming majority.

The victory party was held at a local tavern, and scores of union members and well-wishers attended. Terri was gracious in victory, extending outstretched hands to union members from all backgrounds.

The CJDV, meanwhile, was focused on preparing the community for the Dictado trial, which was scheduled to start in April. The famous – and expensive – Seattle criminal defense attorney John Henry Browne, who had represented Ted Bundy in the infamous string of serial murders of young women, took on Dictado's defense. We speculated, but did not know, whose deep pockets were paying for his defense.

The legal team was still trying to convince the prosecuting attorney's office to charge Pilay and Baruso with the murders. Boy Pilay was missing, and no one seemed to know where he might have gone. Baruso still worked at Boeing, and had little contact with the union since his recall.

The FBI's investigation into the Hobbs Act violation was, not surprisingly, going nowhere. We were still drafting and sending FOIA requests, but had received few documents in response. There was no smoking gun. Still, we moved forward in drafting the complaint which would launch our civil suit against the Marcos regime. Famed trial attorney Leonard Schroeter, a friend of John Caughlan, agreed to participate in our strategy meetings. He brought his superior intellect as well as his considerable experience in challenging government wrongdoing. Len had represented writers, many Jewish, accused of treason by the Soviet government in the 1970s and was instrumental in getting them out of the Soviet Union to Israel. We saw his firm — Schroeter Goldmark and Bender — although not yet officially on board, as the strong, mainstream presence that would add the "respectable types" Bruce Occena wanted.

Liz Schott spearheaded our research into how to sue a foreign government and a foreign head of state. We discovered that under the Foreign Sovereign Immunities Act (FSIA), we could get jurisdiction in a US federal court on a foreign government whose agents had committed a tort (or civil wrong) in the US. The Act provided a solid legal basis for federal jurisdiction, which would allow us to serve process and subpoenas in the case nationally, but the catch was that the trial would be held before a judge, not a jury.

The bigger challenges would be the head of state immunity, which the Marcoses would certainly assert and almost certainly win, and the sovereign immunity of the US government, which we planned to bring in as a defendant. The US government, we reasoned, could be liable for participating in the widespread violation of the constitutional rights of Gene and Silme, as well as the opposition to Marcos in the US, under the Civil Rights Act.

The truth, though, was that we still lacked hard evidence to prove our case. We needed proof that Marcos sent spies to the US to keep track of his opposition. Someone had a vague recollection about a State Department "White Paper" detailing the role of foreign spies, but I could not track it down.

The wait was frustrating. I worked alone, sixty to seventy hours a week, from the tiny former ACWA office on 8th Street, eating dim sum for lunch at the Four Seasons across the street every day and getting even more out of shape. I continued to bring in some fees from cases I had settled or referred out to supplement my small salary from the CJDV. While it was inspiring to work in the same place where Nemesio Jr., Gene, and Silme had plotted their race discrimination cases years earlier, the cramped quarters and loneliness took a toll.

Cindy and I had taken a much-needed vacation in Puerto Vallarta, Mexico, and we'd had fun. But our relationship was struggling. I loved Cindy, but I seemed incapable of doing what was necessary to maintain that relationship. I'd forget to call her, missed important anniversaries, and could not commit to living with her. The usual excuses were piling up like soiled dishes in a bottomless sink that I just wanted to make disappear.

Cindy had flown back to Seattle for the recall, and I had stopped off to visit my mom, Elsie, in Los Angeles. My mom was a women's physical education and social studies teacher who now ran an inner-city occupational learning center, where students from every race, nationality, and income status participated in Elsie's Lab. From her, I'd learned the importance of hard work and sticking up for what you believed in. She believed that cultural and racial diversity was the natural order of the universe and lived that principle throughout her life. She was a powerful influence in my life, and my time with her gave me some needed perspective.

I missed the recall election victory party because of a delayed flight from LA. As I sat in the LAX departure lounge listening to the whoops and hollers of victory over the phone, I wondered if I would ever again have a normal life.

The leadership of the CJDV had decided to stop wearing the bulletproof vests and carrying firearms. We thought they might be necessary again if we ever got Baruso charged, but for now, they seemed like more trouble than they were worth. We were still vigilant about security, but not as concerned that the Tulisan gang would come after us.

The meetings with the CJDV, though, were tough. I was coming under increased criticism during our endless "criticism/self-criticism" sessions at the end of each meeting. The goal of the exercise was to allow each of us to reflect on the meeting and offer any ideas we had on how to make it better. It started with self-criticism, followed by our critique of how others had interacted.

My problem, which others raised repeatedly that fall and which I accepted, was not including everyone in the discussion. I came from a privileged white male background, with a college education and law degree, and I tended to "pontificate" about what I thought was best, without drawing upon the experiences, comments, and leadership of others. Patterns of classism, racism, sexism, and individualism all came to the fore when I discounted the value or importance of what others (mainly women and people of color) were saying.

I remembered how Silme used to call me on my shit. He always said that my saving grace was that I was open to criticism and took it seriously. But he cautioned me, as only a good friend could, that I needed to "put it in my front pocket," meaning I should take responsibility for changing my behavior and not always expect others to correct me when those traits manifested themselves. I missed Silme. My shit was in my front pocket where Silme put it. It wasn't comfortable there, but it was real.

Cindy and I broke up at the end of the year. She expressed her disappointment with my failure to connect fully, and I didn't disagree. Thankfully, it didn't dramatically affect our working relationship.

Terri's call for unity was well received, and in January 1982, she ran unopposed and was elected the first woman president of Local 37 ILWU. Other members of the Rank and File Committee were elected to offices and positions on the executive board.

The decision to go back into the union hall on June 2 had been the right thing to do.

I had cast my lot with this movement, and with Bruce, Terri, Cindy, and the rest of the CJDV. I just had to believe. I was in it for the duration.

CHAPTER SIXTEEN:

ZAVALA

Early 1982
Seattle

As we entered the new year, preparations for the Dictado trial in April were well underway. We heard through Dictado's attorney, John Henry Browne, that his client was willing to enter a plea bargain and "name names," but that the state's prosecutors would accept nothing less than a plea of guilty to first-degree aggravated murder, which carried a mandatory sentence of life imprisonment without the possibility of parole. Dictado and Browne expected better treatment.

The CJDV legal team encouraged Joanne Maida to work out a plea bargain that would guarantee Dictado's testimony against Tony Baruso. Although she didn't rule it out, she didn't seem to jump at the opportunity either.

We were never sure if Browne was being straight with us, but I became convinced that the thought of Dictado turning state's evidence was viewed with great alarm by those who were engineering the cover-up.

Meanwhile, we continued to get disturbing news about the FBI investigation. I was in regular contact with Special Agent Lee Zavala, who expressed frustration at the lack of progress and had been increasingly willing to share information with us. He hinted at the state of the investigation without providing any confidential information about the grand jury proceedings, which had apparently been convened. Then he dropped a bombshell.

Zavala told me he didn't think there would be a federal indictment against Baruso for violating the Hobbs Act, because the US Attorney was considering offering Baruso immunity from prosecution if he agreed to testify against Dictado.

I told him the US Attorney had it backwards. "Why would any self-respecting prosecutor let a higher-up walk in exchange for getting a conviction of the lower level?"

Zavala offered no answer.

Full transactional immunity, meaning no charges could be brought against Baruso for the murder "transaction," would have dealt our justice efforts a fatal blow. The only way to get Baruso to turn state's evidence was getting him charged and threatened with life imprisonment.

I told Zavala that Dictado was going to be convicted in his upcoming trial no matter what. After all, the same proven witnesses – Robert San Pablo, Guy Reynolds, Patricia Wilson, and Jaime Malabo – would testify. We had the same police crime scene investigation and Silme's dying declaration. Baruso's testimony wouldn't add anything, and would likely be viewed with suspicion by a jury given the albatross of guilt that hung around his neck.

In late January 1982, there was more bad news. When Zavala called me on a Monday afternoon with a certain urgency in his voice, I agreed to meet him right away in a dark Irish tavern about ten blocks from the federal building where he worked. I ordered a Guinness, and he had a Diet Coke.

His brow was furled in anger. "You won't believe what happened."

"Try me. I have seen it all in this case."

"First, George Fisher called me on the carpet a couple of weeks ago, claiming that I'd forgotten to secure a key document from the union files. It was a letter on Local

37 stationery that Baruso wrote to folks at Peter Pan, recommending San Pablo as the foreman. Not exactly a smoking gun in the first place, right?"

"I remember turning that letter over to you," I said.

He traced lines through the condensation on the sides of his glass. "Right, but Fisher claimed the original was not in the FBI files. So I went into the office on the weekend to check it out. Sure enough, the original letter was there, just misplaced in the wrong file. So I took the letter, made copies, kept one for myself, and put the original right on Fisher's desk so he saw it first thing Monday morning."

"Good work."

"They were going to scapegoat me for why the investigation hadn't produced results. I'm sure of it." He seemed less than triumphant, so I pressed him.

"But you shut that gambit down. Now you have the proof."

"Yeah, I thought that was the end of it." Lee looked past my Guinness out the window to the now dark alley.

"Now what?" I could not wait to hear the other shoe drop.

"Okay, don't freak out. Late last week I was offered a job as the head of security of Sealand Corporation. It's a better salary. I have a family to take care of and mouths to feed ... so I took it. I'm out of the Bureau."

"What the hell?" I tried to control my rage but still jumped to my feet, knees hitting the underside of the table and nearly knocking over the glasses. "No way. They're buying you off! You're the only FBI agent to do anything on this case."

He shrugged.

"When did you apply for this job?" I was still fuming.

"That's the thing." He hesitated. "I never applied for this job."

"Are you kidding me?" My words hung in the air for a second, then crashed to the sawdust floor. "Let me get this straight. You are the lead FBI agent on a high profile murder investigation. Your boss tries to scapegoat you for not properly investigating, but you bust that ploy wide open. Then a key seafood company makes you an unsolicited job offer to head their security department, and boom, you're gone?"

"Pretty much, yeah." Lee met my gaze, and I saw a hint of regret.

"And you don't see anything fishy about that?"

"There's a silver lining, Mike. I haven't told you the good news."

"I am all fucking ears."

He didn't react to the scathing tone in my voice. "Before I left the Bureau, I took the documents I received from Local 37 and compared them with the documents we subpoenaed from the Union's Health and Welfare Plan. Lynn Domingo had suggested we look at them because she noted something strange."

"And?"

He settled back in his chair. "You know the industry let Baruso run that benefit program with very little insight, right?"

I sat back down, my anger settling. "What did you find?"

"I think Baruso was double dipping. He was reimbursed by the plan for his expenses related to his management responsibility, and then was paid for the same expenses by the union."

"That slimy son of a bitch." I shook my head. "Doesn't surprise me a bit." After a minute, I asked, "So what can you do with that now that you aren't with the FBI anymore?"

"I shipped the documents over to the Department of Labor attorneys who handle welfare plan fraud with a note saying they should look into what I found. They're really experienced in these cases … and they have no axe to grind."

"You pulled an end run around Fisher." I appreciated the effort, though at the time I didn't expect anything would ever come of it to benefit our investigation. The more pressure on Baruso, though, the better.

"I think so," Zavala said. He took out his wallet to pay for my beer. "I need to get home. My wife is so excited. We even get to stay in Seattle. Sealand's headquarters is in Tacoma. It's a really good company."

I nodded and stood with him, shaking his hand. I was sorry to see him go. "Well, thanks for filling me in on this stuff. I'll let the families know you are a stand up guy." I meant it.

Before he turned away, I asked one more favor. "Do you think you can send Norm Maleng a copy of Clevenger's testimony? The whole idea that Baruso was laughing at the size of the bullet holes just might tip the scales and get them to charge him." I was ever the optimist.

Zavala shook his head slowly. "It's out of my hands. It's up to Fisher and Anderson. Take care and good luck." He left the pub, turned right up the alley, and disappeared into the foggy night.

I never saw him again.

CHAPTER SEVENTEEN:

DICTADO'S TRIAL

April 1982
Seattle

The trial of Tony Dictado started in the King County courtroom of Superior Court Judge Terrence Carroll on April 23, 1982. Judge Carroll was a relatively new judge but had earned the respect of the bar for being thoughtful, careful, and well prepared. He granted a motion brought by Jim Douglas, on behalf of the CJDV, to move the trial to a larger courtroom, and our supporters filled the space every day.

From the beginning, the trial went well for the prosecution. The same eyewitnesses who testified at the Ramil and Guloy trial appeared again. When Baruso was called by the prosecution, he invoked the Fifth Amendment's privilege against self-incrimination to any question about the two slain men or the union. Robert San Pablo again testified consistently and effectively about the conversations he had heard about Dictado's intention to kill Gene.

There was dramatic testimony from the Dillingham plant managers, Norm Van Vacter and Denny Plagerman, about how shaken San Pablo was when they announced to the cannery crew on June 2 that Silme and Gene had been killed. According to them, San Pablo was upset and said: "My god, it's not true. I didn't think they would do it." They testified that they had shown him a dispatch list, and he'd circled Ramil and Dictado as the ones who "did it."

After that, Van Vacter said he'd asked San Pablo to identify the Tulisan gang members on the various dispatch lists to make sure they were not sent to his cannery.

Browne repeatedly attacked the credibility of the eyewitnesses, especially those who testified they observed Dictado's black Trans-Am with the golden eagle decal, which had an orange tinge, as it drove away quickly from the murder scene. Browne was relentless in trying to get them to identify Jimmy Ramil's Firebird, which was green, also with a gold decal, or Boyse Campo's black Trans-Am with a different design. But these eyewitnesses held their own.

On May 6, Dictado took the stand to testify under Browne's careful, direct examination. The attorney had the unenviable chore of getting Dictado to testify in ways that would not contradict his sworn testimony in the Ramil and Guloy trial, which had been read to the jury. At the time, Dictado denied having any conversation or argument with Gene Viernes during the May 26 dispatch to Dillingham. He'd said he went to the union hall at Baruso's request on May 30, but denied there was a private conversation in Baruso's office; Baruso just said hello and then invited him to a party with the Dillingham crew. He'd admitted he had a black Trans-Am — a 1980 model with an orange decal on the hood — but claimed his pregnant wife, Carol Williams, had the car on June 1 to shop for baby clothes. He'd stated that he was present at the 514 gambling club on June 1 between four and five o'clock, and that both Ramil and Guloy were also there. He'd testified that the dealers for Filipino gambling games got five percent of the pots in the ID and ten percent in Alaska.

Browne eased into the direct examination by reviewing Dictado's background. Dictado was born in the Philippines and had three children still there. He came to United States in 1975 after working as a prison guard, and he studied political science at a two-year college. He now had a ten-month-old child living in the US.

Dictado stated that he first went up to Alaska in January 1977 and returned in June the same year. He worked at Todd Shipyards in Seattle for a few months, but on April 20, 1981, he quit his job there and began working at the 514 Club. He testified that he remembered having a conversation on May 26 with San Pablo after the dispatch, but not Gene. Mac Callueng, Boy Pilay, Eddie Lopez, and Boyse Campo were present during his conversation with San Pablo. He testified that he never met with San Pablo at the Luna Café, never inquired about the kind of car Gene owned, and had nothing to do with Boy Pilay going to Alaska after the deaths of Silme and Gene.

Then Browne handed Dictado an exhibit, which was a handwritten letter from himself to San Pablo, indicating "Robert, kindly lend me $1,500, I need it very badly for the hospital bill, I need it right away. Let's talk about it later when you come back." The prosecution had used this letter to prove that Dictado expected San Pablo to pay him $1,500 from the Dillingham gambling proceeds, but Browne cleverly used this letter to establish a different story. Dictado testified that San Pablo owed him about $400 and refused to pay him, so he would want Dictado convicted to get rid of him.

Dictado also said that San Pablo lied when he said he would make Dictado the second foreman; he lied when he said Dictado would be dispatched to Alaska; and he lied by claiming Dictado said he would kill Gene Viernes. Dictado admitted that he himself lied about Ramil and Guloy being at the gambling hall on June 1, claiming he had been threatened and had to lie to protect himself.

Then came the highlight of the trial. Browne carefully drew out from Dictado that he knew who had committed the murders and who had ordered them. Dictado testified on direct examination that he still had family in the Philippines, and on re-direct, Browne asked, "Has your life been threatened, Tony?"

Dictado's response was stilted, delivered in his thick Filipino accent. "Yes, sir."

"Your family's life?"

He nodded, thick black hair flopping over his forehead. His eyes darted around at the room's many occupants. "Yes, sir."

"Do you know what's going to happen as a result of your testifying today?"

"Kill my family." Judge Carroll looked up from beneath his thin reading glasses, pen poised over a notepad.

Browne continued: "If I asked you who asked to have the killings done, would you tell me?"

"I cannot told you, sir."

"Why?"

He didn't hesitate, but said, "My family will be dead."

To us, this testimony and Browne's defense were pathetic. He knew but couldn't name those who had killed the pair of activists, but tried to hint broadly it was someone from the Philippines who would kill his family there if he testified. But who? Baruso? Marcos himself? The jury was left to speculate.

On May 12, the jury returned a verdict of guilty on both counts of charges of aggravated murder. The conviction carried an automatic sentence of life imprisonment without the possibility of parole. Dictado was sent to Walla Walla Penitentiary for the rest of his life.

CHAPTER EIGHTEEN:

TAKING STOCK

May 1982
Seattle

Buoyed by yet another conviction, we lobbied Maleng's office to charge Baruso, but to no avail. We discussed with him and Maida the option of providing Dictado leniency if he agreed to testify against Baruso. They did not accept. We reiterated the evidence proving Baruso had prior knowledge of the murder, and that he provided the murder weapon and payment. It fell on deaf ears. We reminded Maida of what she said in her closing argument to the jury at both criminal trials: Baruso and Dictado met on May 30 to plot the murders.

"That was argument," she said. "We need evidence."

The meeting ended. No charges were brought.

The CJDV leadership team arrived at the sober realization that we had gotten as far as the SPD and prosecuting attorney's office were willing to go. The courtroom verdicts against the hitmen and Dictado were victories, but we had fallen far short of what Gene and Silme would have expected of us and what true justice required.

The first meeting after Dictado's conviction was held in the basement of John's house in Madison Park, a well-to-do Seattle neighborhood on Lake Washington. John had made enough money to buy a quaint Tudor house with a nice backyard in the early 1970s, when everyone else was "turning out the lights" in Seattle and houses were cheap. He lived with his wife Goldie, a long-time movement activist for food safety, and their son Sean, then thirteen.

Bruce led off the discussion. "Good try with the prosecutors, you three," he said, pointing at Terri, Cindy, and me, "but I expected that door to slam after the convictions. It's not that the 'fix is in,' as Dale said once. I don't think they have been bought off or approached by anyone and told to prosecute no further."

Dale asked Bruce what he thought had happened. "These folks are just not equipped to take on the interests of who stood behind the murders. And they have the FBI and the US Attorney's office saying that they don't have enough to charge Baruso with a Hobbs Act violation, which is a lot easier than a murder conviction."

I shook my head and settled back in a heavy armchair. It was far more comfortable than anything I had in my house, and I forced myself to stay awake. I could see a similar sleeplessness reflected in the bags beneath everyone's eyes. I jumped in.

"I think when Forsythe tried to throw her trial, Maida might have been spooked. Maybe she checked into his background and found out he's an FBI informant. That would give her pause." I was sure Forsythe's testimony was intended to have an intimidating effect.

Terri, seated cross-legged on the floor, picked at the carpet. "Yeah, but so what? She nailed him anyway."

I shrugged. "And maybe now she's thinking, 'Whoops! What if Forsythe was put there by the FBI or Maheu? Someone wanted to find out how these murders came down. That means there must be much more powerful interests involved.'" I could honestly see her thinking along those lines.

Dale agreed. "That would intimidate any prosecutor, right?"

"It could. And it would explain why she went after Forsythe for being a publicity seeker popping up in big trials, not on his connection to Maheu."

Bruce brought us back to the central point. "Whatever her motive, we have to wrap our heads around the fact that the criminal prosecutions are over and—"

Dale interrupted, "Hey, whatever happened to Pilay anyway? Can't we find him?"

Cindy shook her head. "Lynn's sources on the street say he hasn't been in the ID for months."

"Doesn't his family live in Maryland? Maybe someone can track them down there?" Terri asked.

I made a note, but I was skeptical. It would be great to get the SPD to arrest Pilay and try to turn him, but it would be a long shot. Pilay was long gone.

I turned the group back to discussing the way forward. The first anniversary of Gene and Silme's deaths was coming up soon, and a huge mobilization was being planned.

We saw the one year memorial as a way we could bring together the dedicated group of supporters we had built over the past year, especially those who believed Marcos could be involved. It would also demonstrate to the popular forces – the press, civil liberties groups, and prosecutors – our strength and our resolve to pursue justice. Bruce predicted that these popular front organizations would fall by the wayside as our justice efforts expanded to expose the role of Marcos and multiple US intelligence agencies.

In addition to the memorial, the CJDV was planning an educational seminar in August for the activists who had fought for justice in the 1976 murders of Orlando Letelier and his assistant, Ronni Moffitt, in Washington, DC. Letelier had been the Chilean ambassador to the US under the socialist government of Salvador Allende. He'd been arrested and imprisoned after the 1973 coup that toppled Allende until an international effort to gain his release was successful. He had been living in exile in the US in 1976 when he was killed by a car bomb.

The Institute for Policy Studies (IPS) was running into roadblocks in its efforts to get the US government to cooperate in the murder investigation. The CJDV wanted to put the topic of political assassinations on the agenda for the broader community.

We were geared up for another busy summer and fall. Our thoughts turned to something we could control: our own civil lawsuit.

CHAPTER NINETEEN:

THE PHILIPPINE INFILTRATION PLAN

Mid-1982
Seattle & Washington, DC

Before we could file a civil suit, we needed proof of what we called the Philippine Infiltration Plan: Marcos sending his agents to the US to spy on his opponents, particularly the KDP. Holding him responsible for what happened to Gene and Silme rested on establishing this plan existed.

Our research focused on finding the supposed State Department "White Paper" that explored the role of foreign intelligence agencies in the US. But there was no official record that such a document existed.

The pressure mounted when we found out that Ferdinand and Imelda Marcos were coming to Washington, DC, on a formal state visit with President Reagan in September 1982. The KDP and other anti-martial law forces were already planning huge demonstrations nationally to call attention to Marcos' repression and to protest US support of the dictatorship.

"What if we filed the lawsuit when Marcos comes here on his state visit?" Dale said at a CJDV meeting. "What an embarrassment for the regime!"

Bruce made a note on his pad. "Mike, you guys need to put the rush on so we can get this filed in September. There will be tons of Marcos agents swarming all over DC, so we can document all of the harassment we experience too. It's all part of your conspiracy, right?"

I agreed it was a great idea. It would help prove that Marcos' agents were here to spy on us.

Our FOIA requests finally started to bear fruit, and documents arrived from the FBI and the US Navy. The CIA, NSA, and Defense Intelligence Agency (DIA) remained unhelpful.

The Naval Investigative Service (NIS) operating out of Alameda Naval Air Station in the Bay Area sent us documents establishing that they had obtained an executive order signed by President Ford in 1976 which authorized them to infiltrate the KDP. This was unusual, because Senator Frank Church (D-Idaho)'s Committee report of the mid-1970s prohibited surveillance by the US military against domestic organizations absent an executive order.

One NIS document, written by J. F. Donnelly, stated that the director of the NIS had sent a report to Subic Bay, which authorized the penetration of the KDP and its supporters by an informant who was to be "programmed" to re-contact the KDP in Oakland. It was dated in 1976 and stated:

Katipunan Pg Mga Democratikong Filipin *(KDP) is headquartered in Oakland, CA, and is a revolutionary organization seeking to embrace all Philippine activists who are opposed to US Imperialism and committed to the People's struggle for revolutionary change. The KDP has a hardcore cadre of about fifteen members in the San Francisco area and these individuals are predominately second generation Filipinos. Although the KDP has goals involving the political regime of a foreign nation, its membership and structure subject any operational endeavor involving its penetration by the NIS to the guidelines set forth by Executive Order 11905 and the Defense Investigative Review Council (DIRC).*

Another report stated that on June 23, 1976, Commander H.H. Sowers in Oakland was provided a verbal briefing of an informant's report. The FBI in San Francisco was copied on the report, as was naval headquarters in Alexandria. The report, labeled top secret, stated that the informants'

[P]rimary function for the NIS will be to obtain information relating to efforts by the New People's Army (NPA); Communist Party of the Philippines (CPP) or any other such organization as may surface, to procure US government property from US military bases in the Philippines to support their cause. Any counter-intelligence information obtained regarding these groups or the KDP will be provided to the Philippine authorities or the legal attaché, as appropriate. *The asset will be operated strictly as a "deep cover" source and his identity protected even at the expense of a particular operational endeavor emanating from his information.* (Emphasis added.)

We were all certain that the "Philippine authorities" would have placed a high priority on investigating leaders or members of this "communist" group.

Other documents established an NIS interest in any anti-Marcos activist bringing money from the US to the Philippines to support the opposition. These documents also indicated that "continuing coordination has been maintained with FBI San Francisco during the course of this investigation." It further stated: "This investigation was predicated upon the request of the Commanding Officer, Naval Investigative Service Office, and San Francisco, CA of 7-20-76."

Statements of two confidential informants who were directed by the NIS to infiltrate and monitor the activities of the KDP were included in the files sent to us, but were heavily redacted. We did find evidence that various reports, documents, telexes, and files were provided to the Legat Manila, referring to the legal attaché of the US embassy in Manila, Republic of the Philippines. The NIS neglected to redact the name of one of those informants, Monte Martinez – the navy man that Geline had long suspected.

Martinez had disappeared from KDP meetings after the murders, but his reports provided detailed information about the KDP and its leadership, including Silme, as well as the layout of its headquarters in Oakland, the books and publications produced there, and its events and activities. There were photographs of several KDP members.

There were no documents produced that specifically said that Gene carried money to the Philippines, but Bill's sources had told us those files were missing or red-tagged **Top Secret**, so that was no surprise. Yet the documents we did get confirmed the central tenets of Bill's information:

1. The NIS had an active and deep-penetration investigation of the KDP, authorized by an executive order signed by President Ford in 1976.

2. The NIS was interested in KDP members who opposed the naval base at Subic and who went to the Philippines with money for the opposition.

3. The NIS shared intelligence with the Legat Manila and "Philippine authorities" in Manila.

4. The NIS sent their informants' reports and other files to the FBI in San Francisco.

The FOIA responses from the FBI confirmed all of this. They handed over 1,300 pages on the KDP, but all of the files were heavily redacted. Some pages were completely redacted, with various "national security" and "law enforcement" stamps.

An FBI report from the mid-1970s stated that an informant believed the KDP "was actively channeling funds and supplies through their underground contacts to communist insurgents in the Philippines," and that the KDP was "recruiting military personnel" for this function. There were files from FBI field offices detailing the political associates and activities of the KDP leadership nationally and from ten different cities in the US, as well as photos of KDP members at rallies, events, and teach-ins. Personal details about KDP members' lifestyles, sexual orientations, and living situations were included.

The fact that the NIS had informants inside the KDP and had shared all of this information with the FBI partly confirmed Bill's suspicion that it was Naval Intelligence who did the dirty work for other US intelligence agencies, including the FBI.

It was valuable evidence, but we still had a complex and difficult case. Under the Civil Rights Act of 1864, we needed to prove a conspiracy to violate civil rights—in our case, the First Amendment rights to protest our government's policies. Under this theory, it was not necessary to prove that Marcos himself ordered the murders. Rather, we would prove the "Philippine Infiltration Plan" was the conspiracy, and that Marcos' agents in the US, including Tony Baruso, had committed the murders in furtherance of the goals of the conspiracy. Under established law of civil conspiracy, the overt acts of one or more co-conspirators made other members of the conspiracy liable for the damages caused.

We knew our legal theory was *creative*, to say the least, but based on the research of our summer law clerks, Howard Goodfriend and Sharon Sakamoto, and legal team member Liz Schott, we were confident we had the best available legal precedent. All we needed was the evidence.

In late 1981, I called a Seattle attorney, Bill Bender, who had worked with the leading constitutional and human rights law firm in the country, the Center for Constitutional Rights (CCR) in New York, and asked him to see if the CCR would be willing to join the lawsuit as plaintiffs' counsel. The CCR had pioneered filing lawsuits against human rights abusers from other countries under the Alien Tort Claims Act of 1789, which allowed non-citizens to sue human rights offenders found in the US who had violated the Law of Nations, including torture, genocide, and such extrajudicial punishment as summary execution.

I talked to its executive director, Michael Ratner, about the case and the theory, and the CCR agreed to assist by joining our legal team to file the lawsuit. We were enormously grateful. Since Gene and Silme were American citizens, the Act didn't technically apply, but CCR's advice was crucial. For me, personally, it was a real boost to get such prestigious and experienced human rights attorneys to back our cause.

We were moving forward, but there were still doubts. At one of the leadership meetings, Cindy voiced some of our pessimism. "We're getting pretty grandiose here. Like some court is really going to tell the CIA to stop cooperating with Marcos spies? Wouldn't that result in Marcos retaliating against the CIA spies in the Philipppines?"

"Let's see what the legal team comes up with," Bruce said. "We need evidence that Marcos' spies were here with US knowledge. So filing the lawsuit in conjunction with the Marcos visit, and the demonstrations that will surround it, is ideal. Let's set that in motion."

Terri looked concerned. "Speaking of Marcos spies, who are the plaintiffs bringing this suit? You're not going to put Barbara and me out there by our lonesome, right?" Barbara Viernes was Gene's sister, and represented his estate.

Jim jumped in. "You two shouldn't go it alone, no. Why don't we add other members of the KDP as plaintiffs?" He suggested KDP leadership member Rene Cruz would have standing to sue as victim of the same conspiracy. Dave Della would be a great plaintiff too. After all, they, too, were being threatened, and their free speech chilled, because Marcos' agents were free to operate here.

We all agreed, and got back to work.

In early May 1982, I got a call from Tom Wicker. Tom was an editorial writer for the *New York Times* and someone I greatly admired. He had covered the prisoners' takeover at the Attica Correction Institution in upstate New York in the mid-1970s, and had become involved in successful efforts to negotiate the release of prison guards held hostage by inmates.

"Mr. Withey, Bob Boruchowitz said I should call you about those cannery worker murders in Seattle." Bob Boruchowitz was the King County public defender, and an acquaintance of mine.

I offered to meet him over lunch to tell him about the case, so two days later we got together at the Athenian Café in the Pike Place Market, what I considered the spiritual center of the Seattle counter culture. The Market was a three-block collection of small carrels housing artisans, bakeries, cafes, fish sellers, and fresh produce markets with a commanding view of Elliott Bay. My former law partner, Bob Kaplan, and I had represented many of these small businesses when urban developers tried to replace the market with condos. Victor Steinbrueck had organized the successful "Save the Market Association," and the Market had thrived, growing and drawing hundreds of thousands of tourists a year.

Wicker was obviously interested in Silme and Gene's story and took copious notes. But just when I was explaining how outrageous Forsythe's testimony was, I made a broad gesture with my hand and knocked over his beer, emptying it directly onto his lap.

"Whoa, you got me good," Wicker responded genially, wiping the better part of a pint of beer off his trousers.

I was mortified. "I hope this doesn't affect your story."

"Don't worry, Mike. It takes a lot more than spilled beer to get me off a story I'm interested in. You were saying?" He was a gem.

A few weeks after I met with Wicker, I took a trip to DC, where I had the good fortune to meet with Morton Halperin at the ACLU's office. Halperin was an associate of Daniel Ellsberg at the Pentagon, and had been involved in releasing the Pentagon Papers. Since then, he'd founded a project at the ACLU to combat government secrecy and spying on Americans.

Although generous with his time and advice, Mort had no direct background in Marcos intelligence operations in the US. But he did mention that he believed the Senate Foreign Relations Subcommittee on International Operations had written a still-classified report on foreign intelligence operations in the US, including the Philippines. He told me the Senate Foreign Relations Committee's Chief Counsel Michael Glennon was widely believed to have worked on the report, and was knowledgeable about this topic. But he could not reveal what was in the report because it was still classified.

Mort was clear: it was useless to try to get the report out of Glennon; he had already tried. But he also mentioned that Jack Anderson had written a column about the report in the *Washington Post* in August of 1979. He provided me a copy, which paraphrased the report.

Coincidently, my next meeting was with reporter Dale Van Atta, who had worked for Anderson. I met Dale in his office suite on K Street. Dale asked warmly about the latest in the criminal investigations. He said he received the press releases from the CJDV and had created a file, just in case he wanted to write a story. I mentioned that Tom Wicker had interviewed me and was thinking of writing a piece, hoping to touch some competitive nerve.

I filled him in on the criminal convictions, as well as the prosecutor and FBI's failure to go after Baruso. He said that didn't surprise him: there were few topics that got the CIA and State Department more riled up than reports of foreign intelligence agencies operating openly against their exiled opponents and enemies in the US. He confirmed that the Senate subcommittee staff had briefed its members on six foreign intelligence agencies in the US, including the Philippines, Iran, Taiwan, Chile, and South Korea. The Soviet Union was added for "ideological balance," but its efforts in the US involved mainly classic espionage, not harassment of dissidents.

I asked if I could see the report itself, but he said no. He had one copy kept in a locked file cabinet. After more chit chat, I asked again to see the report, promising I would not let anyone know where I had seen it, nor would I quote from it directly. He smiled and said no.

But then he went to a file cabinet in the corner and withdrew a bulky file marked **Foreign Spies**. It was on yellowed paper, and I saw the seal of the Senate Foreign Relations Committee and the names of its members. He put in on his desk, turned to me, and said, "I have go to lunch. I'm leaving now and will be back in an hour. Let yourself out before that." With that, he left, and I never saw him again.

I picked up the report and read it thoroughly. It was a gold mine of information on the various kinds of harassment and intimidation foreign governments used in the US against opponents of their repressive regimes. The report argued persuasively that the harassment and intimidation of dissidents had a chilling effect on public discussion and attitudes in the US, especially toward governments with controversial human rights records. It stated that the intimidation targeted émigrés, including US citizens, and deprived them of their constitutional rights to free speech, assembly, and association.

This was our exact theory against the Marcos regime.

The report noted that the failure of US intelligence to stop the spies of US allies, including Taiwan, South Korea, and the Philippines, was particularly sensitive. It reasoned that such benign neglect encouraged these countries to continue their behavior.

The report documented that as early as 1973, the Intelligence Section of the Armed Forces of the Philippines (ISAFP) had infiltrated its agents into the US to neutralize political opponents of the Marcos regime. One of those agents had walked into the FBI office in San Francisco with an offer to exchange information. Although the offer was reportedly turned down, our own FOIA requests proved otherwise.

The report also reflected concern that US counter-intelligence agencies had failed to keep track of foreign spies in the country and, even worse, had done nothing to expose and hold accountable those foreign spies who, under US law, were prohibited from operating here. To me, this was the most telling aspect of the Senate report: the FBI was "asleep at the switch" while Marcos agents intimidated and harassed both émigrés and US citizens.

But the report did not go nearly far enough, merely calling for Senate hearings and referral to the attorney general and Department of Justice to encourage the prosecutions of foreign spies operating here. For our allies, at least, it was clear neither of these steps were likely to happen.

We could now confidently allege in our complaint that the Marcos regime had agents in the US operating against its opponents with impunity, in violation of their constitutional rights.

Gene and Silme were the victims of the Philippine Infiltration Plan.

CHAPTER TWENTY:

THE ANNIVERSARY

Summer 1982
Seattle

On June 1, 1982, the CJDV held the First Anniversary Memorial of Gene and Silme's murders, with over five hundred supporters in attendance at a local union hall. Bob Santos and Nemesio Domingo Jr. spoke of our successes and failures during the past year, and we shared our plans moving forward.

The event was heralded in the local press and in the CJDV's *Update* as more than a remembrance, but as a call to further action: we were open about our intentions to press for Baruso's indictment, to pressure the police to find and charge Boy Pilay, and to investigate a civil suit that would lead us to the higher-ups, and even to Marcos himself. The *Update* summed up our past and continued efforts with eloquence.

A full year has now passed since Gene Viernes and Silme Domingo were so tragically cut down in the prime of their lives. Their memory has not faded from our thoughts. We will always remember them for who they were and all they stood for — trade union reformers and progressive leaders whose influence and work were felt by many here in the US and internationally. More importantly, we will not rest with memories. We will renew at this one year juncture our determination to get to the bottom of their murders and to expose the interests which lie behind them.

In Bruce's words, we were "peeling the onion and finding a rotten core."

The *Update* also noted that we needed to take our campaign for justice to a national level by establishing ties to national civil rights, civil liberties, and anti-martial law groups across the US. We announced our goal to unfold the lawsuit as part of the Marcos opposition actions during the Marcos state visit in September.

The memorial was followed by the educational teach-in on the lessons of the Letelier murder. The CJDV brought Isabel Letelier, the widow of the slain ambassador and a senior fellow at the progressive Institute for Policy Studies in DC, to Seattle. Mrs. Letelier had founded, with her husband, the Europe-based Transnational Institute (TNI) to increase international awareness about the struggles of the people in Latin America against poverty, oppression, and military rule. We also invited IPS director Saul Landau, a journalist and filmmaker whose most recent acclaimed work was *Paul Jacobs and the Nuclear Gang*, about the cover-up of health hazards from the nuclear test blast in Utah in 1957. The film earned Landau an Emmy Award and the George Polk Award for investigative journalism.

The teach-in drew hundreds to Seattle University, and it allowed us a time out from the day-to-day struggles and a chance to look at the larger issues of our work. We were inspired by how the families and survivors of the Letelier/ Moffitt assassinations had organized themselves to bring pressure on the US and Chilean governments to share information about Michael Townley, the main suspect tied to the murders. We learned from them to think of the struggle for human rights in cases of political assassinations and summary executions through the telescopic lenses of the long run — understanding that it might take decades to achieve full justice in the murders of these activists.

The Letelier teach-in was followed by a national conference of leading KDP activists and friends, focusing on how to move our justice efforts to a new level. A document from our summation described the impact of the justice efforts as expanding at a rapid rate:

> *The new turn in our work cannot be simply described as going from a local to a national campaign. The real basis for this development is the sharpening of the target of the justice campaign. Whereas in Seattle we began the campaign by targeting the hitmen and noting that there were higher levels of the murder conspiracy as well, we have now clearly identified the upper echelons. This is the Marcos Dictatorship, which initiated the murder conspiracy and carried it out through their agent Tony Baruso and others, with the complicity of US intelligence agencies.*

Experienced KDP activists in the Bay Area, DC, New York, and Chicago were brought in to help build united and popular fronts in their cities and nationally. The CJDV's *Update* became a national newsletter called *Call to Justice*, and we opened CJDV offices in the Bay Area and DC.

Using the energy generated by the memorial, we worked on the lawsuit. We discovered that both Ferdinand and Imelda Marcos had announced at press conferences in 1981 and 1982 that the Reagan administration was willing to back the regime's demand that the FBI and Department of Justice crack down on the "terrorists" in the US who were opposing Marcos. He specifically referred to both the moderate opposition led by Senator Benigno Aquino and former foreign minister Raul Manglapus, as well as the leftists in the KDP. The Marcos regime was pressing Congress to enact an extradition treaty with the Philippines, which would allow Marcos to bring his opponents back to the Philippines to stand trial, or worse.

An outstanding investigative reporter Phil Bronstein and his partner, H.Z. Reza, published an article in the *San Francisco Chronicle* in February 1982 called "Manila Getting Grand Jury Secrets." It exposed the role of the FBI in sending to Philippine authorities the actual sworn testimony from a secret grand jury proceeding that was supposedly investigating the moderate opposition to the Marcos regime, a federal crime.

The moderate wing of the opposition to Marcos in the US, including Steve Psinakis, Jovito Salonga, and Raul Manglapus, had gone public with proof of FBI or Marcos harassment, including burglaries at their homes and offices, surveillance on their families, and threats of violence. Their claims were covered prominently in the Bay Area press and caught our attention because of the similarities between what was happening to them and us.

We believed that these disclosures, coupled with the secret information that Bill's sources provided, were proof the Reagan administration welcomed Marcos' spies with open arms. We were convinced Reagan had authorized US intelligence agencies to cooperate in the Philippine Infiltration Plan. What better way for us to publicly prove these initiatives than to accuse the regime of assassinating two US citizens?

Our work received a huge jolt of energy later in the summer, when, out of the blue, Tom Wicker published a scathing Op-Ed piece in the *New York Times* called "The Manila Connection." In his article, Wicker carefully explained our theory of the murders of Silme and Gene, adding his own editorial flare.

Here is a story of an ostensibly local crime that may be linked to the repressive Marcos regime and possibly lead to high places in Washington .... The charges seem serious enough for Congress to look into, particularly as it weighs the pending US-Philippine extradition treaty. And the House Subcommittee on Asian and Pacific Affairs, which has just held hearings on Taiwan, might usefully turn its attention next to the Philippines and the possible reach of Ferdinand Marcos into the US.

Wicker cited the Senate Foreign Relations Committee Report, as well as Phil Bronstein's article. The publication of Wicker's editorial spread like wildfire within the anti-Marcos movement and heightened national interest in our case. Alex Esclamado, editor of the *Philippine News,* the leading Filipino newspaper in the US, ran the Wicker commentary in full. He intimated that the *New York Times* would not have run the piece unless it believed there was truth to our allegations.

In the middle of this, the legal team was getting ready to file the lawsuit. We had outstanding research and legal theories, thanks to our summer law clerks. We had drafted a highly factual complaint, aided by Jim's editing skills, with what we believed had a solid legal basis to keep us in court. Now we only had to figure out how to serve a copy of the complaint on Marcos during his state visit.

Len Schroeter, who was still providing strategic advice for our team, joined us at a meeting at Jim Douglas' law office. As we were discussing the case, Len dropped a bombshell.

"Listen, gang, I tried to get my law firm to take on this case," Len started. I shifted uncomfortably in my chair. "They're concerned because our offices are on the fifth floor of the Central Building, and the Philippine consulate is on the third floor of the same building," Len said gently.

"We wore bulletproof vests and packed weapons, and your firm is worried about the consulate coming up the stairwells?" I asked incredulously.

"I guess so." Len looked miserable.

"So what, Len?" John looked at him. "You aren't intimidated by anyone."

"I can't be on the pleadings. My firm won't let me."

Out of nowhere, Bill Davis starting singing lyrics from the old Kenny Rogers' song "Lucille." "You picked a fine time to leave me, Lucille," he sang. There was silence, then nervous laughter that quietly fizzled out.

I spoke up. "Len, this is a huge disappointment. We really need you and your firm on this case."

"I am really sorry. They are a bunch of gutless ..." He shook his head, unwilling to say more.

"Then I'm afraid we have to ask you to leave," I said as gently as I could. "If you're not co-counsel, there is no attorney-client privilege in these discussions. You could be asked about them at some point."

We were all sad to see Len walk out of the room. I knew in my heart he wanted desperately to be part of our legal team. I admired him. But we had our work cut out for us, and didn't need distractions.

CHAPTER TWENTY-ONE:

MARCOS SERVED

September 1982
Washington, DC

The National Press Club in Washington, DC, occupied almost an entire block of 14th Street, just a few blocks from the White House. On September 17, 1982, at eleven o'clock in the morning, the national and international press crowded into a briefing room, awaiting the arrival of President Ferdinand Marcos of the Philippines and his wife Imelda.

Outside, Father Bill Davis paced nervously up and down the street. Our committed investigator wore his priest's collar tight around his neck, and he clutched a copy of the complaint and summons in the case called *The Estates of Domingo and Viernes vs. The Republic of the Philippines, Ferdinand and Imelda Marcos.* We also named Secretary of State George Schultz and General Alexander Haig as defendants in order to get injunctive relief against the US to stop aiding Marcos agents.

The Marcoses had arrived in DC on the September 14 for an official, thirteen-day state visit. The night before, they'd been the guests of honor at a formal dinner at the White House hosted by the president and Nancy Reagan. There was also a private meeting between the presidents in the Oval Office, and a series of high-level meetings with Pentagon officials and Schultz.

Although the Marcos regime had gone to great lengths to project an image of political stability, including busing in and paying over a thousand pro-Marcos "supporters" to appear at rallies, the opposition was right on target with a major offensive leading up to his arrival.

A BBC documentary about the Philippines was shown at multiple public screenings throughout Washington in the week before the state visit. The film contrasted the economic hardships of most Filipinos with the Marcoses' lavish spending, and interviewed children who said they witnessed attacks by government soldiers on their parents. One boy said he watched soldiers behead his father, remembering, "They played with my father's head." Amnesty International also issued a report listing details of what it called widespread torture, political arrests, and murders by Philippine agents.

This did not make it easy for Reagan administration officials, who repeated the nostrum that good ties with President Marcos were necessary to protect American military bases in the Philippines and our economic interests. Their message was not always well received. The week before Marcos arrived, eight US congressmen called for cancellation of the state visit, citing the human rights violations. Days later, five US senators released a letter to President Reagan, urging him to use the Marcos visit "to enhance the cause of human rights."

Now that the Philippine president was in the country, Congress Watch and The National Committee to Protest the Marcos State Visit, both organizations led by KDP activists, had brought national attention on Marcos' deplorable human rights record and his role in his military agents' infiltration of the Marcos opposition. Rallies and demonstrations against the regime filled the local news broadcasts, and the national press corps was covering both the visit and the counter-demonstrations carefully.

Throughout the visit, the KDP contingent in DC was under surveillance by Marcos agents. At every picket line, demonstration, rally, and meeting, we saw Filipino bodybuilder types, almost always in pairs, with identical dark pants and white shirts open at the collar – all the trappings of Marcos agents. They stood aside, took pictures, and counted us. They took literature from our tables and threw it away.

More sinister, though, was the continued presence of the bodybuilders after the meetings broke up for the evening. They followed us to the house in suburban Maryland where many of us were staying. We decided to travel in groups of at least three and deployed our own security teams to anticipate and deter any problems. We got out our bulletproof vests and wore them at all times. We took photographs of all of the Marcos agents to use as exhibits in our civil lawsuit. There were many tense moments when the agents saw us taking pictures and approached us menacingly.

In the middle of this, our lawsuit was ready to file. But first, we needed to personally serve Marcos with a copy of the complaint. The summons would hail Ferdinand and Imelda Marcos into federal court in the Western District of Washington (Seattle) to answer for the murders of Gene Viernes and Silme Domingo, and the conspiracy to deprive the anti-Marcos movement in the US of their constitutional rights to free speech, assembly, and association.

As the Marcos entourage of eight black Lincoln Town cars approached, Father Bill slipped into a side entrance of the Press Club. He stood next to a large tree in the hallway leading to where the press conference was being held, hoping this was the path the Philippine delegation would take. It seemed like a long shot, but it was our best shot. If we couldn't get service of process on him, Marcos could legally ignore our lawsuit.

I was on the other side of the city that morning with Cindy, Rene, and other KDP activists getting ready for our own press conference. Back in Seattle, the rest of the legal team huddled around a table in John Caughlan's house, awaiting word from Father Bill to file the lawsuit as soon as Marcos was served. If he was served.

We'd planned simultaneous press events in DC, New York, the Bay Area, and Seattle. We had worked carefully on the statements, placing our lawsuit within the broader context of the Reagan administration's backing of a notoriously repressive and dictatorial regime. We made the case that when our country allies itself with repressive dictators like Marcos, we pay the price here.

We alleged in the lawsuit that Gene's meeting with Felixberto Olalia had been monitored by Marcos agents, as was the ILWU resolution debate in Hawaii. We noted that Marcos had arrested the top leadership of the KMU, including Olalia, and charged them with subversion shortly before he left for the US. We opined that Marcos didn't want the KMU to disrupt the country while he was away, and hoped Olalia's arrest underscored just how dangerous Marcos considered the KMU and its leadership, and why Gene and Silme's work with the KMU came to his attention and concern.

We labored under the somewhat grandiose notion that our lawsuit would color the entire Marcos state visit and could be the chief weapon to expose the regime and change public opinion. We wanted the lawsuit to be the *J'Accuse!* of our movement, imagining an impact similar to what Emile Zola had with his famous 1898 confrontation of the president of the French Republic for the infamous Dreyfuss Affair.

What actually happened was that the Philippines' dismal human rights record created an atmosphere of controversy from the very start of the visit. Our lawsuit used the public characterization of the regime to validate its allegations, rather than the other way around.

I was at the house in Maryland about half an hour after the Marcos press conference was scheduled to start when the phone rang.

"Mike? Bill Davis here." His voice seemed cheery and clear.

"What's the good word, Father Bill?"

"I was in the hallway like we planned, and all of a sudden there he was, walking down the hall with three aides, talking and paying no attention to an elderly Catholic priest huddled in the vestibule. Imelda was way behind him, but you said I only needed to serve the president, so I ignored her."

"And?" I couldn't cage my curiosity.

"Marcos pulls almost abreast of me, looks over, and actually says, 'Good morning, Father.' Can you believe it? I couldn't. I took out the summons and complaint from under my priest's robe and told him I had something he would like to read. I handed him the documents, and he took them, almost instinctively, without looking, and handed them to his aide."

"You got him served, Bill! You got him served!" I was shouting into the phone.

"I left before anyone bothered to read what it was," Bill finished.

"That is so great. Thanks so much. We'll need an affidavit from you describing exactly what you did in case Marcos challenges service of process. Way to go, Bill."

Bill later told me that serving Marcos was one of the highlights of his life. Before we were done, he would also serve Reagan's National Security Advisor Alexander Haig and Secreatry of State George Schultz – a piece of cake after getting to the president of a foreign country.

Our simultaneous press conferences around the country went off without a hitch. The Seattle press covered the filing of the lawsuit, but we were less than thrilled by the reception from the national press. Plenty of reporters attended our event, but most of them took our statements and copies of the lawsuit, created a file, and waited for further developments. The Bay Area conference went well but few showed up in New York.

The lawsuit was filed in Seattle less than an hour after Marcos was served. Our luck that day held, and our case was assigned to Judge Donald S. Voorhees, the jurist we'd hoped for. I never asked Jim how he had managed to accomplish that, and was content with his explanation that it was "just shit luck."

CHAPTER TWENTY-TWO:

BOY PILAY

Autumn & Early Winter 1982
Chevy Chase, Maryland

The evening that we served Marcos and filed the suit, a group of CJDV activists gathered to celebrate in Chevy Chase, Maryland, at the beautiful old Tudor home of Kitty Tucker and Robert Alvarez. Kitty and Bob were leading anti-nuclear activists who had been generous in sharing the lessons of the Silkwood case.

After an early dinner, I noticed a telephone book for southern Maryland sitting on a side table and picked it up. It was a long shot, but I remembered Terri mentioned that Boy Pilay may have family in Maryland.

As I brought the bulky book back into the dining room and started leafing through it, Kitty gave me a hard time. "Come on, Mike, you really have to stop working."

I ignored her, and paged to the name Domingues. That was Boy Pilay's surname. I knew he wouldn't be in the phone book, of course, but hoped to reach his parents to see if he was around. There were four Domingues listings in the greater Chevy Chase and Bethesda area. I called the first number, and the world stood still.

"Hello?" It was a woman's voice, probably older, a little reticent, with a Filipino accent.

"Hello. Is Boy around?" Just like that. No introduction, just straight to the point.

"No, he just left. Who is calling?"

I almost fell off my chair. Waving my hand wildly for silence in the dining room, I thought fast. "Uh, just a friend. I will call back later. Thanks," I mumbled, trying to sound as nonchalant as I could.

I hung up and immediately called Joanne Maida. It was shortly after five o'clock back in Seattle, and I was hoping to catch her before she left work.

When she answered, I jumped in. "Joanne, this is Mike. I'm back east. We filed our civil suit today, but I have something for you. Do you still have a material witness arrest warrant out for Pilay?"

"Yes. Why?" She sounded wary, but intrigued.

"I have an address and phone number in Maryland where he's staying. Can you get him arrested?" I was almost shouting with excitement.

"Whoa, wait a minute. How do we know it's him?" Joanne seemed put off.

"I got a number from the phone book. I called it. His mom answered. I asked for Boy. She said he just left. There aren't that many people called Boy, with last name Domingues, in Maryland." I wanted to be very clear. "We need him arrested, Joanne, and brought back to Seattle to stand trial for the murders."

"Well, if that address is good, the Maryland State Patrol can pick him up. I'll double-check to make sure it's still an active warrant."

I was concerned I might have tipped him off by calling. "We can't wait too long. We might not have another chance." I gave her the address from the phone book and the number I called, then hung up, ready to be disappointed again.

She never called back. I called her again on Monday morning when I was back in Seattle.

"What's the latest on Pilay?" I asked as soon as she answered.

"Looks like we need another warrant to make sure we're solid. I'm working with Tando and Boatman to make sure we put everything we can into the affidavit to secure the warrant. Shouldn't take long."

"You have everything you need. Please let me know. Time is …"

"Sure, Mike. Of the essence. Got it." Joanne hung up abruptly.

"No, time is running out," I corrected her after the line clicked. I sat dejectedly in my office, flipping through the posters and newsletters of the ACWA. Pilay was likely armed and dangerous. He had no reason to be captured and brought back to stand trial. I waited to hear he was picked up safely, but the phone call from Maida didn't come anytime soon.

Weeks passed, and fall was creeping toward winter. Finally, I called Maida again and asked what was going on in Maryland.

"You aren't going to like it," Joanne started slowly, seeming unsure of what to tell me.

"Now what?" I was in no mood.

"We got the warrant issued here in King County and sent it to the Maryland State Patrol. We just heard back from them last night."

"What happened?"

"The SWAT team surrounded the house in the early evening, hoping Pilay would be home for dinner. The way they described it, a man walked out of the house, down the sidewalk in front, got into his car, and drove off. They didn't stop him because he didn't have a limp. Or much of a limp."

"No way."

"That's what they said. So they raided the home with about twenty officers, and Pilay's mom said he had just left. She was scared to death. They're going to stakeout the house for the next few days, but nobody thinks Pilay is coming back. Sorry about that. I'm as surprised as you are."

I wasn't surprised a bit. "This is the most important witness in a case against a foreign government for murdering two US citizens, and you thought getting him arrested was going to be business as usual."

"That's not fair. The patrol didn't want to be charged with false arrest. Plus, Pilay was for sure armed, and they didn't want a shootout in that neighborhood."

"Okay," I said, trying not to let my rage seep out in my tone. This was on her, not us, and not for the first time.

I was still recovering from Maida's news a few days later when Lynn called to let me know that a source in the ID told her Pilay was back in Seattle and hanging out at the 609 Club. We waited until the rumor was confirmed, and then the CJDV leadership team held a major strategy session at John's house.

It was a raw and wintry late November day. A cold front from Alaska bore down on us, giving the impression it was about to snow. That only seemed to heighten the sense of urgency experienced by the group.

In John's basement, in that familiar armchair, I started the discussion. "After we rousted him from Maryland, Pilay came back to Seattle to be with his gang friends.'

"At least what's left of them," Bruce added smugly. With Dictado, Ramil, and Guloy in jail, the Tulisan gang was lying low.

"We can't tell Maida, or she'll tip off the FBI," Jim argued. Nobody disagreed with him.

"Well, there is an arrest warrant out. That we know." I was conflicted. On the one hand, I didn't trust Maida; but on the other hand, only the police could arrest him, and only the prosecutor could charge him.

"It's important to hold the prosecutor's office accountable," John reminded us. "If we find Pilay, they have to arrest him. Otherwise they know we'll claim cover-up." The room filled with murmurs of assent.

"If she tells the FBI, we will never see Pilay again," I said, still pessimistic.

"She will do whatever she wants," Dale said. He was right.

"So how do we find Pilay?" Jim turned our attention to the security problems of establishing a presence near the gambling halls late at night.

I came up with a plan. "I'll talk to Christopher Hershey." He was the investigator who'd completed a thorough dossier on Baruso, and he knew this part of Seattle well. "I think we should set up a stakeout at the Bush Hotel to watch the entrances of the 514 and 609 Clubs. We'll we have a clear view from the relative safety of a hotel room."

The Bush Hotel was built in 1922 and took up close to a full city block on Jackson Street. It was mostly used as temporary lodging for elderly and disabled residents of the International District, and also housed Inter*Im, the ID housing alliance which Bob Santos founded with Elaine Ko. I had visited it before our meeting to make sure it was suitable for my first ever stakeout, and discovered that at least twelve rooms faced south with unobstructed views of the 609 Club.

The plan was simple: watch the clubs until we spotted Pilay, immediately call Maida, watch the arrests, and call a press conference announcing Pilay's arrest. We would feed Dick Clever, an enterprising reporter for the *Seattle Times*, our internal memos on Baruso and Pilay's guilt, then announce that the families of the slain men would meet with Norm Maleng and his assistants to press for charges to be filed against both men. We needed pressure now, not more futile pleas.

Now mid-December, and the weather in Seattle had turned cold and wet. I huddled in room 612 at the Bush Hotel and ate most of the pizza by the time Christopher joined me on the first night of our stakeout.

There seemed to be little reason to watch the streets during the day; our informants had told us Pilay was still laying low and didn't go out until evening.

"What's the word from the front?" I asked Christopher.

"Nothing much, just Christmas shopping and the usual drug buys on Maynard. Lots of folks going in and out of the 609 I don't recognize."

We were both a little anxious about being in the ID, where the Tulisans still patrolled, at night. I had donned my bulletproof vest and packed my firearm for the first time since Dictado was convicted.

It wasn't until the fourth night of the stakeout when something happened on the streets. A small crowd had gathered in the Hing Hay Park across the street from the 609, and the commotion attracted our attention. We opened the window into the frigid night, and a cacophony of angry voices flew up from the streets. Then quiet. Then more shouts. Then quiet.

As the disturbance dissipated, I used the telephoto lens on my camera to take pictures of the street scene below. The next morning, I got the photos developed. One picture clearly showed a car under a street lamp in front of the 609, with two Filipinos standing on the sidewalk. I recognized Baruso's car, and there, as big as life, was Boy Pilay standing behind it. I didn't recognize the other man in the picture. Baruso was not in the shot. But there was no doubt that Pilay was back, and conspiring with Baruso to keep out of the limelight. Or line of fire.

One of our informants was an old-timer who gambled at the 609. We asked him to report any suspicious activity, along with any sightings of Pilay, especially on the nights we were staking out the entrance.

The next evening, Christopher and I started the stakeout early, at about 5 p.m., anxious to see if Pilay or Baruso would return to the street below. There was nothing until about 10 p.m., when a crowd gathered again outside the club under the streetlight. This time I could identify Pilay as one of the bystanders. I passed the binoculars to Christopher and he concurred.

It was Pilay.

I contacted our source inside the 609, and he confirmed that Pilay had been in the club. He wasn't dealing, the old-timer said, just hanging out around the edges. Funtanella Sixto was dealing, and Charlie Penor, the owner, was also present. He said folks started to leave shortly after Pilay arrived, so he left too.

Not wanting to bother Maida at home, I waited until the next morning to call her office.

"Good morning, Joanne. How goes the justice struggle today?" I asked cheerily.

"What do you have, Mike?" she responded curtly.

"I have Pilay."

"What? Where?" She sounded wary. I could hear her fingers tap loudly on her desk.

"He was at the 609 Club in the ID last night at around ten. We have confirmation from two sources, and I saw him personally." I stuck to the facts.

"You shouldn't be out on the streets in the ID," she warned. "Your face is well-known in Tulisan circles."

"I appreciate that, but I was nowhere near the street. The question is whether you can get Pilay arrested if he comes back tonight. I'm happy to tip you off when he arrives." I didn't want to appear too anxious, but I was.

"Yes. Let me give you my home number. Where can I call you?" She seemed earnest, and I had no reason to believe she wouldn't do as she said she would.

"I'll call you. But there is one more thing."

"What's that?"

"No tipping off the FBI. They cannot be trusted."

"I hear you. Let me handle the arrest."

When we hung up, I was convinced that Joanne would have plain-clothes Seattle police officers all over the ID that evening. But the evening came and went, as did the following night. Nothing happened. We didn't see Pilay again among the gamblers going in and out of the club. We saw no police.

When I checked back in with our source, what I heard made my blood boil. He said Pilay hadn't shown up again, but someone else had. He was playing Hi-Q at one of the tables in the 609 when suddenly everyone got really quiet. Two tall white men in identical grey suits and thin dark ties were standing in the front door. They looked completely out of place, the old-timer said, like tourists who were looking for Tai-Tung's Chinese restaurant on the next block.

Addressing no one in particular, one of the guys said loudly, "We're looking for Boy Pilay. If anyone here knows where he is, or sees him come in, let him know we stopped by." They then turned and walked out.

It had to be the FBI making sure Pilay knew he was being sought so he could flee. I called Maida. I could hardly contain my anger.

"You told the FBI about Pilay."

"I had no choice. This is a joint investigation, whether you like it or not. You have no status to complain ... Why, what happened?"

I related what I'd heard, and Maida said nothing. After a moment of awkward silence, she said simply, "That is unfortunate. I'll find out what happened." She hung up.

I called Detective John Boatman at SPD. I trusted him completely.

"Hey, detective. Did you hear Boy Pilay is back in town?"

"That's the rumor. What do you have?" He sounded as interested as always.

"Can't say. Nothing real. But if I find him, will you arrest him?"

"I would love to cuff Pilay."

"You'd have to move very quickly." I hoped he caught my hint that he should not call Maida.

"Right. I'll pull the arrest warrant now."

"Thanks." The line clicked.

When Christopher and I met at the Bush Hotel that evening, I was despondent. There was no way Pilay would show back up at the 609. Someone would surely have tipped him off.

We agreed to suspend the stakeout until we had news that Pilay was still around. We waited a few weeks, and then our source said he saw Pilay on the streets the prior evening. He didn't go inside the gambling hall, but he was seen in the Hing Hay Park across the street with Tulisan gang member Boyse Campo. Birds of a feather.

I called Christopher, who joined me at the Bush Hotel. It didn't take long. At about 8 p.m., Christopher was on the binoculars while I finished off the pepperoni and olive pizza and cold Budweiser that had become our standard dinner fare.

"Lookie here, Mike!" Christopher sounded excited. "In the park right across the street from the 609, big as life." He handed me the well-used binoculars.

"It's hard to tell in the dark." I was not sure.

"Wait until he comes out under the street light," Christopher suggested.

I watched the street below for several more minutes. The man who looked like Pilay was wearing a strange hat and standing in the dark. I could only see his back. Every once in a while someone would approach him, chat for a second, then move on. Finally, the man starting walking toward the corner, heading across Main Street. In the street light, I could make out his face. It was Boy.

I called Boatman at home. No answer. I called him at the homicide division and he answered. Of course he was still at work. "I can see Pilay on 6th Avenue and King Street in the ID, detective. We need to bring it down." I was starting to sound like the cops on *Hawaii 5-0:* Book 'em, Danno!

Boatman told me he would bring in three squad cars, but he didn't have time to get the SWAT Team. "Can you tell if he has a weapon?"

"I can't tell, but you have to assume so." I was concerned about Pilay dying in a police shootout. We needed him alive. "We're going now. Stay off the street and out of our way. We'll get him."

Boatman signed off, and I turned my focus back to the street. It seemed like an hour, but was probably less than ten minutes before three cop cars appeared from three different directions. They surrounded Pilay as he stood on the corner. We heard shouts and threats, but in the end, Pilay thrust his hands up to the sky. Detective Boatman jumped out of his patrol car, pulled Pilay's wrists down, and slapped on the cuffs. He shoved Pilay's head down and into the back seat of the police car. Sirens blaring, the car sped off.

In a flash, Pilay was in jail. We had him.

CHAPTER TWENTY-THREE:

THE COVER-UP WINS AGAIN

Winter 1982-83
Seattle

The very next morning, Terri, Ade, Cindy, Jim Douglas, and I sat in Norm Maleng's office. I carefully summarized the evidence against Pilay and Baruso, based on the twelve-page memorandum I had written the previous August. I argued the evidence and the inferences with the soundest logic, while Maleng and Maida listened passively and without comment. Their body language was stiff and awkward.

I cleared my throat. "You have done a great job with the first two trials, Joanne. We really appreciate all you have done. We had a little kerfuffle getting Pilay arrested, but rest assured Baruso is freaking out right now."

"Norm, there is no justice without full justice," Terri added. She was sitting forward in her chair, framed by the large window that overlooked 3rd Avenue to the west. She stressed our basic point: Everyone responsible must be charged. We reminded them that Maida had argued in both trials that both Pilay and Baruso were part of the murder conspiracy.

"We agree," Terri concluded. "So we don't see the problem. You have had eighteen months to build a case. Baruso is a murderer!"

The prosecutors exchanged a glance, but did not respond.

I cut in. "Pilay is busted. We ran him out of Maryland. We cornered him in the ID. He has no money, no friends, no defense, and no hope. That smells like a plea bargain to me. He will turn against Baruso because he has no choice."

Maleng said, "Believe me, the SPD had its best interrogation team on Pilay all night. If he were going to break, he would have done so. But he said nothing. He's afraid, but not of us."

"Because you haven't charged him!" My pitch was rising as fast as my blood pressure. "We're not asking you to adopt our theory that the Marcos regime is involved. The dispute over dispatch nailed three gang members already. It will nail Pilay as well. But right now he's seeing big time weakness from you, since you haven't charged him or Baruso. He's calling your bluff."

"This isn't a game of poker." Maleng was getting worked up too. "We have to base our decision on the evidence, not the emotions. We would love to see Pilay and Baruso in jail, but we have a responsibility to prove their guilt beyond a reasonable doubt, and in this case, that's not easy." He stood to indicate the meeting was over. It wasn't.

"Norm, let the jury decide guilt or innocence. But don't you even think about letting Pilay out of jail." I was almost shouting. "If you do, he's a dead man."

Now the meeting was definitely over.

We walked out feeling like a huge opportunity was slipping slowly through our fingers.

The police held Pilay for the maximum allowable seventy-two hours without charging him, but then let him go. He disappeared into the foggy Seattle night.

Three weeks later, on January 27, 1983, Teodorico Domingues, also known as Boy Pilay, was found in a clearing underneath a Seattle freeway overpass. He was pronounced dead on the scene with two bullet holes in his head, fired at close range. His car was nearby, his blood and brains splattered all over the front seat.

Within days, two men, Valentino Barber and Esteban Ablang, were charged with the murder. The murder weapon was traced to Ablang, and when I saw his photo in the newspaper, I recognized him as the same man who had stood with Pilay behind Baruso's car during our stakeout. I shared this information and the photo with the police detective assigned to the case, but he informed me that Esteban Ablang had fled to the Philippines the day after the murder.

Valentino Barber was arrested and charged on the theory that it had been a revenge slaying. Pilay was widely suspected of having a hand in killing Valentino's uncle, Jesse Barber, many years earlier. We did our best to convince the prosecuting attorney that Pilay was murdered because he knew too much, and shared the evidence that he was with both Baruso and Ablang prior to the murders. Ablang, we argued, had no interest in some revenge murder of a man he never knew.

Nevertheless, the prosecutors went to trial with the revenge story, and in May 1983, the hapless Val Barber was convicted. Ablang was never caught.

The next CJDV newsletter said it all. By now, the newsletter had wide circulation, particularly in Seattle, the Bay Area and Washington, DC, where offices of the CJDV were located. The headline read, "Justice Has Been Cast in a Deadly Chokehold." The article referenced the actions by the Seattle Police Department, the King County Sheriff's office, and other police departments around the country in detaining prisoners, usually men of color, using a "chokehold" tactic that prevented the prisoner from breathing, often resulting in death or brain damage.

The article read, in part:

"Does this smell of a cover-up, or not?" asked Cindy Domingo, National Coordinator for the Committee for Justice for Domingo and Viernes (CJDV) and sister of Silme Domingo, after the verdict in the Boy Pilay case. "What do you do when for two years you've been giving leads and

evidence to the prosecutor that would further strengthen the case against Baruso and he discounts it as irrelevant material?"

We had followed up our investigation of Pilay in Maryland and located a key, independent witness, Noni Aquino. Aquino had been a close friend of Pilay's while he lived in Maryland and knew his brother and father well. He supplied us with an affidavit which confirmed that:

1. Pilay admitted that he was one of the hitmen in the Domingo/Viernes murders;

2. Baruso had "instructed" Pilay in the murders and promised to pay him $5,000 but never did so;

3. Pilay had returned to Seattle to "turn himself in."

4. Pilay's father and brother believed that Pilay was killed by Baruso because "he knew too much."

5. Pilay said he had lived with Baruso from time to time and was paid regularly by him for odd jobs. They were very close.

Despite this evidence, the prosecutor for Pilay's murder never interviewed Aquino, Pilay's father, or his brother.

Evidence at Barber's trial revealed that Ablang was paid a large sum of money in hundred dollar bills for the hit. The prosecutor never established who paid this money.

It didn't matter. Ablang was long gone. The hope of turning Pilay to testify against Baruso was up in gun smoke. The chances of charging Baruso now were slim to none. Despair ruled my world and that of the CJDV loyalists.

The CJDV held a press conference on May 5, 1983, and leveled serious dereliction of duty charges against Norm Maleng and his office. Cindy stated:

Norm Maleng has long had the image of an objective, liberal and well-respected prosecutor. Recently this image has been tarnished and Maleng's true colors have been thoroughly exposed. As with other supposedly 'neutral' judicial institutions in our society, the prosecutor's office clearly operates with the most profound political biases. Maleng prosecutes to the hilt the common person and petty gangsters. But when powerful interests are threatened, he shirks from his sworn duty ... The Committee for Justice has little confidence that Maleng will charge Baruso.

CHAPTER TWENTY-FOUR:

IMMUNITY

Seattle

Meanwhile, developments in our civil lawsuit were equally ominous. Within a month of being served by Bill Davis, the US State Department brought a Suggestion of Immunity in front of Judge Voorhees. In this pleading, the State Department, represented by the very same US Attorney's office which was obstructing our justice efforts, informed Judge Voorhees that both Ferdinand and Imelda Marcos enjoyed head of state immunity, and that the foreign policy of the US would be adversely affected if the lawsuit against them were not dismissed immediately.

Head of state immunity was widely recognized by the courts to be absolute and not dependent upon the nature of the violations alleged. The State Department's brief was full of assertions of national security, state's interests, and the "train of horribles" that would befall our country if Marcos was required to defend our case. Overall, the State Department's suggestion was as subtle as a sledge hammer.

Our legal team had decided to pursue a more nuanced approach to any suggestion of immunity. We recognized that, in almost all cases, a sitting foreign head of state could not be sued in US court. At the same time, we argued for a Nuremberg exception to immunity, based on the prosecution of Nazi war criminals after World War II. This exception would require even a head of state to appear and defend a lawsuit that alleged serious violations of the Law of Nations, including those prohibiting the use of summary execution as an instrument of state policy.

Summary execution refers to actions by a military or a government that become the accuser, prosecutor, judge, jury, and executioner of political opponents without a just and fair trial. It is a form of extra-judicial punishment and is universally recognized as a violation of the Law of Nations.

We also hoped to develop and push forward the legal doctrine of universal jurisdiction, which had been argued in other cases brought by our co-counsel, the Center for Constitutional Rights in New York. This doctrine recognized that lawsuits or criminal charges could be brought against the perpetrators of human rights violations wherever such person could be located and sued. Since we served Marcos in the US, courts in this country would have jurisdiction over the human rights case against him.

Unfortunately, this doctrine had never been found to trump head of state immunity, and we knew our chances of getting it adopted in our case were admittedly slim. But that didn't prevent our CJDV communications team from going into overdrive. We publicly and loudly decried the assertion of national security and foreign policy interests as a means to avoid taking responsibility for the murders of two American citizens in broad daylight. We pointed out that the US intervention into the case on behalf of Marcos was further evidence of the long-time US support for a foreign dictator who oppressed the rights of his own people.

Judge Voorhees, without even waiting for our opposition brief, granted the State Department's motion to dismiss the Marcoses from the lawsuit "with prejudice." This ostensibly meant they could never be brought back into the lawsuit again. It was a huge setback, but we still had the Republic of the Philippines in the case, and we thought we could still put Marcos in the dock that way.

On January 21, 1983, our legal team received the US government's motion to dismiss our case. Claiming the murders were a result of internal union strife, the motion brusquely brushed aside our claims that the United States itself violated international law as a purely political question and not subject to judicial inquiry. The individually named federal officials boldly asserted that they enjoyed absolute immunity based upon national security and foreign policy prerogatives.

Father Davis had served Secretary of State Alexander Haig with our lawsuit in the dead of winter, both men slipping and sliding on the ice that covered the ground outside Haig's house. Now our case against Haig felt like it was sliding away. He claimed that the parties bringing the lawsuit challenged the US's relationship with the Philippines, which was intricately interwoven into the conduct of foreign affairs.

On February 13, we filed our opposition, citing over 145 separate cases and many articles and treatises which supported our position. Relying on a detailed complaint that alleged specific acts by the FBI, US Naval Investigative Service, and the CIA in surveilling and infiltrating the KDP, and providing false and derogatory information about Gene Viernes to the Marcos regime, the brief argued that these defendants:

(a) Agreed to join and carry out the goals of the civil conspiracy to harass, intimidate, and commit acts of physical violence against the Marcos opposition, including Gene Viernes and Silme Domingo, and to prevent them from exercising their constitutional rights to free speech and association;

(b) Communicated this agreement to the other US and Philippine government defendants;

(c) Directed their agents and subordinates to engage in specific acts of surveillance and intimidation of anti-Marcos Filipinos;

(d) Cooperated with similar acts of Marcos agents;

(e) Carried out a policy of non-enforcement of the criminal laws of the US against Marcos agents; and

(f) Engaged in specific acts to cover up the illegal objectives of the conspiracy.

Over thirty individual, overt acts of conspiracy were alleged and restated in the opposition brief. We pointed out that in 1971, the US Supreme Court had authorized a lawsuit against federal agents for the violation of constitutional rights in a case called *Bivens*.

As to national security and foreign policy immunity, we cited numerous cases holding that those categories are inherently vague and ill-defined, stating that the potential scope of such an exception is boundless. One case stated that "No doctrine that the Court could promulgate would seem more sinister and alarming." We agreed.

That language was the gist of what we briefed, and we hoped the court would quickly deny the motion. Our hopes were dashed.

Months passed without a ruling.

In April of 1983, in response to the US's brazen assertion of national security immunity, the CJDV convened a seminar on national security that featured International Law Professor Dr. Richard Falk of Princeton University, Larry Sarjeant of the National Conference of Black Lawyers, and Rene Cruz of the KDP. Falk was my inspiration for going to law school and spoke eloquently. "This case is not only shocking," he said, "it is, in its way, routine – routine in the sense that where state interests are at stake, dictators dispose of anything that stands in their way."

Sarjeant recounted the abuses of the FBI in COINTELPRO and stated, "We must resolve to challenge such spurious doctrines as national security and foreign policy immunity, which serve only to preserve the power structure. We must retain the belief that while we may at times be deterred, we still not be denied."

Rene detailed the long pattern of harassment experienced by the anti-Marcos movement in the US. "To us, when American citizens are murdered in broad daylight and a foreign government is clearly implicated, we would expect our own government to stand on our side and assist us in getting justice. Instead, with the local US Attorney, with the State Department, and with the Justice Department, we get nothing but a well-orchestrated cover-up. They are siding with a foreign government, not American citizens. If the words 'national security' mean anything, it should mean that Gene and Silme should have been secure in their exercise of their constitutional rights, not that Marcos would be secure in having them killed."

Rene's comments, delivered with spirit, brought the audience to their feet with shouts of support and agreement.

Tony Lee of the Seattle Archdiocese read a statement from the church. "The US government's obsession with 'national security' inevitably results in policies which excuse human rights violations and ignore economic and social injustices because all these other concerns are subordinated to maintaining or furthering the 'security' interest of the US."

The CJDV's community plan had produced tangible results in mobilizing the broadest front against the cover-up, and the anti-democratic legal doctrines the US was asserting in our case.

CHAPTER TWENTY-FIVE:

DISCOVERY

Seattle

Despite all the legal maneuvers we confronted in those early months, we were also able to initiate the first phase of our discovery efforts, which were mainly directed at obtaining documents through *subpoenas duces tecum*. This is a procedure that allows a party in a lawsuit to obtain documents from individuals or companies who are not parties in the lawsuit but who have evidence needed to prove the case. The result was that we could subpoena Baruso and the lower-level conspirators, but discovery against the US and Philippine governments was limited while their motions were resolved.

Though limited, our discovery was well directed. We subpoenaed Baruso's credit card records, his travel agency's flight information, and his bank accounts, including deposits and withdrawals at critical dates. We submitted written discovery questions, called Interrogatories, to his attorney, and the response proved that Baruso was increasingly aware of his trouble.

Baruso's counsel, Tony Savage, announced that his client would assert his Fifth Amendment privilege against self-incrimination to all questions related to the murders, the union, its dispatch procedures, and the like: in short, to all of the questions he had been asked in the criminal trials of Ramil, Guloy, and Dictado. Baruso also denied knowing or having any contact with various Philippine government officials.

We sent formal Interrogatories and Requests for Production of Documents to counsel for the Republic of the Philippines. We sought additional documents from the FBI and NIS, along with other US intelligence agencies. We demanded the FBI's full file on their supposed Hobbs Act violation investigation. We received nothing of value.

Document discovery is notoriously time consuming – a real-life example of looking for needles in haystacks. However, in the case of Baruso's travel and credit card records, the evidence jumped out at us. His travel records showed that he bought his plane ticket for San Francisco on May 4, 1981, the day he got back from the ILWU Convention in Hawaii. We saw that Baruso stayed at the Sutter Hotel in downtown San Francisco, within blocks of the Philippine consulate, on May 16, 1981, for a meeting the following day at the consulate. We also noted that he made small deposits of cash on numerous occasions between June and August of 1981, totaling close to $10,000.

From our earlier investigation, headed by Christopher Hershey, we knew Baruso had traveled to the Philippines on numerous occasions since 1976, and that he had once met with Ferdinand Marcos himself at Malacanang Palace. Lynn Domingo had also found two letters, written by Baruso on Local 37 stationery and buried in the disorganized union files. The first was dated December 15, 1976, and was addressed to *His Excellency President Ferdinand Marcos* personally. He wrote, "I have made known in the United States I was enthused with the progress in metropolitan Manila, the friendly smiles of the people, and the tranquility and admiration of the people toward the government and to Your Honor, the President."

The second letter was written to the Philippine Consul General in San Francisco, Romeo Arguelles. In it, Baruso reiterates his "wholehearted support" of his administration, stating "my feelings for our President is not only one of admiration but of unflinching belief and faith made firmer by the personal contacts and exchanges of views with him ... I would like to reassure you of my support at all times. Allow me should the occasion arise to reciprocate in whatever possible way your kindness."

As we prepared to take Baruso's deposition in mid-January 1983, we convened a meeting of the legal team, plus Bruce, Terri, and Cindy at Jim's law office in the Smith Tower.

Jim summarized what we'd learned.

"So right after the ILWU resolution passed, Baruso comes back to Seattle and immediately buys a ticket to San Francisco to meet with the consulate?" Cindy asked, spinning tight circles in her swivel chair. The window behind her framed a dreary view over the groups of homeless people clustered in Pioneer Square. Grey against a backdrop of darker grey, they stood huddled in threadbare coats that did little to shelter them from the winter winds.

Bruce clenched his hands. "This confirms what Bill's intelligence source said about a meeting in May."

"The theory gets fleshed out a little more," I said pensively, standing up to draw on the butcher paper boards in Jim's office library. "Let's put it together, step by step." I took out a marker and wrote it out, hoping a visual would help.

- Step One: After Baruso publicly supports the ILWU resolution against Marcos, he gets called on the carpet by pro-Marcos forces in Hawaii.

"But who?" John asked.

"Good point. Let's assume at least the union guys, Quitives and Alcaraz, and probably the consul general in Hawaii, Alconcel." Trinidad Alconcel was the former consul general in San Francisco who was involved in the disappearance of Marcos' former press secretary Primitivo

Mijares, who was "salvaged" after threatening to testify in Congress about what he called the conjugal dictatorship.

- Step Two: Someone, probably Alconcel, sends a report on the debacle at the ILWU Convention up the chain to Manila.

John said, "Right. By that time, Marcos and Ver must have received intelligence reports that Gene traveled to the islands, and that he'd carried a large sum of money to the NPA or NDF and had meetings with KMU leadership. That had to raise some hackles."

I leaned forward. "When the news of the resolution arrives, they go operational."

"They are pissed that Baruso supported it," Jim said.

"And that it passed," Terri exclaimed, face flushed.

I continued to write on the butcher paper.

- Step Three: Manila tells Alconcel or someone in Hawaii to get Baruso to San Francisco a meeting on the 17th.

I wondered about going after the cable traffic, NSA intercepts of Marcos communications, and travel plans of senior Marcos military officials. How could we get our hands on those telexes? They were unlikely to still exist, given what Bill told us about documents disappearing.

- Step Four: Baruso agrees, buys a ticket to San Francisco and flies down on the 16th.

"He stayed overnight within blocks of the consulate. Maybe he doesn't know why he's being summoned, so doesn't bother to hide anything."

"We still have to put Baruso in a meeting with the Philippine military," Jim reminded us.

I nodded, hand moving faster.

- Step Five: On May 17th, someone from Marcos's military flies to the Bay Area, and they meet at the consulate.

We reasoned that Baruso was told to take care of the problem that his fellow union officers have created for the regime. Baruso is happy to please Marcos and figures out on his own how to make the murders look like a dispute over dispatch. But he needs to make sure they get both Gene and Silme.

"Yep," Jim mused, scratching his five o'clock shadow – the same one all the men in the room seemed to continuously sport these days. "Killing Gene isn't enough, because Silme would carry on and lead the ILWU delegation to the Philippines."

- Step Six: Baruso hires the Tulisan gang, pays them $5,000 and gives him his gun for the hit.

It was my best guess, but I spoke with conviction.

Jim said, "This theory comports with all of the known evidence. It is compelling."

John was looking ahead. "We need to be careful when we depose Baruso. I bet his lawyer isn't keeping track of all the discoveries in the case, and he doesn't even realize we have this evidence. If Baruso doesn't take the Fifth, he has to have an alibi for this trip or deny it happened. I predict that he will deny it."

"We can only hope." I suspected that Baruso must have learned his lesson about making up stupid alibis and would probably take the Fifth. There was no good way to explain the cash into his bank accounts, but maybe he would try to fool us into believing he had nothing to hide by answering seemingly innocuous questions.

Our first deposition of Tony Baruso took place on January 13, 1983. As predicted, Baruso took the Fifth on any questions directly related to the murders, but he tried to skate on general topics that appeared to be tangential, including his travel and bank activities before the murders.

When I asked him whether he went out of town between the time of the ILWU Convention in Hawaii and the murders, he said he had not. Then he added, "I don't remember." He obviously didn't know what we had.

I asked if he had any reason to be in the Bay Area in May of 1981. He said no. He also denied traveling to Honolulu in December of 1981 to attend a Barrio Fiesta event in the Filipino community, in which Imelda Marcos appeared, although our sources informed us that he was there with a former Seattle consular official, Lourdes "Lulu" de la Cruz. Baruso appeared visibly shaken by the questioning, particularly when I asked whether he and de la Cruz had been seen together at the event with Imelda.

I asked how he got a US national security clearance. He dissembled, claiming it was for his job at Boeing. I tried to see if he would admit calling the US State Department within twenty-four hours of the murders. He said he couldn't recall. I asked whether he had any sources of income in 1981 other than as union president and his work at Boeing. He said no. I asked whether he had deposited a lot of cash into his bank account between the murders and the end of the year. He denied that.

Baruso carried the albatross of guilt like an anvil around his neck. He sagged and sighed and looked peeved at me. He had been ousted from the union, ostracized in the community, and we knew he faced prosecution from the Department of Labor for double dipping from the insurance account. Now he was targeted by our discovery, and we were relentless. I actually enjoyed, if only for the moment, sensing how heavily this burden was bearing on him.

CHAPTER TWENTY-SIX:

THE DIA CIRCULAR

Early 1983
Seattle

As productive as Baruso's deposition was, it was the next development that really got us excited.

Cindy brought it to a meeting of the national CJDV team. We meet at John Caughlan's house in Madison Park on a bright Sunday morning in early 1983, not long after Pilay was assassinated. Lionel Ritchie's "Hello" was playing on the radio as we finished the scrumptious brunch. Everyone was in a good mood.

"We have a confidential source in the Defense Department who heard about our case," Cindy explained. "Maybe he read the Wicker editorial in the *Times*. He wants to leak an explosive document related to the Philippine Infiltration Plan." Murmurs of surprise and encouragement filled the room. Was this the break we were waiting for?

"Who is he and where does he work?" I asked mindlessly.

"Don't ask, because we won't tell," Cindy said, looking askance at my question. "What is that term the spy agencies use? You are not on a 'need to know basis.'"

The room cracked up.

"The source is really nervous about being fired, but is willing to work with us," she explained, serious again. We needed to promise that the CJDV would not release the document directly. It had to be through a "cut out" –

an intermediary of impeccable credentials—who would not reveal where the document came from.

"When can we see it?" Whatever the mystery document said, we would have to authenticate its contents through a witness in order to get it admitted into evidence in our case. But still, it was a lead.

"I'm going to ask Bill Cate to release it," Cindy said, referring to the head of the Church Council of Greater Seattle. "He's beyond suspicion and not closely identified with us."

"If the source provides it to Reverend Cate rather than directly to us, we can keep our fingerprints off it all together," Bruce added.

Reverend Cate convened a press conference to announce that he had obtained a secret Defense Intelligence Agency (DIA) circular entitled "New Philippine Defense Attaché Team Assigned." The document, written by a DIA analyst in July 1982, was explosive. It described five high-ranking officers of the Philippine military, including General Angel Kanapi and Lieutenant Colonel Roman Madella, who had been appointed to attaché posts at the Philippine embassy in DC. The DIA circular featured pictures of Kanapi and Madella and introduced them to the US defense and intelligence communities. Kanapi was described as a graduate of the Philippine Military Academy, class of 1953, "one of two classes most relied upon by Marcos to execute and administer martial law between 1972 and 1981." Madella was widely believed to be one of the most brutal interrogators in Marcos' military, high on Amnesty International's list of suspected torturers.

The circular described the pair as the "highest level" of senior military attachés ever sent to the US by the Marcos regime. It described their close ties to the president and General Ver, and underscored the role they would play in the then-upcoming state visit of Marcos to the US.

The assignment was described as a clear reflection of the importance Marcos attached to the relationship with the US. To us, it suggested the sense of urgency Marcos felt to keep tabs on and suppress the growing movement in the US opposed to his regime.

The circular stated the DIA believed the team would be involved in the delicate negotiations on the US Bases Agreement (Subic Bay and Clark Air Field) set to begin in 1983. But what caught our attention was the way that their additional tasks were described:

The new team is also expected to monitor Philippine dissident activity in the US. Given the background of Colonel Rosales and Madella—the latter was a guard and interrogator of an American incriminated in a series of bombings in Manila in 1980—the attachés will undoubtedly report on and possibly operate against the anti-Marcos Philippine activists in the US.

The CJDV leadership team understood that "operate against" was spy talk for infiltrating, harassing, counteracting, disrupting, intimidating, and committing acts of violence against activists.

The DIA circular was damning evidence that US intelligence approved the Philippine government's use of military attachés assigned to the embassy under diplomatic cover to hide their essential purpose, which was to operate against the opposition. As such, US officials were complicit in the violation of US and international law, which prohibited military officials of a foreign regime from using their diplomatic cover for intelligence gathering and intimidation of their nationals or US citizens in the host country.

The Seattle press covered Cate's release of the document, and we put it before Judge Voorhees as proof, in the DIA's own words, of the Philippine Infiltration Plan. We couldn't trace Kanapi or Madella directly to the murders, but having a US government document prove the essential allegation in our lawsuit gave us hope.

Despite the new evidence, though, on July 14, 1983, Judge Voorhees dealt our case yet another blow: he granted the motion to dismiss the US government defendants, saying we had failed to state a claim upon which relief could be granted. This meant that even if we could prove every fact we alleged, there was no legal theory that would support our lawsuit.

He claimed we had not alleged a conspiracy against a suspect classification. In other words, he said that one group of Filipinos (Marcos and his allies) was not discriminating against another group (the anti-Marcos movement) on the basis of race, national origin, or gender. He said the animus was political, and that was not enough. Judge Voorhees granted the Philippines' motion to dismiss as well, but allowed us to amend the complaint to be more specific.

Although the judge said he did not buy the national security immunity argument per se, he might as well have. We had no case.

We were devastated. Appealing the decision would likely take well over a year. In the meantime, without Marcos and the US as defendants, we had only the government of the Philippines, Baruso, and the hitmen left in the case. We filed a First Amended Complaint and waited for the onslaught of legal motions and diversions.

But then the course of history, like the zig-zags of a tributary flowing to the sea, changed dramatically. It began with another murder, but this time Marcos went too far.

CHAPTER TWENTY-SEVEN:

SENATOR AQUINO

August 21, 1983
Tarmac, Manila International Airport

Senator Benigno Aquino Jr. was widely recognized as the leading Filipino political figure who could threaten Marcos' rule if he were ever allowed back in the country.

But that was a big if.

Hailing from one of the leading oligarchical families in the Philippines, Aquino grew up watching both his father and grandfather serve presidential administrations. Aquino himself moved up rapidly in politics, serving as the youngest governor of his home province of Tarlac before becoming a leading senator in the Liberal Party. He was widely assumed to be a shoo-in for president when Marcos' last term in office was set to end in 1972.

But instead of giving up his office, Marcos declared martial law and abolished the legislature. Senator Aquino was arrested, tried, and convicted of sedition by a military court. He was imprisoned in solitary confinement for nine years under a sentence of death by firing squad.

Aquino responded with a long hunger strike that attracted world-wide attention, but also adversely affected his health. He developed a serious heart condition, which led to two heart attacks in 1980. Filipino military doctors were unable to perform the life-saving bypass surgery he needed, so they permitted him to travel to the US. After successful surgery,

Aquino taught at Harvard and headed the Movement for a Free Philippines, the moderate wing of the anti-Marcos movement in the US.

Throughout his exile, Aquino always said he planned to return to his country, hopefully to oust the Marcos regime. By 1983, Aquino decided it was time. Ferdinand Marcos had developed lupus and was weakened both politically and physically. The economy was failing, and the opposition, led by the NPA in the countryside and the KMU in the cities, was gaining ground rapidly.

Aquino was fully aware of the dangers that awaited him. Warned that he would either be imprisoned or killed, Aquino answered, "If it's my fate to die by an assassin's bullet, so be it. But

I cannot be petrified by inaction, or fear of assassination, and therefore stay on the side." The statement proved prophetic.

On August 21, 1983, Aquino boarded a flight from Los Angeles to Manila with his supporters, including his brother-in-law, Ken Kashiwahara, an ABC-TV journalist from the Bay Area. He and his entourage were jovial, as Aquino talked about how much he looked forward to again being on Philippine soil. Ken filmed the entire sequence of events.

As soon as they landed in Manila, military gendarmes boarded the plane to escort Aquino from the plane. The officers barred anyone, including Ken, from leaving with him. As Aquino stepped onto the tarmac, a hail of bullets from his military escort struck him in the back of the head, and he landed face down, never to rise again. Soldiers loaded his body into an armored personnel carrier and hauled him away before his supporters could react.

Another man on the airport tarmac, Rolando Galman, was shot dead as well. The Marcos government claimed Galman was Aquino's assassin, hired by the communists, but no one believed them.

Aquino's funeral procession, held on August 31 in Quezon City, was presided over by Catholic Archbishop Jaime Sin and included the senator's widow, Corazon, and his five children, who had all flown to the Philippines from the US. Over two million people filled the street to view Aquino in his open casket, his face still bearing the scars inflicted by his assailants.

An ocean away, the murder of Benito Aquino Jr. was a time for reflection and rededication. The CJDV never doubted that we were up against a ruthless regime, willing to commit summary executions in broad daylight.

Aquino's death only confirmed our theory that Ferdinand Marcos was willing to use "any means necessary" against his opposition. But it also reminded us of just how desperate the Marcos regime had become, and how dangerous our path forward was.

CHAPTER TWENTY-EIGHT:

THE FORSYTHE DEPOSITION

1983
Port Orchard, Washington

We had to quickly turn our attention away from the Aquino assassination in order to prepare for the deposition of LeVane Forsythe. We continued to suspect that Forsythe was an informant for one or more US intelligence agencies, and we wanted to find out who had sent him to the scene of the murders on June 1, and/or who had asked him to testify for the hitmen. Either answer would prove he was involved in a cover-up by sinister forces who might have had pre-knowledge of the murders.

The legal team knew we would probably only get one chance at a deposition, and that Forsythe would likely plead the Fifth Amendment since he had clearly perjured himself in his testimony at the Ramil and Guloy trial. But we were prepared for anything.

To help me prepare, I contacted Hal Rhoden, the probate attorney from Southern California who represented Noah Dietrich, the man Howard Hughes had named as the executor of his estate in many of his wills, including the one in question. Dietrich and Rhoden had litigated the Mormon Will case on behalf of Melvin Dummar. Dummar had claimed the will had been left in his gas station by a mysterious courier: none other than LeVane Forsythe.

Forsythe's testimony stated Hughes handed him an envelope at the Bayshore Inn Hotel in Vancouver, British Columbia, and told him to follow the instructions in the envelope when he passed away, which he did. Forsythe claimed he did not know it was a will.

Forsythe said he had flown with an architect friend from Seattle, Alex Bertulius, to San Francisco, where he then rented a car and drove to Utah. This drew my attention because Forsythe claimed in Ramil and Guloy's trial that he was trying to call an architect friend, Alex Bertulius, when he was at the phone booth across the street from Local 37.

As we'd heard in Ramil and Guloy's trial, Forsythe passed numerous lie detector tests when asked whether Hughes himself had given him the will, whether he delivered it, and to whom and where. Bertulius confirmed Forsythe's account of the trip to San Francisco, but he did not accompany him to Utah. The fact the judge didn't believe Forsythe was a source of surprise and consternation to Rhoden, whose effort to get the will probated was unsuccessful.

I tracked down Mr. Bertulius near his office in the Madison Park neighborhood of Seattle, and asked what he knew about Forsythe. He merely said, "He's a spook. CIA." We engaged in small talk, but he wouldn't say anything else about Forsythe.

The only other lead I had to help me understand Forsythe came from his trial testimony about his connection to Robert Maheu, an infamous member of the "invisible government" or "deep state" — personnel in or formerly in the CIA, FBI, NSA, Department of Defense, or the military contractors who comprised what President Dwight D. Eisenhower called the "military industrial complex" who sought to secretly guide US national security doctrines. These agents and their activities could not be traced to particular agencies in any formal or accountable way, and so were used for black bag jobs, like the Watergate break-in and other secret crimes.

There was ample evidence that both Forsythe and Maheu worked as bag men for Howard Hughes, delivering large sums of cash to politicians and leaders of community and business. Maheu was also the person the Kennedy administration used to contact John Roselli and Sam Giancana of the Mafia about assassinating Cuban president Fidel Castro, and he was suspected of so many other undercover deeds for the US and for Hughes, there was widespread concern within the US intelligence community that Maheu would spill the family jewels if he were ever indicted. So he wasn't.

This fact was borne out by a memo from the House Intelligence Committee, authored in 1976, that related its staff's conversation with CIA officials. The memo stated that one CIA official believed the prosecution of Maheu would lead to exposure of sensitive information related to the abortive Cuban invasion in April 1961 – the Bay of Pigs fiasco – and would result in damaging embarrassment to the United States government.

And Forsythe, under pressure from Maida in her cross-examination, had named Maheu as someone in the Hughes empire who could vouch for him.

In their takeover of Las Vegas in the late sixties and early seventies, Hughes and Maheu had befriended the then governor of Nevada, Paul Laxalt, an up-and-coming Republican who later became a senator from Nevada and a close personal friend and confidant of President Reagan and his wife. Was there a connection there? I had a long list of names to ask Forsythe about, including Laxalt.

We convened his deposition in a court reporter's office in Port Orchard, just a ferry boat ride away across Puget Sound from Seattle and just south of the navy town of Bremerton and the Puget Sound Naval Shipyard.

Forsythe was helpful without trying to be. He was cagey, secretive, and knew when to dissemble. He struck me as someone without any moral compass.

He testified that he was a paid informant for the FBI as part of a presidential task force run by the FBI, IRS, and DEA, and had been for many years. His control agent was Ralph Hernandez, who operated out of Cucamonga, California. Forsythe never mentioned working for the local Seattle FBI office. He claimed he had been tapped by the FBI to conduct a number of top secret projects, including placing sophisticated electronic surveillance equipment into the noses of commercial aircraft heading from Anchorage to Japan, flying over North Korea and the Soviet Union. He testified that he had over twenty pseudonyms and aliases he used when he was a courier and bag man for Howard Hughes.

He seemed to be on a first-name basis with a number of Hughes' lieutenants, including Maheu, Nadine Hensley, and Johnny Meier. He claimed to have met Laxalt, and handled some

confidential matters for him as well. As in his trial testimony, Forsythe testified that he helped his son get a job working for a Hughes-run business.

I asked him about his modus operandi as an informant. He testified that he would be called by someone, not always Hernandez, and told to go to a particular location. He'd observe what happened, write or dictate a report, and send it to whoever hired him. Beyond that, Forsythe could not be pinned down about critical details. In his testimony, he said that he was "not trying too hard to remember" certain things, including where he sent his report about Gene and Silme's murders. He repeatedly scolded me for "not asking the right questions," and even admitted talking to fellow task force members about his testimony in the Ramil and Guloy trial.

He reiterated his story about being present at the site of the murder. He swore he handwrote his report on the ferry, and that he showed a copy to and discussed what he witnessed on June 1 with his wife and a neighbor, who he identified as Mark Williams. He claimed Mark was a naval officer who worked in intelligence at the navy yard in Bremerton. When I took Rebecca Forsythe's deposition, I found out the neighbor's real name was Mark Williamson. Why would Forsythe lie about his name?

We entered a copy of his report as an exhibit to the deposition. Who did he send it to? He wasn't trying real hard to remember.

Rebecca Forsythe, in her deposition, confirmed the essential details of her husband's story, including that he informed her and Mark Williamson on June 1 that he had witnessed the shooting in Pioneer Square. She seemed to be telling the truth about her husband. Not that I believed him, but I believed her. He had told her what he saw.

By the end of the depositions, I was convinced that Forsythe had been present at the murders. He seemed comfortable describing the scene of the murders. To have been there on the exact day and time, he had to have been sent by someone with knowledge of the murder conspiracy, and probably even the Marcos regime's role in it. This black bag operative wanted eyes and ears on the ground to make sure everything went according to plan.

My leading suspect for this role was Robert Maheu, who I thought would have relished another soiree into the operational world. The other suspect was someone in the FBI.

Of course, the problem remained that Judge Voorhees had dismissed the US government defendants from the lawsuit, and we had little chance of getting them reinstated. So we weren't sure how we could use Forsythe's testimony at trial, if at all.

Our subsequent deposition of Forsythe's control agent, FBI Special Agent Ralph Hernandez, was also revealing, though we were limited in our questioning to three substantive areas.

Was Forsythe was an informant for the FBI?

Answer: Yes.

Was he considered to be a reliable informant?

Answer: Yes.

Was he used as a confidential informant for the FBI even after he testified at the Ramil and Guloy trial (where he knowingly perjured himself)?

Answer: Yes.

We also put forward Interrogatories and Requests for Production of Documents to the Republic of the Philippines. Their lawyers responded with little of value, mostly objections and obfuscations. They were likely distracted by the events unfolding closer to home. Ferdinand Marcos and General Ver were having a hard time convincing the world that they had nothing to do with the murder of Senator Aquino. Their effort to implicate Rolando Galman blew up in their faces when it was revealed he was taken to the airport by Marcos' military intelligence officers, who then killed him for the murder. Talk about a cover-up!

CHAPTER TWENTY-NINE:

THE QUIET YEARS

1983-86

By the end of 1983 and for a few years after, our lawsuit hung by a thread. Our discouragement put a dark pall over our justice efforts. The initial flurry of constant meetings, security threats, and anxiety over the cover-up had taken its toll on all of us emotionally and physically.

Still, we hung on to that thread for dear life. As dark as those days were, we always felt that help was on its way.

The CJDV continued to host widely attended memorials in June of each year, and the impending overthrow of Ferdinand Marcos in the Philippines became an effective rallying point for our ongoing justice effort.

The IPS's Saul Landau, who had provided us with important analysis and support years before, was featured at the 1985 memorial. When he took the podium, Landau drove his lesson home. "When you hear these two words – national security – you know two things are certain. First, that a crime is being committed, and second, that it is being covered up."

A 1986 CJDV newsletter contained extensive analysis of the crisis engulfing the Marcos regime:

The public outcry in the Philippines over the assassination and continued human rights violations has not subsided; in fact, it has grown to include a significant sectors [sic] from the business community, middle-class and people from Marcos' own camp. Significantly, this opposition has not only called for an end to the Marcos regime but has begun to target US Support for the dictatorship and the presence of US bases at Clark Air Base and Subic Naval Base.... [T]he sheer breadth of the anti-Marcos movement gives them wide political initiative. In particular, the growth of the insurgency and the influence of the left-led opposition, as demonstrated in the formation of BAYAN, a broad-based coalition of groups and individuals sympathetic to the program of the National Democratic Front.

Cindy assumed day-to-day operational control of the CJDV and had turned her efforts to raising money from foundations and church groups. CJDV activist Kris Melroe was a great asset in the fundraising efforts. Ade, Nemesio Jr., and Lynn continued to work on CJDV and Local 37 matters, even as Nemesio Sr.'s health deteriorated. Terri was firmly established as the president of Local 37, even as the union weathered years of "concessionary bargaining," which resulted in significant wage cuts in order to salvage the contracts it maintained.

The CJDV's work was still demanding on Terri. She shouldered the burden without complaint, though that certainly didn't make her home life any better. Ligaya and Kalayaan, six and eight years old by 1986, were raised by the movement. Emily continued to live with them, and many meetings of the Local 37 team convened in their Beacon Hill house. The kids seemed used to the constant stress and pressure that Terri felt, but still suffered emotionally from the loss of their father.

My own life changed in the quiet years as well. The money from Gene and Silme's life insurance policies ran out in 1984, and I was forced to seek a new job. I was lucky to have great friends at Schroeter Goldmark and Bender, including Len Schroeter and Paul Whalen. Len had always chafed at not being able to convince his law firm to take the Domingo case, and Paul was one of its leading rain makers. The firm had recently taken up litigating hundreds of personal injury cases involving asbestos-related lung diseases, and they invited me to be part of it.

As a condition of joining the firm, I insisted that they allow me to bring the Domingo case into the office. This raised some eyebrows. During my interview, one of the partners suggested it would take an overthrow of the Marcos regime in the Philippines for us to win, noting that their screening criteria did not usually include the need for revolution in a foreign country.

I answered their concerns, accepted their job offer, and in October 1984 started taking and defending depositions in asbestos injury cases, winning the "Deposition King" award for attending fifty depositions in my first month on the job.

Soon after I started at the firm, I met my future wife, Alison Rooks, at a local tavern, the Red Onion, in Madison Park near John's house. She was there with a close Filipina friend who had heard of our case. I'd headed there after hearing the Steely Dan song "You Gotta Go Back, Jack, and Do It Again." A believer in the guiding mesh of the spiritual world, I interpreted this as a sign that it was time to let somebody into my life again after years spent in the dating wasteland. I hadn't had a serious relationship since I mangled things with Cindy. I also heard the Eagles lyrics from "Desperado:" *You gotta let somebody love you before its too late.*

It was getting really late. As we started to talk, I was drawn to Alison's calmness and serenity, something that I had not had much of for the last three years. I tried valiantly to get her phone number, without success. I offered her my card, but she said, "Don't count on my calling you." As they drove away in Alison's VW bus, her friend rolled down the window and yelled, "She works at the Bon Marché."

The next morning, I tracked Alison down in the Bon Marché, a department store in downtown Seattle. When she knew I was interested, she did her due diligence on me and called her uncle, a King County Superior Court judge. When the judge passed me, she accepted a date, and remained together. When we married, John Caughlan and Paul Whelan stood as my best men. I needed two.

My kids were doing well, attending Garfield High School, in Seattle's Central District, as Advanced Placement students. My relationship with Alison improved my relationship with them, and the four of us started spending more together.

With a new job and a wonderful relationship, I stopped drinking and drugging. I hadn't really planned on quitting completely, but when I stopped, I felt better. I decided to stay clean and sober. I went cold turkey, without any counseling or treatment, in 1986 and remained sober. The healthier relationships I had with my children, others, and with myself held. I was on a new and better track in life.

Meanwhile, on the other side of the world, by 1985, the official Philippine investigation into the Aquino assassination, headed by a sitting justice of the Supreme Court, Corazon Agrava, had tentatively implicated General Ver and his military underlings, although formal charges were not forthcoming.

Senator Aquino's widow, Corazon Aquino, had organized rallies and demonstrations for justice ever since her husband's death, and a political movement to oust Marcos had grown stronger and stronger. The People's Power Revolution – the revolution that surprised the world – was a sustained, non-violent campaign of civil disobedience and mass resistance against the regime's systemic pattern of violence, human rights violations, and electoral and financial fraud. The movement used yellow ribbons, and sometimes called themselves the Yellow Revolution or the EDSA Revolution, after the *Epifanio de los Santos* Avenue, a main thoroughfare in Metro Manila where the majority of demonstrations took place. Over two million Filipino civilians – led by political, military, and religious leaders – joined these mass protests.

The growing opposition pleased the US ambassador to the Philippines, Steven Bosworth. The United States seemed to have grown weary of coddling Marcos and was wary of continued support for a failing dictator.

Bosworth's predecessor, Ambassador Michael Armacost (who was my Pomona College Internatioanal Relations professor), had first signaled the shift in relations. By late 1983, Armacost's speeches became implicitly critical of Marcos. At the Rotary Club Convention held in Manila that year, he said, "Powerful and able leaders need the discipline, and they need the competition of a democratic system and a free press. Competitive markets and competitive politics go hand in hand."

Armacost openly called for a fair judicial inquiry into Aquino's assassination, and US embassy officers attended the public Agrava Commission inquiries. Articles in the American press pointed to the "shift" by the Reagan administration away from Marcos, citing the attitudes expressed at a high-level three-day conference at the US War College in 1985 featuring Philippine experts from the State Department, CIA, and DIA. A conference participant stated, "Nobody in the administration is beating the drum for Marcos anymore. And no one thinks it does us any good to have him there."

In an October 1985 visit to Manila, Reagan's personal envoy Senator Paul Laxalt communicated to Marcos that the US wanted democratic reforms. The International Monetary Fund (IMF) withheld a $453 million loan citing Marcos' failure to carry out promised economic reforms that threatened the interest of his crony capitalist allies. Laxalt and Marcos initiated a steady, almost daily communication about the growing unrest. Marcos was living on borrowed time.

On November 3, 1985, Marcos announced that a presidential "snap election" would be held in the spring – a year ahead of the regular schedule. He was advised by a well connected Republican party lobbyist and political consultant, Paul Manafort. This was a brazen effort to legitimize his declining control over the country, but the unicameral congress, the Regular Batasang Pambansa, legalized the ploy, and the elections were set for February. The opposition movement persuaded Corazon Aquino to run for president and to select Salvador Laurel as her running mate under the banner of the United Opposition Party (UNIDO).

After a spirited and often violent campaign, elections were held on February 7, 1986. The official, regime-controlled election canvasser, the Commission on Elections (COMELEC), declared Marcos the winner, with over ten million votes to Aquino's 9.2 million. The final tally for the National Movement for Free Elections (NAMFREL), an internationally accredited poll watcher, had Aquino winning with 7.8 million votes to Marcos' 7 million.

There were accusations of widespread violence against oppositionists and election tampering. Thirty-five COMELEC computer technicians walked out of their workplace to protest the deliberate manipulation of results to favor Marcos. That spark ignited a general conflagration and led the Catholic Bishops' Conference of the Philippines to condemn the elections. The US Senate followed suit, and even President Reagan issued a statement calling the election fraud reports "disturbing."

On February 15, COMELEC proclaimed Ferdinand Marcos the winner. Fifty opposition members of parliament walked out in protest, and the Filipino people refused to accept the results.

Both Marcos and Aquino took their oaths of office, with Aquino enjoying greater support in civil society, demonstrators on the streets, and the international press.

Claiming electoral victory during her inauguration address, she called on the country to engage in coordinated work stoppages and a mass boycott of the Marcos-controlled media. The Catholic church hierarchy issued a declaration that stated, in part, "When a government does not of itself freely correct the evil it has inflicted on the people, then it is our serious moral obligation as a people to make it do so." The declaration continued, "Now is the time to speak up. Now is the time to repair the wrong. The wrong was systematically organized. So must its correction be. But as in the election itself, that depends fully on the people, on what they are willing and ready to do."

A newly formed Reform the Armed Forces Movement (RAM) set into motion a military coup, but Marcos discovered it and arrested the key military plotters. The Armed Forces' vice chief of staff, Lt. Gen. Fidel Ramos, and Defense Minister Juan Ponce Enrile – both close friends of the US Department of Defense — resigned from their posts in protest and joined the opposition. Their support helped turn the tide of public opinion against Marcos, who promised retaliation.

The leading authority in the Catholic church, Cardinal Jaime Sin, used his independent airwaves on Radio Veritas to encourage his followers to go to the street to support the defections of Enrile and Ramos and to prevent the Marcos military from arresting them. Tens of thousands responded to this call, coming out of their barrios to join the throngs that filled the *Epifanio de los Santos* Avenue with protestors. More defections from the military were announced; Marcos and Ver could no longer count on their military to defend them from the mass insurrection occurring in the capital.

At three o'clock on Monday, February 25, Marcos called Laxalt, asking for advice from the White House. Senator Laxalt explained that his support in the country and military had evaporated, and that if Marcos and his wife wanted to live and not face a firing squad, he must relinquish his office and flee. Laxalt's exact advice was to "cut and cut clean," to which Marcos paused for a long time, and then expressed his disappointment at the lack of US support. Marcos then called Enrile, asking that he, his family, and General Ver be allowed safe passage out of the country.

At midnight, the Marcos entourage boarded a US Air Force helicopter and flew to Clark Air Base, then proceeded on a US Air Force DC-9 to Guam before finally arriving at Hickam Air Force Base on the island of Oahu, Hawaii.

Marcos may or may not have understood what coming to the US meant for him legally. He was not granted asylum or other special status, which may well have been the Reagan administration's way of ingratiating itself with the new government in the Philippines, which had an interest in recovering their former dictator's ill-gotten wealth, the proceeds of years of kickbacks and payments for government contracts. Marcos potentially was even vulnerable to having the US file criminal charges against him. Fleeing to Malaysia (or Indonesia, as General Ver did) would have made holding Marcos accountable far more problematic.

Marcos was specifically permitted to collect and bring his financial documents to Hawaii, which the former president deemed essential to allow him access to his many secret and off-shore bank accounts, including in Switzerland, where he had hidden his net worth, which at the time of his exile exceeded $30 billion.

There was Marcos, sitting in Hawaii with his financial documents. To me, he was a sitting duck.

CHAPTER THIRTY:

THE SMOKING GUN

1986
Seattle

The overthrow of martial law in the Philippines threw our justice efforts back into high gear. A few days after Marcos fled, Cindy arrived at my office in the Central Building, and we walked down two flights of stairs to the Philippine consulate's office.

Introducing herself as the sister of slain activist Silme Domingo, Cindy told the clerk that she believed the consulate had documents that would implicate the Marcos regime in the murder of her brother. She demanded to see their diplomatic cables and intelligence files related to the time period of May through September of 1981. She also asked for any evidence that former consul general Ernest Querubim had left behind related to his relationship with Tony Baruso or the murders.

The officials refused to provide her anything, saying they needed instructions from the new government, but Cindy's determination to see those files was inspiring. In the five years since her brother's murder, she hadn't lost an ounce of the fire in her belly.

John Caughlan stepped in to assist. He had traveled to the Philippines in the late 1970s to attend a World Peace Through Law (WPTL) conference in Manila, where he'd met and established close ties with Senator Jose Diokno, a Philippine politician and human rights advocate.

The new Aquino government had appointed Diokno to head a human rights commission to investigate the Marcos regime's treatment of political opponents and to allow victims to have a voice of reconciliation in the new government. John reached out to him, and the three of us had many late night telephone conversations. Diokno was intrigued by our case, and John was at his very best in describing it. Through his persuasive intercession, Senator Diokno announced that the Aquino government considered the Domingo and Viernes murders to be one of the top three human rights cases his commission would investigate, along with the assassination of Senator Benigno Aquino in 1983.

President Aquino and her cabinet also created the Commission on Good Government, dedicated to tracking down and recovering the billions of dollars Marcos had stolen and hidden in Swiss bank accounts and other unknown locations around the world. Cindy had strong ties to the head of the new commission, former senator Rene Saguisag, and we were encouraged by his determination to recover the stolen funds.

With developments moving quickly, the legal team and CJDV leadership met to assess how to best take advantage of the tremendous opening that the change in governments and Marcos' ouster created for us.

Our strategy had three interrelated prongs: (1) use our subpoena power to obtain documents and a deposition under oath from Marcos; (2) meet with representatives of the new regime to get evidence of Marcos' role in operations against the US-based anti-Marcos movement; and (3) eventually ask the court to reinstate the Marcoses as defendants in our case.

We moved quickly to issue a subpoena requiring Marcos and his wife Imelda to sit for depositions in our civil suit, and to produce their papers and financial documents, along with any intelligence files related to the murders and/or the Philippine Infiltration Plan. US Marshals served him with a subpoena *duces tecum* as he walked out of Hickam Air Force Base on Oahu in late February 1986. The US Customs Service, acting at the request of the new Philippine government, had seized those same documents already, so we slapped a subpoena on the Customs Service to make sure we saw everything Marcos had brought with him.

Prodded by the late Senator Aquino's brother-in-law, reporter Ken Kashiwahara of ABC News in San Francisco, the national and local press were also trying to track down where Marcos had hidden his money. Gary Rebar at KGO-TV, the ABC affiliate in San Francisco, called me out of the blue and said his station wanted to do a story on our case. I reviewed all of the details of the case with him, and he aired a two-part series on the murders and the role of US intelligence in supporting the Marcos regime. His work was spectacular, and the story was a huge hit in the Bay Area.

In the meantime, the US Customs Service released a major document dump of everything they had obtained. They sent copies to Congress, the Reagan administration, the public, and press. The CJDV received its own copy because of our subpoena.

The documents arrived from FedEx in two large Bankers Boxes, and I tore into them like an eagle swooping down a river in search of salmon. Alone in my office, I brushed aside my 150 current asbestos case files and started pouring through bank record after bank record. There were thousands of transactions, involving scores of banks and secret deposits.

I was startled when the phone rang. It was Gary Rebar.

"Mike, do you have the Marcos financial documents?"

I kept digging through the files. "Yeah, they just arrived. It's going to take some time to copy them and send them to you. Can you re..."

"I have them already. Got 'em from Customs."

"Great. Let's give ourselves time to read them and then talk, okay?" I didn't want to be quoted on something I wasn't fully up to snuff on.

"Well, that's fine, but I think you're going to want to look at one financial document in particular."

"What do you have?" My hands grew still.

"Didn't you allege that Baruso traveled to the Bay Area on May 16 and 17 and stayed near the Philippine consulate?"

"Not only alleged it, Gary; we have his travel records and credit card receipts. Why?"

Gary paused. "Well then, I don't think it is a coincidence. You better read this yourself. Let me find the BATES number." BATES is a system lawyers used to keep track of the page numbers of documents produced in legal proceedings.

"Okay, it's 01638. Find it."

I took out the second box and rifled through the documents until I found the document he referenced and read it slowly. I was standing by the time my gaze had panned halfway down the page.

The document was marked **Strictly Confidential** and stated it was a "Statement of Expenses" as of February 16, 1982, of the Mabuhay Corporation. At the bottom of the page, there was an unsigned, handwritten portion that stated "I acknowledge having received $1M from PNB for intelligence purposes minus $762,478.52 withdrawn by the AFP by authority of the Chief of Staff, leaving a balance of about $230,000."

Given the poor quality of the handwriting, it wasn't clear whether there was a missing second page. But it was clear that PNB referred to the Philippine National Bank, the AFP was the Armed Forces of the Philippines, and the chief of staff was none other than General Fabian Ver.

The document itemized exactly how that $762,000 was spent. Political campaign contributions of over $175,000 were made to politicians in national races, as well as a few in California. The Mabuhay Corporation made $50,000 in campaign contributions to both President Jimmy Carter and President Ronald Reagan. There were also itemized expenses for "Special Missions" involving meetings that the Marcoses attended in Honolulu, New York, and Cancun. But the most sinister column was called "Advances to C.G. (Special Security Projects)" and included fifteen figures, totaling over $500,000.

"Holy shit," I said when I found my voice again. "Is this what I think it is?"

I could hear him shuffling papers on the other end of the line. "Okay, now look under Special Security Projects in the middle of the page at number twelve and check out what it says on May 17."

"A $15,000 expense on May 17, as well as a second expense for Pulong-Pulong, USA." I read aloud. "Whatever that is."

"Mike, could that 15k be the payment to Baruso?" he blurted out.

"Jesus Christ." I paced to the window and back again. "Baruso pays $5,000 to the hitmen and keeps ten grand. This is amazing. We've been wondering about that trip since we got Baruso's credit card records."

As grandiose as my vision for this case could sometimes be, I never dreamed we would find a document that itemized a Marcos-run slush fund expenditure that paid for the murders of my friends. Here's our smoking gun and it was still hot!

"We're going to go with this story on air, Mike. I need to interview you right away," Gary said. He sounded excited too.

"Hold on, let me see what we have in Baruso's bank deposits after May. Give me a second." I was breathless as I walked over to the cabinet where another twenty boxes of pleadings and documents waited.

I was paging through the voluminous bank records when Gary interrupted. "I talked to a source at the *Philippine News*. You know Alex Esclamado's paper, right?"

"Sure, very helpful guy." I nodded, although he couldn't see me.

"Pulong-Pulong was a two-way video transmission between Marcos in Manila and his supporters in the Bay Area held on May 17. It was telecast at the San Jose Convention Center, and tons of Marcos supporters attended. So those expenses may be legit. But what about that fifteen grand?"

"Let's see. Baruso's bank records show cash deposits in various amounts from June 3 through the end of the summer. Some less than a hundred, others like eight hundred." I was still reading when Gary cut to the chase.

"Close to 10k?" he asked excitedly.

"Let me get a calculator out." I started adding the deposits, more than fifteen of them total, and realized it was going to be close. "Okay, the final deposit is about $9,752."

"No shit, close to ten grand. He keeps a few hundred for pocket change. Baruso is going to have some 'splainin' to do." Gary was ebullient.

"I asked him about those deposits at his deposition. I figured they might be bribes he took, except by June of 1981, Rank and File did the dispatch and nobody needed to bribe anyone to get to Alaska. Hang on." I was reaching for his deposition transcript in another box. A sense of triumph filled me as I read. "Okay, I think we've boxed him in. I never showed him the bank records. He denied having any source of income except his paychecks from Boeing and the Local. I asked if he had come into any money after the murders, and he said no. Then I asked if he had made any cash deposits into his bank account after the murders, and he said no. So no 'splainin' is going to get him out of that box."

I set a time to talk to Gary again after we both looked through the rest of the documents. After I hung up, the doubts started to creep in. The document was not signed. We might need a handwriting sample. What was this Mabuhay Corporation? The fifteen thousand could have been for something else related to Pulong-Pulong. But then why two entries? And Pilay claimed Baruso never paid the hitmen the five thousand he promised. So what happened to that money? But then, who could trust Pilay? He could have been lying.

I came back to my basic intuition: It all fit together so well. I called Terri. I called Cindy. I called Jim and John and the other members of the CJDV. I called my wife. I called my kids. I called ... myself home.

CHAPTER THIRTY-ONE:

THE AFTERMATH

March—July 1986
Seattle, San Francisco, And Honolulu

Armed with the Mabuhay statement of expenses and the political momentum from the ousting of Marcos, the CJDV leadership and legal team went into overdrive. We still had to follow the money.

We needed to figure out who authored the Mabuhay document, and then subpoena the relevant documents of that individual, as well as the corporation and its bank accounts at the Philippine National Bank. We would then need to take their deposition and add them into the lawsuit as defendants. And we needed to do all of the discovery about the Mabuhay Corporation right away, before we deposed Ferdinand Marcos.

Our ultimate goal was still to get both of the Marcoses reinstated as defendants in our lawsuit. Marcos had hired Richard Hibey, a renowned criminal defense lawyer from Washington, DC, who specialized in white collar crime and racketeering cases. He'd also represented Jonathan Pollard, the Israeli espionage agent who turned over US intelligence secrets to Israel. No chump for sure.

Hibey filed a motion in the US District Court for Hawaii seeking to quash our subpoena and prevent the deposition. He maintained that the court in Seattle had found Marcos to be immune from suit as the head of state, and he should not be required to answer any questions about the same lawsuit. The assertion of absolute immunity from providing testimony was novel. Previous courts had ruled that even an incumbent US president, Richard Nixon, had no absolute privilege from disclosure of presidential conversations in discovery. President Gerald Ford was required to testify when he was in office because he was a witness to a crime against him. So it wasn't a surprise when the US magistrate appointed to hear the case in Hawaii denied the motion, but Hibey still appealed to the district court.

On June 18, 1986, Judge Harold Fong issued a ruling allowing the deposition to go forward, stating that "[A] former foreign head of state cannot expect to enjoy broader immunity than that enjoyed by a former President in his own country." The judge went on to note that we wished to depose Marcos on topics that "appear to be outside Marcos' official duties as President." He also noted that Marcos would be entitled to assert any privileges allowed by law, including questions that might jeopardize the national security interests of the Philippines or his privilege against self-incrimination.

With this ruling in hand, I worked and reworked my proposed questions to try to avoid any occasion that would allow him to assert these privileges. Fat chance. I also made it my purpose to never refer to Marcos as "president," only "mister," in recognition of the undeniable fact that he was no longer the president of the Philippines and deserved no special treatment or recognition.

By prior agreement, we were set to take the deposition in two two-hour segments (one in the morning, the other in the afternoon) over a period of two days. This arrangement was in recognition that Marcos needed to use a kidney dialysis machine between segments due to his deteriorating medical condition.

While all of these negotiations were being worked out, we tackled Mabuhay. We hired an ace investigator, George Barron, in the Bay Area. I'd known Barron since law school, and met with him twice—on April 24 and May 13, 1986—in the office of Charles Morgan, the attorney I'd worked for then. Barron quickly discovered that the incorporator of the Mabuhay Corporation was one Dr. Leonilo Malabed, a sixty-three-year-old medical doctor who had a small practice in San Francisco.

Our friends in the Philippine Solidarity Network in the Bay Area, including Geline Avila and Cathy Tactaquin, knew Malabed well and called him the eyes and ears of Marcos in the US. A childhood friend of the former president, Malabed was a staunch ally who was known to angrily drive his Rolls Royce into anti-Marcos demonstrators and picket lines outside the consulate office. Geline also told us that *Mabuhay* was Tagalog for "May you Live!" or "Welcome." The corporation opened its first bank account on July 7, 1977 (7-7-77), another telling sign. Marcos had publicly disclosed that he believed the number seven to be lucky.

Malabed published a pro-Marcos newspaper, *Philippine American,* and had attempted to purchase KJAZ, an FM radio station in Oakland, for pro-Marcos propaganda. He owned significant real estate and businesses in the Bay Area and was the chairman of the board of directors of the Mission National Bank in San Francisco, which served a largely Filipino clientele. George found out he was also a director, along with Marcos' Defense Minister Juan Ponce Enrile, of the PNB, which provided the funding for the Mabuhay Corporation.

In short, it looked like Malabed was ideally situated to operate an intelligence slush fund.

Alex Esclamado, the anti-Marcos publisher of the *Philippine News* in the Bay Area, was also a source of inside information about Malabed. Alex told me "everybody knows Malabed's a front for Marcos." So we tasked George with investigating a number of key Malabed/Marcos supporters in the Bay Area, including former consul general Romero Arguelles, Lieutenant Colonel Edmundo Mendigo, and Lito Gorospe, Marcos' press secretary who frequented the Bay Area and was reported to be close to Malabed. The investigation would try to establish whether any of these Marcos men were involved in the payment of $15,000 to Baruso on May 17, and get further background on Malabed's ties to the regime.

Even before we started issuing subpoenas, the press had a field day with the Mabuhay statement of expenses. Noting that it was illegal for foreign nationals to contribute to the campaigns of American candidates or conceal the source of those contributions, the *New York Times* ran an in-depth article titled "Doctor Denies Using Marcos Money," which focused on Malabed's campaign contributions. According to the article, Malabed was "in seclusion." The article went on to quote Malabed as stating, "I am not a conduit. All of the money I contributed was my own." The various campaigns affirmed that they had received contributions from Malabed, but of course denied they knew the funds were from Marcos.

Similarly, the *San Francisco Examiner* produced a series of articles on March 20 and 21 of 1986 in which Malabed said he was "shocked" at the allegations, and that the Mabuhay Corporation was used only to try to purchase the KJAZ radio station. According to the article, he said it disbanded when the deal fell through. However, while the radio station purchase fell through in October of 1979, Malabed continued to pay the corporate fees for two more years, through 1981.

Malabed, through his counsel, dismissed the Mabuhay document as meaningless, stating, "Who signed it? If it is not signed, let us treat it as a useless document. Everything is false." Malabed insisted that the corporation had held one meeting of the board but never effectuated any of the business plans, stock subscriptions, financial dealings, or other activities referred to in the minutes of their meetings (obtained through our discovery) or in the statement of expenses. In another interview, Malabed embraced Marcos, calling him "my best friend ... I have adored his brilliance over the years we have known each other."

Armed with many of the publicly-available corporate documents obtained from our discovery against the Philippine National Bank, as well as those we had subpoenaed, we were scheduled to take Malabed's deposition on May 15, 1986, in San Francisco. When his attorney tried to quash our subpoenas in early May 1986, Judge William Orrick of the US District Court in San Francisco held a hearing and promptly denied the motion, stating we were seeking relevant information into a wrongful death case.

During the depositions of Malabed followed, Patrick Hallinan, the able son of famed radical San Francisco labor lawyer and criminal defense counsel Vincent Hallinan, appeared as Malabed's counsel. Given Vincent's strong pedigree and left-wing politics, it struck us as a strange but telling choice, seemingly designed more to protect Malabed from criminal prosecution than to defend a civil deposition or lawsuit.

Throughout the proceedings, we narrowed in on Malabed's ownership and/or directorships of various financial institutions. Hallinan instructed Malabed to assert his Fifth Amendment privilege against self-incrimination to every single question I asked about the statement of expenses, with the exception of expenses related to the purchase of the radio station. He even took the Fifth to my questions about whether he had made any of the statement attributed to him in the *New York Times* and *San Francisco Examiner* articles.

Aware that Malabed had denied writing or signing the statement of expenses in those interviews, I asked him for a handwriting sample, including various terms and words used in the document, as well as the sentence: "We hold these truths to be self-evident that all men are created equal." I thought the Hallinans would appreciate that. Malabed dutifully wrote those words out.

I asked Malabed about his knowledge of or any recent communications with Marcos and various Marcos allies. Malabed admitted he and Marcos had spoken a few days prior to his deposition, but claimed that they did not discuss the deposition or the Mabuhay document. He admitted he had met with Marcos during the president's state visit in September 1982. He admitted he knew and had contact with Lieutenant Colonel Edmundo Mendigo, Consul General Arguellos, Juan Ponce Enrile, and Tex Balmeceda, a Philippine military attaché in the consulate in Hawaii. He denied being involved in any of Marcos's security details or being given a flag insignia to designate him as part of a community protective task force for Marcos when he traveled.

Malabed denied knowing Tony Baruso and claimed he had only read about him in an article in the *Philippine News* after the murder convictions in Seattle. Then came an interesting exchange.

I wanted to pin Malabed down on whether he saw Baruso in May 1981. In the midst of his deposition, I leaned across the table with my hands clasped and met his gaze directly. "I take it, then, you deny having met with Mr. Baruso in May of 1981?"

The tall man seated across from me shifted nervously in his seat. He glanced at his attorney. "I am not denying it. I just know I never met him."

Mr. Couenhover, Malabed's co-counsel, prodded, "You can answer it."

Malabed shook his head resolutely. "No. He said deny. Deny, that means that could have happened, but that does not mean you couldn't say it is."

Sometimes a trial lawyer just gets a feel for a witness, not based on the actual words used, but the body language, fumbling, evasiveness, and dissembling. Right then I knew that Malabed not only knew Baruso, but met with him in May of 1981. I also knew our case might turn on proving that Malabed and Baruso, as leading pro-Marcos allies on the West Coast, knew each other.

Our investigator George Barron was going to be busy. With that non-denial denial answer, I adjourned the deposition, promising to reconvene after we had obtained the documents we needed to prove that the Mabuhay Corporation was a slush fund used to pay for the murders.

Malabed lost no time in trying to save face. Patrick Hallinan convened a press conference to claim that Malabed had been "victimized" into signing a document as a favor for his boyhood pal. He stated that Ferdinand Marcos had pressured Malabed to write and sign a message at the bottom of an already-drafted document four years earlier to vouch for its authenticity.

This struck me as odd, since the financial document we had was not signed. We repeatedly asked Hallinan for any copy which had a signature, to no effect. I was outraged that Hallinan had gone to the press with such a lame excuse, and I was determined to make him regret it.

I shipped the expense statement and deposition transcript to Bonifacio "Boni" Gillego, a principal investigator for the Commission on Good Government. As an active member of the Movement for a Free Philippines (MFP), Gillego was highly recommended by our contacts because he was a career military intelligence officer who had broken with the Marcos regime.

I sent the deposition transcript and attached exhibits to Gillego to review and analyze as an expert in intelligence. I wanted to see if he could offer any new insights into a connection to the murders and Marcos' efforts to suppress his opposition in the US.

He spent some time with the material and came to the conclusion that the Mabuhay Corporation was used as slush fund, or conduit, for Philippine intelligence operations in the US. He stated, "The middle-level conspirator [Malabed] stands at the nexus of our investigations of both Marcos' extraordinary wealth and his fascist activities in the US, including murder." He stated to me, and publicly said months later at the Fifth Annual Memorial of the CJDV, that "all of the charges against Marcos are true."

Gillego wrote us a scathing report called "The Spy Network of the Marcos Dictatorship in the US." His report went well beyond what we knew from the Senate Foreign Relations Report and the DIA circular. It began, "Yes, Virginia, there are spies of Marcos in the US." It then went on to name more than fifteen members of the Armed Forces of the Philippines (AFP) who were assigned to various diplomatic posts in the embassy and various consulates under diplomatic covers such as *trade attaché* or *cultural attaché*. Calling the DIA circular the "tip of the iceberg," Gillego's report unwrapped the covert side of the Philippine Infiltration Plan, explaining how military attachés acted as case officers to recruit potential informants and agent provocateurs in various anti-Marcos organizations in the US, including the KDP. They reported the leadership, activities, and proposed events of each movement.

Boni was a charming man, full of twinkle in his eyes, and I made a note to make sure to call him as an expert witness if we ever got to trial. With the DIA circular, the Mabuhay evidence, and Boni's opinions, the proof of the Philippine Infiltration Plan was solid. But we needed Marcos to top it off.

CHAPTER THIRTY-TWO:

THE COCKROACH OF TRUTH

July—August 1986; March 1987
Honolulu
Preparation for the Marcos deposition seemed to last lifetimes. We started by pulling almost every press account that quoted what Marcos had said publicly about every possible deposition topic, including his relationship with Ronald Reagan, his concerns about the KMU and its leadership, his military intelligence operation in the US, his knowledge of developments in the Marcos opposition in the US, what he said about the NPA and NDF, his statements about his intelligence agencies keeping track of tourists and visitors from the US, and the like. I read his books about the New Society. I wanted to control Marcos with documents – quoting back at him the statements he had made in the press and asking follow-up questions if he answered.

Our work was aided by the fact that the Diokno-led Human Rights Commission had already begun investigating who was involved in the assassination of Senator Aquino. We secured copies of the Agrava Commission Report, which found Brigadier General Fabian Ver, General Prospero Olivas (Metropolitan Command), and General Luther Custodio (Aviation Security Command), along with twenty-two other low-ranking military officers, were involved in the murder plot. The supposed lone gunman, Rolando Galman, was not implicated. Jurist Corazon Agrava dissented from the findings, claiming only seven military officers, not including Ver, were implicated. We saw this assassination as a crucial piece of evidence and I wanted to be prepared to question Marcos about it, despite knowing he would likely take the Fifth Amendment.

Marcos was still active in exile in Hawaii, rallying his supporters, promising to make a comeback, and encouraging his allies in Hawaii to bring large sums of cash into the Philippines to support an uprising. Marcos exhorted his followers in Manila to rise up in protest against the Aquino government, which he charged with "the biggest robbery in political history. I am your legitimate president." Marcos loyalists organized and paid scores of poor squatters and unemployed workers to attend protests against the new government.

In the wake of a reported coup plot, US Undersecretary of State for Political Affairs Michael Armacost, former ambassador to the Philippines, urged Marcos to keep his hands off Philippine politics and warned him that he would be violating US law if he tried to export weapons to his former country. Even Secretary of State George Schultz weighed in, according to NBC News, saying, "He is causing trouble, and some of it goes beyond argument."

Marcos taped a video of himself with his shirt off, flexing his muscles and urging his supporters to take up arms against Aquino and to overthrow her government when he returned. A copy of the video found its way into the hands of Boni Gillego, who promptly turned it over to the press and played it for the CJDV. It made Marcos look weak, even ridiculous, and the fact it was leaked caused him great embarrassment.

The deposition was scheduled for July 14, 1986, and I spent the entire month prior preparing exhibits. Each of the press clippings that quoted Marcos on a deposition topic was copied, given an exhibit number, and pre-marked by my court reporter, Jan Van Pelt. The Agrava Commission Report was pre-marked as well. Jan's husband Dale had been a radical labor activist with the United Farmworkers Union in the Yakima Valley. She was the best and most reliable court reporter I'd ever worked with, and I trusted her completely.

We knew that Marcos would most likely take the Fifth Amendment to questions about his knowledge of Gene and Silme's activities and politics and murders, as well as the Agrava Commission findings, so our goals were more modest. First: get Marcos to agree that he had kept close track of the anti-Marcos movement in the US, and that he had taken steps to counteract their influence. Second: get Marcos to concede that if an American associated with the anti-Marcos movement in the US (like Gene Viernes) came to the Philippines to meet with the KMU, NPA, or NDF, his intelligence agencies would have known about it and taken steps to counteract it.

If we could prove that Marcos initiated or joined a civil conspiracy to monitor and operate against the anti-Marcos movement in the US, including the KDP and Gene and Silme, and undertook specific and overt acts to carry out the goals of that conspiracy, including the use of physical violence to neutralize, intimidate, and liquidate the opposition, such a civil conspiracy was clearly actionable. Foreign governments cannot legally harass and intimidate American citizens in their exercise of rights guaranteed by the US Constitution. In fact, it is illegal for foreign governments to spy on Americans at all.

Then, if we could prove that the Mabuhay intelligence slush fund was used to pay for the murders, we would have a decent chance of holding Marcos liable in a court of law. But first we had to prove that Marcos authorized the creation of the Mabuhay Corporation, or knew of and approved of its use as stated in the document.

The Aquino government had issued a decree declaring that Marcos was not entitled to assert head of state immunity. This effectively removed a huge legal hurdle for us.

It was going to be fun.

When our entourage gathered in Honolulu, the general feeling was one of excitement and optimism. Terri, Jim, Jan Van Pelt, and I all travelled together and stayed at the Reef Hotel in Waikiki, the same hotel that the Local 37 team had used during the fateful 1981 ILWU Convention. Jim and I shared a room and watched the all-star game in our hotel room the night before the deposition began. Jim rooted for the Giants players on the National League team. I made fun of him. Baseball seemed so out of place with the enormity of what was at stake.

The next morning, we got in a cab to take us to the deposition. As we were leaving Waikiki, I noticed a t-shirt stand on the side of the road and asked the driver to stop.

"Mike, what are you doing?" Terri was peeved at the delay, nervously drumming her fingernails on the open window of the taxi. Warm, salt-flavored air swept into the space, ruffling her hair.

I grinned at her. "Don't worry, I'll be right back." I jumped out of the car and jogged up to the stand.

When I came back, I proudly displayed my purchase. I had bought every last shirt, which had the yellow McDonald's arches and the phrase "McMarcos: Over 30 Billion Stole."

The cab erupted in laughter.

The Marcoses were staying at a lovely beachfront house in Honolulu. When we arrived, an aide led us into the spacious living room. Wide glass doors opened onto a veranda. I sat in one of the plush, Rococo-style armchairs and stretched my feet out, noticing that the tips of my toes were within thirty feet of the beach. The opulence didn't surprise me, but I shook my head softly as the videographer and court reporter set up their equipment. We had decided to videotape the deposition so we could play any revealing portions to jury and give them the full measure of Marcos the man.

Paul Bernstein, a local lawyer, was present to represent the new government of the Philippines.

Marcos finally appeared from a long hallway, wearing a pale yellow shirt and dark pants. He seemed unsteady, his hands wavering as he sat down, adjusting the microphone on his shirt lapel. Shorter than he appeared on television, seemingly docile, he seemed like a grandfather, a husband, just another Filipino. He joked causally about putting on his microphone and smiled comfortably. I was disgusted by his presence: he was responsible, at least in part, for the death of two of my best friends. Terri shifted anxiously in her chair.

He looked like he was ill, but as soon as he opened his mouth, I had the impression he was mentally sharp, well prepared, and ready for battle. This was it.

I had divided my questioning into six main subject matter areas:

(1. His response to our subpoena *duces tecum* to produce documents;

(2. His personal history and the powers he had assumed under martial law, including the consolidation of intelligence functions within NISA under General Ver;

(3. The public statements he had made to the press about a wide range of topics, including his treatment of the KMU, NPA, and the moderate opposition, his concern about the Marcos opposition in the US, his use of military attachés and informants in the US, his close friendship with Ronald and Nancy Reagan, and his history of human rights abuses;

(4. Senator Aquino and his assassination;

(5. The Mabuhay Corporation and Dr. Malabed; and

(6. The DIA circular and his intelligence operation in the US.

The questioning was routine until I got to the topic of why he declared martial law in 1972. I asked him to describe his reasons. He said there were seven attempted assassinations of himself, plus the bombing of the Constitutional Convention

Hall, the planting of dynamite in the Supreme Court, and attempted kidnappings of his ministers. The armed forces were crying for martial law.

I then handed him a book he had written called *Marcos Reader: Selected Essays and Speeches of Ferdinand Marcos.* His throaty tenor cleared as he read the selected passage. "Philippine society before September 1972 had reached a condition that a powerful few, the national's oligarchy, held in their hands the lives and fates of millions of other citizens." I then asked whether reducing the power of the oligarchy was also a reason for declaring martial law. He agreed.

I asked him whether, under the Philippine Constitution of 1936, then in effect, he was limited to two six-year terms, which were set to expire in the fall of 1972, and was therefore prohibited from running for a third term.

He hesitated, and in that second of hesitation, a large, flying Hawaiian cockroach flew into the room and landed on Marcos' left shoulder. Being intent on the questions and answers, neither Marcos nor I noticed it. The videographer did and started focusing on it. Marcos's answer came evenly. "No, no, that is not true."

I asked again whether the Philippine Constitution he was elected under had a two-term limit, to which he responded, "Hold the phone, hold the phone." Just then I first saw the cockroach and watched it heading for Marcos' neck. I thought that it would bite him if he lied.

In that moment, it was the cockroach of truth.

Richard Hibey abruptly swiped his hand toward it, knocking it away. Without missing a beat, Marcos said, "Was that the wrong answer?"

As uncomfortable laughter fluttered through the room, this became the only light moment in the two-day deposition. In the end, though, we made important headway by getting Marcos to make a number of damaging admissions, including:

1. Marcos acknowledged that if someone from the anti-Marcos movement in the US came to the Philippines to meet with the opposition and was believed to carry funds to support them, every branch of his intelligence services would have monitored and reported on that person's activities. When asked who had responsibility for surveillance of such a person, Marcos answered, "Well, everybody, the whole government."

2. Marcos claimed the KMU was infiltrated by communists, and he had banned the federation and had its leadership arrested and charged with sedition and rebellion.

3. Marcos claimed he had seen evidence that "foreign money" was used to support the KMU. He claimed such evidence was found in the books of the KMU and believed the amount was "more than hundreds of thousands of dollars."

4. His government was concerned about the growth of the NPA in 1980.

5. He was concerned about outside material and financial support for the NDF coming into the Philippines.

6. Philippine intelligence agencies and consular officials in the US (including military attachés) collected, disseminated, and analyzed anti-Marcos opposition groups in the US.

7. He had a "special office" that he refused to name, which processed all intelligence reports and was similar to the National Security Agency in the US. General Ver headed the NISA and was the chief of staff of the AFP until he took a leave of absence after the Aquino assassination.

8. Marcos knew each of the military attachés identified in the DIA circular but claimed it was an "exaggeration" to say they were sent to monitor anti-Marcos Philippine activists.

9. He ordered the arrest of Benigno Aquino, Raul Manglapus, and other opposition leaders in 1981 because he believed they were behind a series of bomb attacks in Manila in 1980.

10. He did not contest a report in the press from early 1981 that the Philippine military authorities were tightening their watch on incoming tourists from the US. He said the program was headed by General Olivas, head of AVSECOM (Aviation Security Command) with jurisdiction over Manila Airport.

11. He acknowledged stating publicly in 1981 that his government was gathering evidence to go after the US-based opposition.

12. He recalled a trip that Alexander Haig made to the Philippines in June of 1981, in which they discussed the need for an extradition treaty between the US and the Philippines. That treaty would have allowed Marcos to indict and extradite his opponents from the US to the Philippines, but it was opposed by many members of Congress.

13. He was informed that certain anti-Marcos organizations in the US were supporting his opposition in the Philippines, but refused to answer any details due to "security reasons."

We agreed to stop the first deposition after two days, but reserved the right to reconvene at a later point to finish questioning him. We felt that with Marcos' answers and his assertion of the Fifth Amendment to any and all questions about the murders, the Mabuhay statement, the Agrava Commission, and his financial dealings, we had more than enough to name him as a party defendant and ask the court to reinstate him in the lawsuit. In a civil case, unlike a criminal case, the jury was instructed that a defendant's assertion of the Fifth Amendment allowed them to draw adverse inferences (i.e. that any answer would incriminate the witness).

As soon as the deposition was over, we held a news conference, and our assessment of the deposition was covered by the press; in particular, the *Philippine News* in San Francisco. We stated that Marcos had made damaging admissions about the role of many intelligence agencies operating in the US, and we decried his use of the Fifth Amendment to shield himself from questions about the murders. "What does Marcos have to hide?" was a refrain the press picked up.

Marcos' lawyers brought a motion before Judge Fong to terminate the deposition, claiming that there was ongoing "collusion" between the plaintiffs and the Republic of the Philippines. Marcos claimed that both Terri and I made statements to the press following the deposition which caused "annoyance, embarrassment, and oppression." Judge Fong transferred the motion to the federal court in Seattle, where the case was pending, and the motion was assigned to Magistrate Judge Phillip Sweigert.

Magistrate Sweigert heard the motion on August 29, 1986, and found there was no improper collusion between the plaintiffs and the Philippines. He reaffirmed that the prior grant of immunity to Marcos by Judge Voorhees did not encompass testimonial immunity, stating, "Marcos is no longer a head of state or representative of the government of the Philippines, and he is not immune from giving testimony in this case." Finally, the magistrate found that Marcos was a "public figure whose testimony regarding his actions as president of the Republic of the Philippines are of public interest," and he had not established that any of the press comments made by Terri or myself caused him any oppression. An appeal to Judge Voorhees was unsuccessful, and we were free to proceed with the second portion of his deposition and use the videotaped transcript at trial.

The continuation of Marcos' deposition was held in March of 1987, again at his home in Honolulu. Marcos was then represented by John Bartko from San Francisco, but Richard Hibey was still his chief counsel. When we arrived, Imelda was in the living room, sitting at the piano. She started playing and singing "Bring in the Clowns" as soon as we entered. We took it in good humor.

The second deposition produced more of the same: general admissions about Marcos' security agencies' capacities and their targets, but assertions of "national security" and Fifth Amendment privileges to any question that bore on the murders, the Mabuhay Corporation, Dr. Malabed, or his financial dealings. I framed the questions in such a way as to allow a judge or jury to infer from the invocation of the Fifth Amendment that the answer, if given, would be adverse to Marcos' interests.

For instance, I asked, "Mr. Marcos, were the funds provided from the Philippine National Bank to the Mabuhay Corporation for intelligence purposes used to conduct acts of physical violence against the anti-Marcos opposition in the United States, including and up to the use of murder, political assassination, and summary execution, sir?"

Marcos took the Fifth, thus allowing a jury to infer that the answer to that question would be *Yes*.

In the middle of the second deposition, I noticed Imelda pacing outside the deposition room. I asked Mr. Marcos if his wife wanted to join us. Marcos looked a little confused, then seemed to realize that he should let her come in, and he said yes. As soon as she was seated, I asked Ferdinand Marcos to identify all of the positions of responsibility his wife held in his administration. It was like asking a husband the date of his wedding anniversary. He fumbled, then starting naming governmental departments, like the Ministry of Human Settlement, that she had nothing to do with.

"No, no, no, that's not it. It was Ministry of Culture," she almost shouted. I watched with amusement as Imelda corrected and argued with him. Finally, their counsel told Imelda that Ferdinand had to answer the questions, not her, stating, "Don't provide him any answers."

She said, "Well, why did you invite me in here then?" She got up in a huff and left.

Paul Bernstein, a fine attorney from Hawaii, again attended the deposition on behalf of the Republic of the Philippines, which was still a party defendant in the lawsuit. I was pleased that the new government was able to question Marcos under oath, but Marcos provided little of value and asserted the Fifth Amendment to Paul's questions as well. He was mainly interested in finding out about where Marcos had hidden his money, but Marcos was having none of it.

Imelda's videotaped deposition was also taken, but produced only one answer of any value. Between her grandiose statements glorifying her husband's administration – stated always in threes: "love, beauty, and justice" – she admitted that seven was their lucky number. The license plate of his car at the Presidential Palace was numbered 777, a fact Mr. Marcos confirmed in his second deposition. I realized that the first of June would equal seven if we added the number of the day and the month together. Another clue of Marcos' involvement.

There was also an interchange that I thought was very suspicious. I'd heard through Philippine government sources that Imelda had given a very expensive gift to the Malabeds in May 1981. Whether it was a payoff for Malabed's handling the funds for the murders was not clear. But when I asked her about it, Imelda Marcos completely came apart. She hesitated and looked like a deer in headlights. She then mumbled something incoherent, with a perplexed look on her face. Although not really captured in the written transcript, I was hopeful her evasion was clear on the videotape. She never answered the question.

I'm sure it was hard on Terri to sit through the long interviews with the people she believed were responsible for her husband's murder. But it was also an amazing accomplishment. Most heads of state, and even CEOs of *Fortune* 500 corporations, are never required to answer questions under oath in an adversarial proceeding. Just making the Marcoses sit for a deposition was a victory. But we were not satisfied until we saw justice. In order to accomplish this, we would have to go back to the source.

CHAPTER THIRTY-THREE:

A NIGHT IN CAMELOT

September 1986
Manila, Philippines

I couldn't breathe. My lungs burned hot ... humid, wet, smoky. The dark exhaust of a thousand jeepneys filled my lungs. I was going to pass out.

It was midnight at Manila International Airport. My baggage on the claim carousel spun around and around. My knees buckled, and my head grew light. I slumped down.

"Are you all right?" Rene Cruz asked.

I tried to mumble, "Sure, just jet lag." But only a faint gasp came out of my mouth. The heat and fumes were unbearable. I was dying of carbon monoxide poisoning. My shirt was soaked.

"You look terrible. Do you want some water?" Rene asked.

"Sure, thanks." I took his cup of water and poured it over my head. Rene was calm. He wasn't even sweating.

"Cindy's at the Camelot," he said simply. "She'll meet us there. You can get some sleep. Looks like you need it."

I picked up my luggage and headed to Rene's car, dragging one foot after the other. It seemed like miles. Throwing my suitcase and legal attaché case in the back, I sat in front and rolled up the window to avoid a blast of exhaust from a bus on our right as we headed toward downtown Manila.

I spent the next forty-five minutes rolling my window up and down: first to get fresh air and then to avoid the next blast from passing buses and jeepneys.

Cindy and I were in Manila to take advantage of the new, progressive government's political opening. We were seeking documents and possibly witnesses who could verify that Gene Viernes was under surveillance by Marcos intelligence on his trip to the Philippines in 1981. Marcos had established that he "would have been" surveilled, but we were hoping for proof positive from NISA, Metro Command, AVESCOM, or the NBI that Gene's meetings with the NPA and KMU were monitored.

The Camelot Hotel looked like a medieval Arthurian castle, complete with towers and long, dark halls. I fumbled for my room key, entered the room, flopped onto my narrow bed, and passed out. But I was plagued by nightmares. I dreamt I was running up and down the dark corridors escaping Marcos loyalists, and exchanging gunfire with Marcos rebels in the hills. I spent hours tossing, waking, sleeping, and barely reaching consciousness.

The phone rang across the room. I imagined I jumped up and bounded over to it. In fact, I didn't move. My legs felt like tree trunks, my arms dead branches. Eighth ring, ninth ring. I didn't move. It stopped ringing. I fell back asleep and dreamt of Marcos agents and rebels some more.

The phone rang again. This time I inched across the floor and picked it up.

"You hungry?" Cindy asked. "You slept all day."

"I have no idea. I can't wake up. I can't move. Where are you?" I was semi-conscious.

"At dinner. We planned to start our planning tonight."

"Okay, I'll come right down," I said apologetically.

"You'd better not try going down. Your room is on the first floor." She laughed.

Groaning, I rolled out of bed. "On the way."

Rene Cruz had spent months in Manila after Marcos' ouster, meeting with his comrades in the National Democratic Front. He and Cindy sat at the table drinking coffee, deep in some intense conversation. They looked up at me as I approached and started laughing out loud.

"Jet lag?" Rene asked. "All activists get it here."

I thought about Vice President George H.W. Bush saying he must have had jet lag when he spoke at a conference with Marcos, praising his "love and adherence to democracy."

"No, no jet lag. Whiplash. I was dodging bullets from Marcos agents and running up and down these corridors all night long. This place is crawling with agents." They looked appalled.

Rene changed the subject. "Okay, here's the plan. Tonight I need to use your room, Mike, while you and Cindy…"

"What for? I asked.

"A meeting. You and Cindy will go to see Senator Diokno, and…"

"A meeting with who?" I asked.

"With the chairman of the National Democratic Front," Rene replied nonchalantly. "Now, as you know, Diokno heads the new Human Rights Commission…"

"Wait, wait a minute. You want to have a meeting with the head of the Leftist front in my hotel room?" I asked. Cindy didn't look nearly as at ease as Rene did anymore.

"Yes, it's more secure there, less likely to be bugged. They don't bug the rooms of US lawyers," Rene explained.

"No, the Marcos loyalists just run armed agents up and down the corridors."

Rene's irritation at me slipped into his tone. "You were having a nightmare. The political situation is very different now, but I need your room."

I knew that Colonel Hosanan, a former military officer, was in the countryside, mobilizing to lead an armed rebellion against the Aquino government. He had attempted a coup once before, but was unable to topple the government and had to retreat to the hills. The press accounts I read speculated that Hosanan was also trying to recruit military officers still on active duty in the Aquino military to join him for another coup attempt.

"Okay, if you insist." It was the best response I could manage, but I was still not totally convinced it was a good idea.

We paused to order the lumpia and pork adobo, and then Cindy explained that Senator Diokno needed to see us at his house because he was feeling ill. We would not stay too long. We would meet with Senator Saguisag at the Presidential Palace the following morning. After that, Boni Gillego and Raul Manglapus were trying to set up an appointment with General

Fidel Ramos, a former Marcos chief of staff who had defected to the opposition and was now the chief of staff for the Aquino military.

It seemed inconceivable that Ramos knew nothing of the thousands of "salvagings" and human rights violations that the Marcos military perpetrated. I was never sure why Filipinos called summary execution "salvaged." In Latin America, people were "disappeared," and were known as *desaparacedas*. "Salvaged" sounded like someone found salvation, rather than the business end of an automatic weapon.

The meetings with Diokno and Saguisag went well. These human rights advocates were dedicated public servants who wanted nothing but the best for us and our case. There was little they could do to help with our discovery, but they promised to put in the good word with the new government.

Rene and Geline's advance work paid off, and the meeting with Ramos was approved. On the scheduled day, Cindy, Boni, Raul, and I set off for Fort Bonifacio, full of hope and trepidation.

That same day, by coincidence, the morning newspapers were full of articles about a Philadelphia lawyer, Robert

Swift, who had filed suit against Ferdinand Marcos and the current Philippine government (which legally remained liable for the crimes of the prior regime), seeking compensation and punitive damages for the ten thousand victims of Marcos's terror. Swift had asked a court in Manila to order the Philippine military to turn over, among other things, the location of "safe houses" used by the military to interrogate and torture human rights victims.

As we left the choking, exhaust-filled air of metro Manila and entered the stately and well-groomed grounds of Fort Bonifacio, our discussion ceased. I gazed on the lush Philippine countryside and thought about Gene's trip five years earlier, and his description of the beauty that he saw.

With rumors of a *coup d'état* in the air, the headquarters was a heavily armed camp, surrounded by troops armed with M16 assault rifles on lookout for a possible attack. The guard at the gate asked for all of our papers and delayed our entry onto the base. Boni's face tightened as he informed the adjutant of our identity and the purpose of our visit. Our military escort conducted an extensive search of our persons and belongings. My pocket Dictaphone didn't pass the inspection, and I never saw it again.

In the outer office, Raul Manglapus, who was close to President Aquino but no friend of the military, chatted quietly with one of the secretaries. She was a town mate whose father had fled after martial law was declared. She said she was honored to meet the former foreign minister and that her dad would be proud.

Time passed. We looked at old *Time* magazines and the local newspaper. More time passed. Cindy and I speculated that Ramos might be too busy with the potential of an armed uprising to see us. But suddenly the door flew open, and a colonel asked us to step inside.

The room was large, ornately decorated, and a welcome relief from the noonday sun. General Ramos sat at his desk, piles of paper in front of him. He did not rise. His eyes were dead cold, his jaw tight around a short, fat cigar. Smoke billowed in all directions.

The colonel asked us to sit at a small table perpendicular to General Ramos' enormous desk.

Was this the desk that General Ver sat at when he ordered Aquino's assassination? I wondered. After all, this was Ver's headquarters before he was thrown out. There was no food, no drink, and no small talk. Ramos said nothing.

Tension mounted until finally Raul spoke, in English. "Thank you, General Ramos, for taking time from your busy schedule and your important duties in defending the People's Power Revolution against our domestic enemies." Ramos looked sternly at Manglapus, unmoved by the polite formalities. Raul continued. "With me is Bonifacio Gillego, a former intelligence officer in the Armed Forces of the Philippines; Cindy Domingo, whose family comes from Cebu. She is the sister of Silme Domingo, who was killed in Seattle. And this is her attorney, Mike Withey of Seattle. We have come to ask you to direct your subordinates to conduct a search for documents of the military that might help Cindy and Mike present their case to the American courts. They have the backing of Senator Diokno ..."

"What you ask for, no military would ever agree to," Ramos interrupted, taking the cigar from his mouth.

"I'm sorry, General?" Raul responded with some confusion, although we heard every word.

Ramos shot back. "We cannot give you what you ask for. It would compromise our security. It's unthinkable."

In just two minutes, the primary goal of our trip had gone up in the general's cigar smoke. Then Cindy spoke, hesitantly at first, but stronger as she hit her stride. "You see, General. It's just ... they killed my brother, Silme Domingo, and our friend, Gene Viernes, and we think Marcos knew about ..."

Ramos was glaring at Raul Manglapus and interrupted Cindy without looking at her.

"I'm sorry about your brother, miss, but we will never turn over to the American courts, or the Philippine courts for that matter, the location of our safe houses. Some of them are still being used. We need them. You should go home!" He got up as if those were the final words, and we were dismissed.

Safe houses?

Cindy spoke. "No, General, we would never ask you for the location of your safe houses. The security of the Aquino government is important to us too. You may have us confused with the case in Philadelphia. That's a different case." Raul and Boni nodded and murmured in agreement, filling the open spaces. I was still too dumbstruck to say anything.

Ramos turned his gaze to me for the first time. "I thought you were the lawyer asking for the locations of the safe houses."

"No, General," was all I could manage to get out.

Ramos looked around the room. "In that case, attorney, tell us what you want."

I pulled myself together. As I began to explain our case and our request, the tension oozed right out of the room. Ramos turned to his adjutant. "Colonel, get our guests some *pupus* and coffee." Suddenly the room was full of attendants. Soft drinks and *merienda* appeared out of nowhere.

Smiling broadly now, Ramos came out from behind his desk and joined us at the table. After hearing what happened to Gene and Silme, and what Gene was doing in the Philippines, he asked us to prepare a detailed list of documents, and identify which agencies should conduct the searches. I had prepared a mental list prior to our visit and quickly wrote down the highlights, including MetroCom surveillance reports for April and May 1981 and the dates of Gene's meeting with the KMU. Ramos told his adjutant to fully cooperate with our request. When he walked us to the door a half an hour later, he reached to shake each of our hands, promising to do whatever he could.

I knew our chances of getting the documentation we wanted was slim, and that Ramos' abrupt change in demeanor was an expression of his relief that we were not there to press for his safe house locations. But for us, it was still a mission accomplished.

The last night of our trip, Cindy, Rene, and I relaxed in the restaurant of the Camelot Hotel. We ate a large Filipino meal and chatted with some of the other hotel guests. Before long, the guests, fulfilling a Filipino tradition, began to sing. Cindy encouraged me to play the upright piano on the side of the dining room.

I wasn't sure what songs the guests might want to sing, so I tried out a medley of Beatles tunes. In unison, the whole dining room stood, flocking around the piano, and sang "Yesterday," "With a Little Help from My Friends," and "Fool on the Hill." Somehow, the songs seemed appropriate, given the circumstances. The crowd roared their approval, and we all sang long into the night. The nightmares from my first day in the Philippines had become a distant memory.

The following morning dawned cool and fresh. I had an hour to kill before our departure, so went to the hotel pool and sat on a lounge chair. A small boy approached and asked if I wanted to buy a newspaper. Handing him some change, I unfolded the paper and read the front page headline

Marcos Loyalists Convene Confab at Camelot Hotel. Seek Return To Power.

CHAPTER THIRTY-FOUR:

SETTING THE BEST CONDITIONS

1987—89
Seattle

After taking Marcos' second deposition, we asked the court to reinstate him and Imelda as defendants in the case. Richard Hibey and his co-counsel, John Bartko, went ballistic, stating the obvious: Judge Voorhees had dismissed the couple with prejudice in 1982 due to their immunity, and they could not be brought back in to stand trial.

We had a narrow pathway to get them reinstated, and it all depended on how Judge Barbara Rothstein, who was replacing Judge Voorhees after he succumbed to a long illness, read Federal Rule of Civil Procedure 54(b), which stated that where one party is dismissed but there remain other parties or other causes of action, such dismissal is "subject to revision at any time." Since Marcos was not the only defendant in the case, we argued that the court could revise Judge Voorhees' Order of Dismissal "at any time."

The rule also stated that a party gaining a dismissal can move the court to make that order a "final and appealable" order. If the State Department or US Attorney had done so in 1982, the court would undoubtedly have granted that motion. There was no "just reason for delay" in Marcos' appeal, and we would have had to appeal his dismissal. That appeal would certainly have failed while Marcos was still the head of the Philippine state. But the US government's attorneys had never asked Judge Voorhees to enter a final and appealable order. They must have thought a dismissal with prejudice was all they needed. But then Marcos was overthrown and lost his head of state immunity, and the dismissal order was subject to revision.

We wrote the brief and filed it with our Motion to Reinstate the Marcoses as defendants. Then we held our breath. Judge Rothstein struggled with what Judge Voorhees meant by "with prejudice," but eventually granted our motion in June of 1987. She denied the Marcoses' motion to dismiss. She stated:

The failure of both the United States and Philippine governments to request immunity for the Marcoses underscore the court's rationale for refusing to extend head of state immunity here ... Head of state immunity serves to safeguard the relations among foreign government and their leaders, not as the Marcoses assert, to protect former heads of state regardless of their lack of official status.

The Marcoses appealed this order to the Ninth Circuit Court of Appeals, but that court also held that Marcos was no longer entitled to head of state of immunity since it is the government, not the individual, who "owns" the immunity or privilege. The Philippine government had declared that the Marcoses were not longer entitled to head of state immunity and we were the first to take advantage of this development by getting a court to make a specific legal finding to this effect. It set a useful precident for others. Victory prevailed.

The second task was adding Dr. Leonilo Malabed as a defendant, which we also undertook in September of 1987. Malabed's counsel, including Patrick Hallinan and Kate Alfieri, argued the statute of limitations had long run out, because we had not sued him within three years of the murders. We argued, successfully, that the statute is only triggered when the plaintiffs discover, or should have discovered, a basis of holding Dr. Malabed liable for the murders. Since the Mabuhay Corporation was a cover for a secret intelligence operation, there was no way we could have discovered it was used to pay for the murders until the files were released in 1986. The judge agreed, and Dr. Malabed was added as a defendant.

Curiously, Malabed's counsel did not ask for a jury trial. Thus his case would be tried to Judge Rothstein, not a jury. But the trial would occur at the same time as the trial of Marcos. We were delighted. This gave us two bites of the apple: even if the jury found the Marcoses not liable, the judge could hold Malabed liable. But if the jury found Marcos liable, we were convinced that Judge Rothstein would hold Malabed liable as well.

The third major pre-trial development came in 1988, when we tentatively settled the case against the Republic of the Philippines. This legal maneuver proved tricky. Our sole basis of jurisdiction in federal court was that we had sued the Republic of the Philippines under the Foreign Sovereign Immunities Act (FSIA). Liz Schott took primary responsibility for researching, briefing, and arguing the FSIA cause of action, and we all weighed in on whether we could retain federal jurisdiction if we dismissed the Philippines from the lawsuit. We all assumed we could not, that the case would be dismissed and we would have to re-file in state court. This meant we would have to re-serve the Marcoses and Malabeds with a new state court lawsuit, and they would argue that the three-year statute of limitations had run its course, and we would be out of court and potentially out of luck.

Despite earlier difficulties with obtaining anything useful, we persisted in our efforts to dislodge documents from the US State Department. I scheduled a meeting with Michael Armacost in the summer of 1987. I didn't know at the time what a pivotal role he'd played in Marcos' ouster, but Armacost had been my International Relations

Professor and faculty advisor at Pomona College, and he had encouraged me to apply to law school.

Armacost brought his assistant to the meeting, and everything was very cordial. We spent a few moments reliving the days we spent shooting hoops in the gym before my basketball practice with the college's team. I described our case and our frustration with getting anything of value from our own government, and he expressed neutral sympathy. As we shook hands to bid adieu, outside the earshot of his assistant, he looked at me intently and said quietly, "Keep pressing, Mike, keep pressing."

Fortunately, in the summer of 1988, we hired a fearless and creative second year UW Law School student, Yvonne Ward. She claimed there was legal precedent for a federal judge to retain subject matter jurisdiction over a case that had long been litigated in federal court, even when the legal basis for federal jurisdiction no longer existed. Our legal team expressed our cynicism about that approach, even claiming that there was "no way" Yvonne could be right. To her credit, she stuck to her guns, and after reading her cases, I agreed with her and asked her to write our brief to preserve federal jurisdiction.

Judge Rothstein agreed with Yvonne's analysis and retained jurisdiction in an order we obtained in early 1988. Congress later passed a federal rule that allowed federal courts to do exactly what Yvonne had argued.

After that, we needed to complete our discovery against the Philippines and the US governments. Our settlement with the Philippines in mid-August of 1988 kept the Philippines in the lawsuit in order to obtain their cooperation in obtaining documentary evidence, including the surveillance by the Metro Command counter-intelligence units in Manila who monitored the KMU in 1980 and 1981. Judge Rothstein impressed upon the counsel for the Philippines, Steve Bomse and George Greer, the importance of making sure this was provided to us. In addition, the new government agreed to compensate the plaintiffs in the amount of $340,000, which the estates used to prepare and try the case against Marcos and Malabed.

Bomse and Greer traveled to Manila in October of 1988 and personally sorted through intelligence files in the dusty shelves and attic spaces at Fort Bonifacio. I don't know whether General Ramos had anything to do with producing the documents, but what we recovered from the Philippine military was extensive, filling at least two Bankers Boxes. They proved that General Prospero Olivo, head of Metro Command, who was implicated in the murder of Senator Aquino, had directed a military intelligence operation against the KMU, including Felixberto Olalia and other KMU leaders, from at least May 1, 1980, through September 1982, when Marcos had the KMU leadership arrested. The files contained transcripts of Olalia's speeches, extensive electronic and physical surveillance reports of their meetings, pickets, and demonstrations, and an in-depth assessment of the KMU's strengths and weaknesses.

Felixberto Olalia's letter to the ILWU, brought to Hawaii by Gene Viernes, was part of this evidence. Although there was no mention of Gene, per se, the surveillance reports in the files corresponded to the dates and times Gene visited Olalia and the rally he attended in April. We provided them to Boni Gillego, our expert witness in the intelligence operations of the Marcos military, in the hopes that Boni could "connect the dots" and show that Gene's presence and activities were picked up by Metro Command's surveillance team in Manila.

Although the meeting with Armacost seemed inconsequential at the time, when we finally started receiving additional State Deparment documents in 1988, it achieved greater significance. When we received a supplemental response to our document production requests from the State Department, we were amazed. There was an **Eyes Only** cable, dated August 10, 1979, from the deputy undersecretary of state for East Asian affairs, Richard Holbrooke, to the then ambassador of the Philippines, Robert Murphy. The subject line read, "Philippines Intelligence Agents in the US." Holbrooke called on Murphy to make sure a demarche — a diplomatic maneuver in which the ambassador takes strong objection to an action or policy of a foreign country – was communicated directly to Marcos. *Reading the riot act* might be another, less diplomatic expression.

The cable read, in part, "[I]t is hard to believe that the Marcoses do not understand the sorry lessons of the past few years," regarding the matter of Philippine agents operating in the US. Holbrooke seemed to be referring to the Koreagate exposure from the mid-1970s, which revealed South Korean agents operating openly in the US, causing grave embarrassment to both countries. In paragraph three of the cable, Holbrooke used terms like "strong belief," "resentment by Imelda," and "finding additional ways to warn the Philippines at every level."

A second **Eyes Only** response cable from Ambassador Murphy to Holbrooke was dated August 16, 1979. The cable related that the opposition movement in the US was having a negative impact on the Marcos government, and that the US intelligence agencies believed all areas of violence – including intimidation, strong-arm teams, assassinations, and kidnappings – could be used. This echoed a similar statement contained in the DIA circular that stated Marcos agents might "operate against" oppositionists in the US. The State Department document further stated that all actions of Philippine intelligence agents in the United States were taken at the directive of General Ver and under the overall guidance of Marcos. This was important evidence that Marcos controlled this operation.

As incredibly important as these cables were, there was an even bigger surprise. Murphy wrote the following to Holbrooke:

Imelda sent word to me a few days ago through mutual friend of her unhappiness over my having advised the President against approving the "desire of a few Ilocanos with American wives to start a newspaper in the US which would feature pro-Marcos material." I replied to her through same channel that:

A. *US law requires registration with the Department of Justice anyone acting on behalf of a foreign power.*

B. *Our laws are clear and strict, affecting foreign financing of the media.*

C. *Any subterfuge in this matter would inevitably come to light, if for no other reason that as result investigative efforts by Marcos critics in the United States. This would be counter-productive and embarrassing to both our governments.*

Dr. Malabed's wife, Yvonne, was American. We knew that Dr. Malabed was involved in purchasing newspapers. Now, here was the ambassador to the Philippines warning Marcos and Imelda not to break the law by funneling funds to the US for propaganda operations, almost certainly Malabed's, two years before the Mabuhay Corporation was used to pay for the murders of two opposition activists.

The warnings to Marcos were communicated in 1979, when Jimmy Carter was president. As Imelda told Psinakis in 1980, Reagan would change things.

The pre-trial proceedings (involving the filing of motions, briefs, orders, court deadlines, and the like) consumed ten volumes of pleadings in the district court clerk's office. We were still proceeding to trial on two basic theories: civil conspiracy and negligence. We had to prove that Marcos had initiated a civil conspiracy to monitor and operate against the anti-Marcos opposition in the US, including through the use of threats, physical violence, and intimidation. We had to prove that Malabed, Baruso, and the hitmen were members of this conspiracy. We needed to prove that the creation of the Mabuhay Corporation and the murders of Silme and Gene, along with the assassination of Senator Aquino, were overt acts of that conspiracy.

Under our negligence theory, we needed to prove that Marcos had created the Philippine Infiltration Plan, but his control and supervision of this plan fell below the standard of care of a foreign leader to prohibit his agents from using acts of violence. We had to prove that such negligence proximately caused the murders.

These two theories did not require proof that Marcos himself had ordered the murders.

The CJDV, through Cindy's leadership, had actively prepared our supporters and the broader community for the trial. Her fundraising skills, with the help of CJDV activist Kris Melroe, were at their finest, and we could pay all necessary trial expenses. None of the lawyers would be paid unless we won the case and collected a verdict, but the expert consulting fees, travel, and lodging and board expenses of our witnesses were significant, not to mention all of the costs we incurred in taking over fifty depositions.

Through Len Schroeter, I became active in the Trial Lawyers for Public Justice (TLPJ), a national public interest law firm. TLPJ agreed to join our civil case legal team as cooperating counsel and asked Richard Ben-Veniste, a DC-based lawyer who had worked on the Watergate case, to assist us in taking the depositions of the officials selected by the FBI, State Department, Naval Intelligence, and the DIA. We were overjoyed at TLPJ's involvement and couldn't have been more pleased that somone as experienced and prestigious as Ben-Veniste would help us in our thorniest depositions.

I was still at Schroeter Goldmark and Bender, and by 1988, I'd won a number of million-dollar jury verdicts and worked my way up to partner. The TLPJ executive director, Arthur Bryant, asked me to take depositions in the Iran-Contra scandal case, including that of Donald Gregg, the national security advisor to then vice president George H.W. Bush. It was an adventure and an honor, and it helped to prepare me for the Marcos trial.

As the trial neared, we assembled the respectable legal team that Bruce Occena had tasked me with assembling eight years before. Joining me in presenting our case was not only my steady and reliable co-counsel, Jim Douglas, but also Jeffrey Robinson, a partner at my law firm. Jeffrey was a criminal defense attorney and one of the best trial lawyers in town. He took major responsibility for trying the case, and having him at my side was unbelievably helpful. As I looked at the team, I thought about how proud Bruce must be. He was no longer active in the CJDV or leftist politics, and I missed his leadership and insight.

As we approached the November trial, all of my waking hours were dedicated to preparing witnesses, planning cross-examination, and getting ready. Then, on September 28, 1989 – a day before my forty-third birthday – the phone rang early in the morning.

"Mike, did you hear?" Cindy sounded breathless, as if she'd run a marathon.

I checked my alarm clock. "I was sleeping. It's only six in the morning."

Cindy hardly let me finish before blurting, "Marcos died. It's all over the papers."

"That son of a bitch!" I sat up straight in my bed, throwing the covers to the side and letting cool air rush over me. Beside me, Alison stirred and asked what was wrong. I told her to go back to sleep, but I was reeling. We knew Marcos wasn't well, but had no indication he was ready to pass away.

Just when we had him in our sights, he kicks.

Cindy was distraught. "What does it mean for the trial? I'm not sure we can stand another continuance."

I wished I could reassure her. Instead, I cursed. The trial would probably be postponed. We would need to move to substitute Marcos' estate as a defendant, but first, someone would need to be appointed as the executor. Then the executor would be entitled to weigh in on the strategy for the defense and its counsel.

"There's less than two months, and that's not nearly enough. We may have to bring our case in whatever court probates his will. Maybe in the Philippines. Oh shit, this is bad." My mind was racing. "We need to pull together an emergency legal team meeting. All hands on deck to figure out our strategy."

When we met, we realized that there was little we could do; the ball was in Richard Hibey's court. We prepared a simple motion to change the caption listing the defendant as "Ferdinand Marcos" to "the Estate of Ferdinand Marcos," as if that was all it took. There was actually no "Estate" yet.

And then, as it turned out, that really was all it took. In early October, we brought our motion to change the language, which was not opposed and quickly granted. The Marcoses' attorney apparently never grasped the legal significance of his client's death in our case. Rather than moving for a continuance of the trial to allow the estate time to appoint an executor, select a court to probate Marcos' will and estate, and allow that executor to hire separate counsel to defend our lawsuit – and in the many others proceeding against Marcos around the world – Hibey acted as if Marcos was still a defendant. We all prepared for trial as if nothing had happened.

Between the US government's failure to make Marcos' dismissal a final appealable order and Richard Hibey not seeking a trial continuance, Ferdinand Marcos was not well served. Not that we shed any tears. We were delighted to take advantage of these avoidable mistakes. Sometimes you make your own luck. We had an uphill battle to win with the jury or Judge Rothstein. We needed them to believe our theories about the conspiracy. And we needed some luck.

CHAPTER THIRTY-FIVE:

THE TRIAL

November 20, 1989
Federal Courthouse, Seattle

The trial of the *Estates of Domingo and Viernes, Plaintiffs v. Ferdinand and Imelda Marcos, Dr. Leonilo and Mrs. Yvonne Malabed and Tony Baruso, Defendants* began on Monday, November 20, 1989, in the federal courthouse on 5th and Madison Streets in downtown Seattle.

Unable to sleep much over the weekend, I went over and over my witnesses' detailed outlines of the testimony. At seven o'clock on Monday morning, I put on my best dark suit, a conservative tie, and checked my reflection in the mirror.

I looked worried.

Saying goodbye to Alison, I gave our two-year-old son Cameron a huge hug. They both expressed a assurance that restored the confidence I had started to feel in myself.

Our trial was held in the seventh-floor courtroom of the Honorable Barbara Rothstein in the federal courthouse. Rothstein was appointed to the federal bench by President Carter in 1980, and I had heard from attorneys active in the federal bar the ultimate compliment for a judge: She lets you try your case.

Her courtroom was magnificent, a trial lawyer's dream. It had high ceilings and plush, thick brown leather chairs, with ample space for counsel and ten long rows of benches for those attending the trial.

When I arrived, the courtroom was already full of supporters. I greeted Terri and Barbara Viernes warmly and asked them to sit with us at the counsel table. Jeff and Jim walked in shortly after I did, and we exchanged hugs. "Let's do this," I said, and was surprised my voice was calm.

We greeted defense counsel warily, but were respectful enough to smile and shake hands before taking our seats. As lead counsel, I sat at the table closest to the podium. Jeff was second chair and sat to my right, unless he was questioning witnesses, in which case we switched places. Jim was our scribe, document guru, and timer. He sat at the counsel table next to Jeff, with Terri and Barbara on his right.

At 9:30 sharp, the door behind the judge's bench opened and Judge Rothstein emerged. The clerk's voice was easily audible in the space, but somehow did not echo. "All rise. Hear ye, hear ye, hear ye. The United States District Court for the Western District of Washington is now in session, the Honorable Barbara Rothstein presiding."

"Are plaintiffs' counsel ready to try the case of Estates of Domingo and Viernes vs. Marcos *et al*?" Judge Rothstein was formal, resolute, and looked directly at me.

I rose from my chair. "Plaintiffs Terri Mast and Barbara Viernes are ready, Your Honor."

"Thank you, Mr. Withey. Good to see you again, Mr. Robinson. Mr. Hibey, are you ready to proceed?"

"Yes, Your Honor."

"Thank you, Mr. Hibey. Ms. Alfieri, are you ready to proceed?"

Kate Alfieri, the Malabeds' attorney, indicated she was ready, but raised the fact that she had recently discovered new documents, in addition to the ten exhibits which were provided to plaintiffs' counsel on the Friday before trial. "It was in a research file that should have had nothing to do with

Dr. Malabed's case. I was not looking for it or searching for it," she said. With that, she handed me the exhibits.

One of the new exhibits was the copy of the Mabuhay Corporation statement of expenses signed by Malabed, which we'd been asking for ever since Malabed's lawyer mentioned it in the press conference. Another purported to be a receipt for $15,000, signed by Lito Gorospe on May 17, 1981. I wasn't too concerned about that, since Gorospe was a Marcos operative; if he gave the money to Baruso for the hit, both Marcos and Malabed would still be liable. We did not object to the "newly discovered" evidence, and it was admitted.

However, the court was not happy. "I'm telling you something, Ms. Alfieri. I'm very, very troubled by this whole thing ... You know, I just can't believe – I mean, this isn't a minor case, Ms. Alfieri."

We then proceeded to jury selection. This is a lot quicker and simpler in federal court than in state court because the judge, rather than counsel, conducts the majority of the questioning. Judge Rothstein asked prospective jurors a set of background questions: whether they had been jurors or parties in lawsuits before, had heard of the case or the murders, had been in the military or law enforcement, had owned a firearm, had worked in a cannery or for the seafood industry, were active in social or political organizations, and the like. A few jurors reported they'd heard of the murders but had not formed opinions. Counsel was allowed to ask a few follow-up questions and exercise our preemptory challenges, but by early afternoon we had a jury.

Judge Rothstein gave the jury some preliminary instructions and asked my able second chair Jeffrey Robinson to proceed with opening statements.

Jeff was magnificent. He started with the murder scene, the hitmen, Silme's valiant efforts to name his assailants, the murder weapon, and the police investigation proving Ramil, Guloy, Dictado, and Pilay's involvement. He was clear, strong, and confident. He then moved on to describe Gene and Silme's upbringings, their outlooks, and the work they did in the union and the KDP. He described Gene's trip to the Philippines and the ILWU resolution. He then posed the essential question:

Who is responsible to the Domingo and Viernes families for June 1st of 1981? Who paid for these murders? Who supplied the gun that was used in these murders? The responsibility for June 1, 1981 lies squarely in the lap of Ferdinand Marcos, the ex-president of the Philippines, Imelda Marcos, his trusted wife and assistant, and General Fabian Ver, the leader of the Armed Forces of the Philippines.

Jeff described the details of the Philippine Infiltration Plan. "This was a plan to have secret undercover military attachés in this country monitor, harass, attempt to silence, and intimidate the anti-Marcos organizations in this country, which led directly to the murders of Gene and Silme on June 1, 1981." He described the unlawful techniques used in vivid terms and introduced the witnesses and evidence that proved our case. He then went into even greater detail about how much of the work of Gene and Silme was known to this operation.

We knew we were on thin ice in describing the role of the US government: what it knew about the Philippine Infiltration Plan; the fact it did nothing to shut it down, and that they had even aided and abetted this illegal foreign intelligence operation. The US had been dismissed from the case early, and Judge Rothstein made it clear we could not present evidence of US involvement. There would be no mention of LeVane Forsythe in this trial.

So Jeff took another tack: he used what the US government knew to prove the existence of the conspiracy. He asked the jury, "Can the US government help at all in establishing the existence of this operation? You bet it can, and we'll present you evidence to that effect." He then cited the DIA circular, FBI reports showing Marcos' intelligence receipt of FBI files on the KDP, and the two secret State Department cables from 1979.

Jeff described Baruso, his trip to San Francisco on May 16-17, and the payment of $15,000 out of the Mabuhay Corporation slush fund. He described how Baruso set up the murders by employing the Tulisan gang. He conceded that both Baruso and the gang had their own interests in seeing Gene and Silme dead, but stressed that the critical element was the Philippine intelligence operation and the payment for the murders out of the Marcos/Malabed-controlled slush fund.

Next, Jeff turned to damages. He described Kalayaan, now nine, whose name means *freedom* in Tagalog, and Ligaya, twelve, whose name means *happiness*. Both were fatherless children. What had they lost?

With that, Jeff completed his opening statement and yielded the podium. The judge instructed and excused the jury, and the first day of trial was over.

We retired to my office to assess the day. We were upbeat, happy that Jeff had done such a great job in laying out our case, and pleased that Hibey's opening statement would not be heard until the morning. Jeff would handle the testimony of the crime scene witnesses when the opening statements were over, and we hoped to get to Terri's testimony by the afternoon as well.

We had a pretty good idea from our discovery and the pre-trial order what the Marcoses' defense was. First, Hibey would claim that this crime was solved nine years ago by the Seattle Police Department and King County prosecutors. It was a dispute over dispatch to protect high-stakes gambling in Alaska. Second, he'd say that Gene and Silme's activities would never have risen to the level of the president of the Philippines – that Gene and Silme weren't important enough. Third, he'd argue that there was absolutely no proof that any "Philippine Infiltration Plan" had ever existed, let alone targeted Gene and Silme.

Hibey's strong opening statement bore out our predictions. He detailed the lower level of the murder conspiracy, focusing on the threat Gene and Silme posed to the Tulisan gang's gambling proceeds and Dictado's outburst at Gene at the May 26 dispatch. He acknowledged Baruso's clear complicity in the murders. But he said the evidence would show that the dispatch was the sole motive for the murders. Hibey met the jury's gaze head on as he said:

We expect the evidence to show that there was a massive investigation undertaken by not only the Federal Bureau of Investigation, but also the Seattle Police Department. They pursued all of the leads that were given to them and supplied by the family and the lawyers and in the end we expect the evidence to show that Ramil, Dictado, and Guloy were convicted of the murders of these men and sentenced to life imprisonment without parole.

I was always concerned that the defense would rest on the undeniable reality that neither the FBI nor the King County prosecutors had charged Baruso with the crimes, let alone any higher-ups. Hibey made this point exceedingly well. But then he did more than that. He stated unequivocally that Baruso never met Malabed, that there was no evidence Baruso received $15,000 from Malabed, and there was no linkage between the "special security project" of May 17 and Baruso.

He told the jury that Baruso had been convicted of fraud and embezzlement of union funds in 1983. He claimed that Baruso's deposits of close to $10,000 in cash occurred during the time period when he was embezzling funds, and that Baruso had also deposited cash into the same account as early as March and April 1981 – well before the May 17 payment.

Although he said he was not defending the politics of the Marcos regime, Hibey told the jury that the testimony of Mauro Domingo, a supposed military attaché at the Seattle consulate in the relevant years, would dispel any notions the regime had even heard of Gene, Silme, or the KDP, let alone "operated against" them, as stated in the DIA circular. In this, Hibey was exploiting what he knew to be a central hole in our case: we didn't have any witnesses to connect the Philippine consulate in Seattle to surveillance of Gene and Silme.

Then Hibey made what I thought at the time was a critical mistake, but one we'd anticipated. He stated that the plaintiffs were offering proof of four "summary executions," or "political talk for political killings," including Senator Aquino, and contrasted them to Gene and Silme. He elaborated:

These [other] killings were of visible leaders in the national leadership opposing Marcos. They wrote books, they gave speeches, they made public appearance, they gave testimony before the Houses of Congress regarding the situation in the Philippines. We expect the evidence to show the Messrs. Domingo and Viernes did none of this. What we expect the evidence to show is that they labored in a smaller vineyard dedicated to union reform and the improvement of lives who went off to those canneries and that reform was extremely important, especially when it was not being accomplished at the speed with which they wanted it.

Jeff nudged my ribs underneath the counsel table. Hibey was saying that, unlike Aquino and the rest, Gene and Silme were not important enough to merit Marcos' attention, let alone ire. It put Gene and Silme's outstanding character and their anti-Marcos work into question, and we were not going to let it pass. We had prepared our witnesses specifically to rebut this defense.

Alfieri submitted her opening argument to Judge Rothstein in writing, since the jury was considering only the liability of the Marcos defendants. Dr. Malabed's defense was even simpler: the Mabuhay Corporation's "special security projects" were not in the least bit sinister. The funds were used for the publication of the *Bataan News*, a pro-Marcos paper in the Bay Area, and Marcos had asked Malabed to author a document showing what those expenses were. He staunchly denied ever knowing or meeting Tony Baruso, and said he gave the $15,000 to Marcos' press secretary Lito Gorospe on May 17, 1981.

The testimonial portion of the trial began in earnest with Jeff calling the crime scene witnesses who had testified in both criminal trials. He questioned Frank Urpman, Henry Gruber, Dr. Oreskovich, Medical Examiner Dr. Rhea, the medic driver Richard Ford, the state ballistics expert Frank Lee, and SPD Officer Tony Delgado, who recovered the murder weapon.

Late in the afternoon, I called Terri to the stand. For this appearance, we'd agreed to limit her testimony to damages, keeping the door open for later testimony about the events surrounding the murders. This was unusual, but was necessary in order to accommodate expert witnesses whose schedules were not flexible.

Terri was strong and resolute. We had prepared meticulously for these few critical moments, but she was not looking forward to being cross-examined by Marcos' attorney. She began by describing her background and her work, then her personal relationship with Silme. Sitting high and tall, she spoke of him with affection and pride. Her love for her daughters shone through, and it moved me; and I hoped the jury as well. She testified:

He was a good father. With Ligaya, of course, he was nervous, like a lot of first fathers and with Kalayaan. He was very excited about having another child and he cared a lot for the kids and had a lot of expectations for them. Whenever Silme would go away, he would always make it a point to bring something home for Ligaya. One time he had brought her this purse from Las Vegas and we were at a movie one time and she left it there and she got so upset. It was like she had lost something really, really important or worth a lot, and it was just this little purse but she felt so bad that he went back to the movie theater later to find it.

She continued, a faint sheen of tears glossing her eyes:

He wanted his kids, he wanted his family to be like his, very loving and supportive, and we would tell stories about how his mother made sure that the kids, even though they didn't have a lot of money or things, that they got to go to different cultural events and be exposed to a lot of different things. Silme liked to cook. He was a good cook and did most of the cooking in the family.

Terri shared how Ligaya always wanted her daddy, not anybody else, to cook for her on her birthday, and to make a cake for her, wrap her birthday presents, and help her open them.

When she was done, we called Barbara Viernes to talk about Gene's life and work. Barbara was clearly fond of her older brother. She recalled how Gene and their brother Stan would wrestle for hours without a pin. She discussed his avid interest in his heritage and his book about the Alaskeros.

There was one more day of testimony before the Thanksgiving break, and we wanted to make it count. As boring as some depositions may seem to jurors, our videotaped deposition of Raul Manglapus was critical: it established the basic contours of the civil conspiracy we had to prove; in particular, the way Marcos intelligence operations in the US had targeted him and the Movement for a Free Philippines (MFP).

Raul had been appointed secretary of foreign affairs of the Republic of the Philippines by the Aquino government in 1987, and I had taken his videotaped perpetuation deposition in 1989 when he was in New York to attend the United Nations General Assembly. After describing his education, upbringing, law degree, and employment, Secretary Manglapus discussed working for General Douglas MacArthur in broadcasting. He was arrested when the Japanese entered Manila and was imprisoned for two years before he escaped to join the guerillas. He rejoined MacArthur's forces and was present with him when Japan surrendered in Tokyo Bay, ending World War II in the Pacific.

When Marcos declared martial law, Raul – by then a senator – was again arrested, this time by his own military. Again, he escaped from prison. He left the Philippines, and went to Malaysia, and then eventually to the US. There he joined with others to found the Movement for a Free Philippines (MFP), which advocated for a peaceful restoration of the democratic process in the Philippines. The MFP addressed human rights violations, especially acts of intimidation by Marcos agents directed against the exile movement and family members of those involved in the opposition movement. They advocated for total withdrawal or symbolic reductions of US support.

Manglapus was involved with the US Department of State and Amnesty International in publishing reports regarding the human rights situation in the Philippines. He testified that Bonifacio "Boni" Gillego went into hiding after martial law was declared, and Manglapus helped plan Gillego's escape route through Malaysia. When he arrived in the US, Gillego was given the director of intelligence position in the MFP. Heherson Alvarez and Steven Psinakis also joined the movement.

Manglapus stated that Marcos posted agents in the US to closely watch the opposition movements. Suspected Marcos agents took pictures at picket lines and demonstrations. Gillego and others recognized members of the Marcos intelligence corps. The MFP published reports of these incidents and informed the FBI.

Manglapus testified about the indictments Marcos brought against the opposition in 1982, which named him, other MFP members, and KDP leader Rene Cruz as defendants. He testified that this was an effort to retaliate against oppositional activities in the US, and to provide the

Marcos government with a basis for asking that the FBI direct an operation against the opposition, and to push through a US-Philippines extradition treaty. The harassment scared many Filipinos away from the anti-Marcos movement. Manglapus pointed out that it was significant that Rene Cruz, a close comrade of Gene and Silme, was also indicted. It showed Marcos was concerned about the KDP, and that its leaders did not "labor in smaller vineyards," as Hibey claimed.

Having established Secretary Manglapus' expertise and bona fides, I asked him to state his opinions. Based on his experience, background, and training, he said he believed that the Marcos regime established an intelligence apparatus in the US to be used against the Marcos opposition, including both the MFP and KDP, that was operational between 1972 and 1986. He testified that the apparatus harassed and intimidated the Marcos opposition, including acts of physical violence and threats of assassination.

He stated that it was an improper use of a foreign service, and that those operatives who had allowed themselves to be so misused had been dismissed from the service that he now headed. He believed that the Marcos' seizure of economic power in the Philippines was related to his political and military power.

I was pleased with the jury's attention to the testimony. They seemed impressed with the foreign minister, and I didn't worry that Richard Hibey's cross-examination would shake that impression.

During his cross, Hibey got Manglapus to admit he'd never met Silme Domingo or Gene Viernes, and did not attend their funerals. However, the secretary testified that he had heard of the case, and that the present government of the Philippines and its solicitor general considered the murders a significant human rights violation by the Marcos regime. He testified that he had seen General Angel Kanapi, referred to in the DIA circular, attend various anti-Marcos rallies and demonstrations in the DC area.

On redirect examination, I drew out that the secretary believed that from 1980-82, there was an intensification of harassment towards the anti-Marcos movement. This was when Senator Aquino joined the MFP, and Marcos was in hot water at home as the economic crisis began to intensify, and Marcos felt he had to take "extraordinary steps" in order to silence the movement abroad.

When Manglapus' testimony was over, Judge Rothstein ended the testimony early to let everyone get home for Thanksgiving.

We reconvened on Monday. Our first witness was Steve Psinakis, another key MFP oppositionist who had direct testimony about the Marcos operation in the US. He described the disappearance of Marcos' former press secretary Primitivo Mijares. Psinakis also testified about his own experiences after he joined the MFP; in 1980, a man stuck a gun in his face in his San Francisco restaurant and told him to stop his activities.

Psinakis recounted a four- or five-hour conversation he'd had with Imelda Marcos in December of 1980 at the Waldorf Towers in New York City. She told him, "Your man Jimmy Carter is out and our friend Ronald Reagan is in, so you'd better really stop your activities against our government, or we're really going to hurt you." He later described this meeting in a book he wrote, *Two Terrorists Meet*.

We then worked to establish that Gene and Silme were significant leaders of the anti-Marcos movement in the US. Psinakis pointed out that Gene and the KDP had made a close connection with the KMU, which represented as many as a million Filipino workers, something his moderate operation did not have. He testified that the passage of the ILWU resolution was front-page news in the US and Philippines.

So much for lesser vineyards.

Hibey didn't accomplish much on his cross-examination. He drew out that in his original statement to the FBI about being threatened with a gun, Psinakis didn't use the phrase *If you don't stop your activities* to describe what the gunman said. Nor did he claim the assailant had a silencer. On redirect examination, Psinakis explained that he recalled the gunman stating, "If you don't wise up," which he felt meant stop his anti-Marcos activities. His demeanor and body language made it clear to the jury that Psinakis had been in fear for his life, which Hibey did nothing to shake.

Our next witness was Geline Avila. As the founder of the KDP and Anti-Martial Law Alliance (AMLA), Geline had collected information for years about the harassment visited on her organization at the hands of Marcos' military and allies. She described activists who were threatened, and the effects that had on the movement and her work. She detailed the harassment she experienced personally when distributing leaflets at an Oxon Hill, Maryland, church. Thirty-five to forty "bodybuilder" types – she assumed Marcos agents – came from three directions and encircled her group, trying to push them off the premises. Among them was a Filipino man in a white military uniform whose name badge read "Kanapi." She testified it was the same Kanapi pictured in the DIA circular.

Geline was able to situate Gene and Silme's work within the broader context of the political and economic crisis emerging in the Philippines, as Marcos felt his grip on power ebbing away. She described the role that Gene's trip to the Philippines played, explaining that he planned to present the information he gathered not only to the ILWU convention but also in speeches to other labor unions and community organizations in the US.

In a meeting she'd had with Gene in May 1981, shortly after the convention, she testified that she had advised him to be vigilant, particularly when discussing his trip or the resolution. That was the last time she saw Gene.

As we broke for the day, we were pleased with how our case was going. Geline made a good witness. She was strong and passionate about her beliefs, and able to share the inner thoughts of Gene and Silme and the importance of the work they were doing. As qualified as Hibey was as an attorney, he was not prepared for the kind of detail and passion that Geline brought.

On the morning of November 29, we called former Filipino consular official Lourdes de la Cruz – known as Lulu. We used her testimony to establish how close-knit the pro-Marcos community was in the US, and how routine it was for the consulate to report on the activities of the opposition. We suspected, but could never prove, that she'd had an affair with Baruso around the time of the murders, and believed she acted as a key link between Baruso and the Marcos administration.

Jeff skillfully guided her through the many important Marcos allies she'd worked with or for, including Consul General Trinidad Alconcel, Bart Alcaraz, Benny Quitives, Dr. Malabed, and others. In fact, Malabed was her child's godfather. We made a point to draw out that Lulu knew every person connected to the prior surveillance on Gene and Silme and the murders. It laid the foundation for our argument that there was no way Malabed and Baruso did not know each other.

I then called to the stand Mr. Ken Kashiwahara as a witness to the summary execution of Senator Benigno Aquino. We alleged that this assassination was a particularly egregious, overt act of the very same conspiracy that killed Gene and Silme.

One of the many emotional highlights of the trial came when Ken presented a dramatic description of what he observed on that fateful flight into Manila in August of 1983, and we played Ken's video of the events. Ken explained that the senator, despite being warned of possible assassination plots, had cast his fate willingly by returning to the Philippines.

The video showed a jovial Senator Aquino, speaking with broad smiles and animated gestures to his aides and supporters. As soon as the plane landed, the aircraft doors tore open and five armed military officers charged into the plane. They demanded the senator come with them. Panic and chaos ensued as the officers escorted Aquino toward the exit. The camera was jostled, and no more than a few seconds passed before the unmistakable sounds of gunshots rang out, followed by anguished cries and loud denunciations.

Ken gave an emotional description of his efforts to get to the bottom of the murder. His impact was palpable. The jury seemed jolted, like Ken was an electric current.

We introduced into evidence the full report of the Agrava Commission, which gave us ammunition to argue that if a regime was so brutal that it would assassinate its leading opponent in broad daylight, while in military custody, the second he set foot on Philippine soil, it would do the same to rid itself of opponents like Gene and Silme.

The next phase of the trial included testimony about the various documents obtained in discovery about the Marcos regime's intelligence operation in the US, and how the US government had responded to it. We called two witnesses: ex-CIA agent Ralph McGehee and James Nach, a career State Department diplomat who had served at the US embassy in the Philippines in the early to mid-1980s.

A graduate of Notre Dame, McGehee was an amiable ex-football player who wore the role of a CIA operative like a glove. He'd spent a quarter century as an intelligence officer in the Philippines and beyond, and then had learned the hard way what happened when you took on the CIA. McGehee wrote a book about his experiences called *Deadly Deceits: My 25 Years in the CIA*. He had to submit the manuscript to his former employer prior to publication, and when he received it back from its censors, a significant portion was redacted because it was deemed a violation of his security clearance. Undeterred, he published the book with the redactions, showing everyone how much of his life the CIA didn't want anyone to see.

I asked McGehee to identify Exhibits 184 and 185. These documents included the two State Department cables between Richard Holbrooke and Robert Murphy. McGehee testified that the first document, the one describing a "demarche" to warn Marcos against operating his agents in the US, was significant because it confirmed that Philippine agents were operating in the US. He testified that this action seemed extremely unusual, and that most diplomatic cables dealt in more ambiguous terms and steered away from strong adjectives. McGehee specifically pointed out that the ambassador had been instructed to warn others in the Philippine government hierarchy, not just the head of state, about sending spies to the US. To undercut an ally like Marcos by going to his underlings demonstrated a great deal of concern, McGehee reasoned.

McGehee explained to the jurors that the ambassador warned Marcos and Imelda not to break the law by funneling funds to the US for Malabed's propaganda operations two years before the Mabuhay Corporation was used to pay for the murders of two oppositionists, along with other "security projects." McGehee testified that, based on his review of all the available documents, Marcos and Ver continued to operate Philippine intelligence agents in the US between 1979 and 1986. Marcos also funded propaganda operations through Malabed, all of which directly violated the US ambassador's 1979 warning.

Finally, I had McGehee discuss Exhibit 138A, the Mabuhay Corporation statement of expenses. He testified that this appeared to be an ideal example of a "proprietary" organization, controlled by Marcos with a cover or "cut-out" to give him plausible deniability. McGehee testified that, in his opinion, it was unusual to see such a document because one doesn't usually find the financial accountings of foreign intelligence services. Since the whole purpose is to avoid detection, records were not usually kept.

Richard Hibey did a good job on the cross-examination of McGehee, drawing out that none of the documents he testified to directly showed that either Silme or Gene were targets of the supposed intelligence operation. Hibey then got personal. He pointed out that McGehee had sued the CIA over the redactions in his book and implied that it was hypocritical to publish his book yet also accept the CIA's Career Intelligence Medal. But McGehee was prepared with the perfect response: he accepted the Career Intelligence Medal so his children could be proud of their father, to not embarrass the person who nominated him, and to lend credibility to any criticisms of the agency he might make in the future.

After McGehee's testimony, I read to the jury the deposition we'd taken of US State Department official James Nach. Nach was stationed in the Philippines between 1980 and 1986, serving as the Internal Affairs attaché under Ambassadors Murphy, Armacost, and Boswell. He stated that during his time in the State Department, Marcos was never authorized to operate an intelligence network in the US against the opposition. Upon reviewing the DIA circular, which outlined the attaché team assigned to the US, Nach testified that he believed that the document would have caused some alarm to the State Department. Nach agreed that in 1981, Marcos still heavily controlled the Philippine press. He believed that the declaration of martial law played a very large part in developing the Marcos opposition in the US. He also believed that the status of these opposition movements was an issue for Marcos. We closed the first full week of the trial on that note, satisfied our case was going well.

CHAPTER THIRTY-SIX:

THE HEART OF THE CASE

December 1989
Seattle

That weekend, the legal team, aided by Cindy and Terri, assessed how we were doing. We had proved the basic contours of the Philippine Infiltration Plan and proved, we thought, that the conspiracy we alleged truly existed. But we needed to bring the case back Gene and Silme and how the Marcos operation affected them and the KDP. We needed the emotional heart of our case to tie it all together.

Before our last witnesses testified, we put into evidence the depositions of the key Marcos operatives in Hawaii, including Trinidad Alconcel, Arturo "Tex" Balmeceda, Benny Quitives, and Bart Alcaraz. Their testimonies established that the Marcoses set up a "community protective task force" to provide them with security when they traveled to Hawaii. To our great satisfaction, the exhibit listing the members of this "task force" was admitted without objection and proved that we were on target. The task force was headed by Alconcel and included none other than Bart Alcaraz, Tex Balmeceda, Benny Quitives, Lulu del la Cruz, and even Dr. Malabed himself, who had denied under oath that he was part of any such group. It further showed how close knit the pro-Marcos forces in the US were, and that our assertion that pro-Marcos Filipinos were involved in efforts to defeat the controversial ILWU resolution was reasonable.

We brought Barbara Viernes back to talk about Silme and Gene's work, their struggle for racial equality, their leadership of the reform movement, Gene's trip to the Philippines, and Silme's winning ways with workers.

Cindy testified about the origins of the CJDV, and how after the murders, a number of friends and political associates insisted that there was much more to the tragedy than conflict over union reform and gang violence. She described the drama that unfolded at the ILWU Convention, and the actions of the KDP and anti-martial law forces. It all added to the texture of the case and showed the jury what these men stood and fought for. She explained how the murders led to a great deal of intimidation to those still working in Local 37, as well as those who were participating in anti-Marcos activities.

Cindy also described her close relationship with her nieces, Silme's daughters, and the effect their father's murder had on their well-being. She related that Ligaya was withdrawn and fearful, still had to be accompanied by a family member when going out, did not like to be left alone, and cried when there was a delay in a relative or friend's return from out of town. She said Kalayaan was very affectionate to the point of being overly so to strangers, particularly men. Both daughters required attention that they did not always receive, considering their now-widowed mother and her ongoing work with the union and CJDV.

Bob Santos, the universally respected "unofficial mayor" of the International District, was called to the stand to describe Silme's work in the community. He recalled one particular demonstration in the mid-seventies at the Filipino consulate office in Seattle, when three peaceful picketers had water, garbage, and debris dumped on them from the third-floor consulate windows.

We recalled Terri to complete her testimony. She described how her work with Gene and Silme aimed to bring uncensored information to the Filipino community in the US and especially to Local 37. At the canneries, they encouraged conversations about current events, as well as the anti-Marcos movement. She stated that Tony Baruso made it very clear that he did not want Marcos' martial law to become a topic of debate in Local 37, and how he took steps to exclude them in the union.

Terri explained the ILWU's progressive history regarding the support of worker's rights, both in the US and internationally, and that the KDP hoped the resolution would lead to a stop-work action, such as shutting down the ports to products imported from the Philippines. The ILWU had done this in the past, bringing national attention to the issues. She described the dispatch system in the union and why the "dispute over dispatch" motive did not fully explain the murders. She testified the second dispatch would have sent most of the Tulisan boys to Dillingham anyway, and the Rank and File Committee was not interested in stopping gambling in the canneries.

She described her actions on the day of the murders, and how she thought it was odd that Tony Baruso did not come to the hospital right away. She detailed the events that led to Baruso's recall, and how in the fall of 1981, around the same time he was being implicated in the murders, he was also given an award by the Philippine government for being an outstanding US citizen.

As I listened to her, I reflected on the fact that history had served up a strange coincidence: Here in the US, Terri ousted and then replaced the man (Baruso) who killed her husband. In the Philippines, Cory Aquino also ousted and then replaced the man (Marcos) who killed her husband. Now Terri was in the process of holding both men accountable for their summary executions. These were two incredibly brave and valiant women who fought for what they believed in and prevailed against long odds.

Terri explained the union's investigation of improprieties during Baruso's term of office. They found that he was double dipping, with accounting irregularities covering a span of five years. In total, she estimated he netted about $5,000, always paid by checks that were verified and submitted to the Department of Labor. They also found that Baruso falsified documentation in order to get health benefits for his non-union uncle. Neither their investigation nor the Department of Labor's inquiry uncovered any cash that was paid to Baruso as part of his scheme. Hibey's double-dipping excuse for Baruso's cash deposits was blown.

A jury had convicted Baruso of fraud in the double-dipping case brought by the Department of Labor, but Terri bemoaned the fact that he spent little time in jail and reiterated that he should have been tried and convicted of his role in the murders.

We also put Dave Della and Ade Domingo on the stand to further fill the jury in on Silme's personal and political history. The jurors seemed moved by their quiet dignity and obvious love and respect for Silme.

Having introduced Gene and Silme to the jury in a thorough and respectful way, we turned to the conspirators who caused their murders. We'd decided that trying to force Imelda Marcos to appear in court would have made our trial into a circus, but we could put Baruso on the stand.

Jeff made the most of what he could with a reluctant witness who repeatedly took the Fifth Amendment. It turned into one of the highlights of the trial.

Baruso's defense counsel, Tony Savage, who was well over six feet tall, stood awkwardly behind him at the witness stand to make sure he asserted the Fifth Amendment to all potentially incriminating questions. It was no secret to anyone by then that he had a lot to hide. So after each question, Savage tapped Baruso on the shoulder if he wanted him to take the Fifth.

Jeff was savvy and used Baruso's assertion of the privilege against self-incrimination strategically. *Did you know Boy Pilay was murdered? Did you ask Mac Callueng* *to bring Dictado to your union office on May 30, 1981? Did you deposit almost $10,000 in cash into your bank accounts after the murders?* His questions, and Baruso's refusals to answer, did plenty to elicit skepticism and distrust among the jurors.

Jeff asked Baruso about his personal feelings toward Marcos. Baruso claimed he had no close ties with the former president. He described the photo in his former office of him shaking hands with Marcos as something every delegate on a foreign trade mission received.

Jeff then had Baruso read aloud the letters that he wrote to President Marcos and General Romeo Arguelles, where he described not only "admiration but ... unflinching belief and faith made firmer by the personal contacts and exchange of views." Another letter written in December of 1976 reassured the Philippine president of his support and willingness to "reciprocate his kindness in whatever possible way." Jeff let the implication hang in the air: Baruso had found a way.

Jeff pointed out that Baruso claimed in his deposition that he'd never asked Ade Domingo who the members of the KDP were, or referred to them as *Mao-Maos*. So he asked Baruso, "And you have expressed to Ade Domingo that people who belong to the Union of Democratic Filipinos were *Mao-Maos*, is that correct?"

Baruso took the Fifth.

Later, Jeff returned to the same topic. In the courtroom, Jeff asked Ade to stand up in the audience. She complied and Jeff then bore down on Baruso asking if he asked Ade Domingto who were members of the KDP. Baruso said, "I was not interested in who were the members of that Democratic Filipinos."

"Are you saying you never asked Ade Domingo that?"

"I did not ask anything."

"So, if she said, in this courtroom, under oath, that you asked her those questions, she's again a liar?"

"She's lying."

The words seemed to hit the floor and ricochet loudly throughout the courtroom. Jeff let the implication – the murder mastermind telling the mother of the victim that she was a liar –reverberate for at least ten seconds. Finally, he turned to another to topic, but the damage was done. Baruso would never recover.

Baruso's memory seemed to finally return to him about his trip to San Francisco in May 1981. After denying it under oath for years, he'd testified in a final deposition, taken only a month before trial, that he went to California to attend a meeting of the Grand Lodge of the *Caballeros de Dimas-Alang*, a Filipino fraternal organization for which he was the Grand Prosecutor. He claimed an "all-womens' chapter" needed his help getting set up.

In response, Jeff drew out that Baruso had no letter, no invitation, no minutes, no documents, and nothing in writing to substantiate his recently created recollection.

When asked whether he attended the Pulong-Pulong video event in San Jose, he dissembled. "I don't know what Olong-Olong or what have you," he blurted in a lame attempt to mispronounce the name. When he repeatedly denied having ever met "Dr. or Mr. Malabed," it seemed forced, at least to me.

At that point, neither he, Alfieri, or Hibey knew we had a rebuttal witness, Wayne Alba, who could put Malabed and Baruso at the same receptions on two occasions, and even saw them talking to one another. Legally, we did not have to identify rebuttal witnesses until we needed to use them to counter testimony.

After Jeff released Baruso, the jury was read Malabed's deposition and we showed selected segments of the videotaped depositions of Ferdinand and Imelda Marcos. We tried to keep it focused, certain that the jury did not want to hear dozens of hours of anyone's testimony, even a former head of state and first lady. We focused on showing the jury how Marcos had admitted to basic background information about the role of his intelligence agencies, his concern that money from abroad was financing the KMU, and his powers as president. The jury laughed out loud when they watched Marcos's attorney knocking the "cockroach of truth" off his shoulder.

Imelda Marcos, on videotape, droned on about her glamour days at Malacanang. We had designated less than two hours of her deposition, but only a few minutes in, the gavel banged and the judge asked, "Would counsel please approach the bench?"

We all gathered at the sidebar for a simple but off-the-record discussion.

"How much more of *that woman* do I have to listen to?" Judge Rothstein asked me.

Stifling a laugh, I hemmed, "Well, we should be done in about an hour and a half."

The judge's eyes turned into saucers. "Can you cut it back?" she asked.

"Well, it's hard to edit the videotape now," I said apologetically.

"Well, you have to do something."

I turned and looked back at our counsel's table, helplessly. Jeff and Jim had no idea what was happening.

"I have a solution," I said finally. "We could mark her deposition as an exhibit and offer it into evidence without showing it, as long as I can play for the jury one short portion,where she is asked about a gift I believe she gave to the Malabeds in May 1981. Her reaction to the question is critical."

Hibey objected. "That would draw too much attention to that portion, Your Honor."

"You could play as much as you want in your case, Mr. Hibey."

I returned to my seat as if nothing happened and cued to the part with Imelda hemming and hawing. I then pulled the plug on the videotape. So much for Imelda.

Our final witness, not including rebuttal witnesses, was Bonifacio Gillego. Boni was a crucial expert witness, well qualified to explain the extensive investigation of the KMU by General Prospero Olivo's Metro Command in Manila. We could prove the outlawed union federation was under heavy surveillance when Gene met with its leadership in April 1981, but we needed Boni to testify that it was likely such surveillance had detected Gene's presence there, and that this would have caused the unit to inquire about what the US intelligence agencies had on him. Marcos, in his deposition, had admitted the same.

Boni testified that the Naval Investigative Service reports described its infiltration of confidential informants into the KDP, and that the many FBI reports on the KDP would likely have been provided to Marcos intelligence. He testified that both Gene and Silme would have been identified as labor leaders in the KDP, and Gene as a likely source for the transmission of funds to the KMU or other opposition groups that concerned Marcos.

He further explained that the Philippine consular officials and military intelligence officers in Hawaii, including Alconcel and Tex Balmeceda, were alarmed at the ILWU resolution and its passage. He opined that Alconcel provided the data and rice production figures that Alcaraz and Quitives used in the floor debate, and that a report of the ILWU Convention debacle would have been communicated up the Philippine chain of command to the level of General Ver and Marcos himself. Boni believed that Baruso's role in supporting the resolution would be looked upon by Marcos as a betrayal. He reasoned that an ILWU investigative team traveling to the Philippines offered nothing but bad press and more labor trouble for the embattled regime.

Boni had reviewed Baruso's travel records and the Mabuhay documents, along with Malabed's testimony. He concurred with Ralph McGehee's testimony that the corporation was used by Marcos to fund his intelligence operations in the US. He pointed out the use of certain familiar code words in the exhibits Malabed's attorneys had turned over the day the trial began. These included "codes" such as "33 reinvigorating vitamins," which would mean *$33,000*. The word "tablets" was used in a receipt as a code word for *cash*. These exhibits, some of which were produced on the first day of trial, far from being exculpatory, conferred an even more sinister purpose to the entire Mabuhay operation. Boni testified that the document proved that the NISA, under General Ver, had complete control of the Mabuhay funds.

Hibey did his best to discredit Boni's testimony, calling attention to his staunch anti-Marcos political beliefs and his support for the CJDV. But in the end, the documents and sworn testimony were unimpeachable, and Boni was unshakeable.

We called Wayne Alba as our final witness. He was an excellent rebuttal witness, with no axe to grind or interest in the outcome of the trial. Alba stated that as a member of various Filipino community fraternal organizations, including as a board member of the *Caballeros de Dimas-Alang* (CDA) organization that Baruso claimed he was visiting in San Francisco in May 1981, he came to know both Tony Baruso and Dr. Malabed. Alba stated that Baruso did know Dr. Malabed, and that Alba had seen them interacting at two CDA events in Manila. He said Zoilo Inacay, another CDA officer, told him that Baruso said he was going to see Leo Malabed during a convention, and he stated that Baruso had discussed Malabed on several occasions. There was "no question," Alba said, that Baruso was pro-Marcos.

With that testimony, the plaintiffs rested.

Hibey called no witnesses. He played one additional portion of James Nach's deposition, which we considered uneventful. He then said, "The defense rests."

I looked up and saw Juror 6's jaw literally drop when she realized the trial was suddenly over. I looked up her name on our roster. Linda Barber. I had a feeling, a courtroom intuition: she was on our side.

I had already prepared my closing argument, but I spent the night before editing, moving sections around, and finalizing the most important argument I would ever give. I practiced it in front of my mirror at home with Alison watching. She'd taken the day off work to come watch the closing arguments, and I was grateful for all of her support.

In court the next morning, it was difficult to sit still through the reading of the court's jury instructions. Judge Rothstein gave the standard instructions that the plaintiffs had the burden of proof on their claims—that the jurors must find by *clear*, *cogent*, and *convincing* evidence that the civil conspiracy we alleged existed and that, "by the preponderance of the evidence," the Marcoses were negligent.

I gave my closing argument to the jury on December 14, 1989.

Ladies and gentlemen of the jury: It was made to look like a dispute over dispatch. Hot-headed Filipinos shooting it out in the local union hall, vicious thuggery. No one was supposed to survive that hail of .45 caliber bullets, no one was supposed to live to tell. The gun they used was good for one thing: executing people.

It would be cheap, it would be easy, it would be over with. No one would know who did it and no one would tell. But someone did live, someone did live long enough at least to tell. That was something that they didn't count on.

As his whole life passed before his eyes in the seconds after that burst of gunfire, Silme Domingo had one thing in mind. "There's one last thing I must do. My life must not be in vain. The principles and ideals I fought for were worth living and dying for." *Because Silme Domingo said to himself that the perpetrators of this foul crime must be brought to justice; it was his last wish and we must answer it.*

Imagine the incredible courage of Silme Domingo to get out of his chair with .45 caliber bullets, four of them, to see his best friend Gene Viernes dying on the union floor, to get out into the streets to hail down a fireman, to say those words that would eventually unlock the mystery of what happened on June 1, 1981. Those two words: Ramil *and* Guloy. *It was at that instant that this murder plot began to unravel, not just for the hitmen, not just for Ramil and Guloy, not just for Pilay and Dictado, but for those who put them up to it, for those who stood in the shadows, to those who covered their tracks, to those who are responsible for these murders, the defendants on trial here ...*

Because after Ramil and Guloy were arrested, the tracks began to be uncovered, the gun was planted, fingers began to be pointed, and the cover story that it was just a dispute over dispatch began to unravel, and that's why we're here today. But, of course, it did not unravel by itself. The other thing the perpetrators of this murder did not count on was the courage and tenacity of Terri Mast and Barbara Viernes, and their determination that justice would be done to get to the bottom of these murders.

And what better example of who Gene and Silme were than the fact that these young women have fought for eight and a half years, despite many obstacles, to bring this case to trial ... It is to them that we have dedicated this trial, because it comes down to you, ladies and gentlemen of the jury, because it was made to look like a dispute over dispatch, but after three and a half weeks of trial in this courtroom, do you still buy that cover?

I let those words — *Do you still buy that cover?* — sink in. I then turned to explain why the jury system is such an important democratic institution, derived from the Magna Carta in England, where common citizens ,with no particular expertise, come into court to sit in judgment of even the most powerful. In this, they express the conscience of the community.

I asked, "Did the defense fulfill the promises they made on opening statement?" I reminded the jurors that Richard Hibey told them Detective John Boatman would testify the case was closed with the convictions of the hitmen. But Boatman was never called. Even Mr. Savage, while Baruso was on the stand, admitted the case was still open. I reminded the jury that Hibey stated that the union was in the ravages of bribes, kickbacks, thuggery, and violence, and Gene Viernes was out to stop the gambling. There was no such evidence. He claimed Gene and Silme gave no public speeches. Wrong again. The defense couldn't ignore or deal with the most important speeches either man ever gave, just weeks before their deaths, at the ILWU Convention. Those speeches, I said, sealed their fate.

Hibey claimed Malabed and Baruso never met each other, but he didn't know about Wayne Alba. I pointed out that it stood to reason that the leading pro-Marcos community leader operative in Seattle knew the leading pro-Marcos operative in the Bay Area.

Addressing the jury instructions, I pointed out that the evidence of the conspiracy had been proven through the overt acts of the defendants, the unrebutted evidence of the military intelligence operation against the opposition in the US, the murder of Senator Aquino, the infiltration and harassment of the KDP and MFP at their rallies and protests, the Mabuhay intelligence slush fund, and the expert testimony tied it all in together.

I pointed out that all three defendants took refuge in the US Constitution and its guarantee of the privilege against self-incrimination. "American soldiers have died, face down in the mud, to defend Ferdinand Marcos' right to assert his Fifth Amendment, and he has the absolute right to do so." I then repeated the questions that Marcos had asserted the Fifth to.

"Was the Mabuhay Corporation opened on 7/7/77 to insure its good luck?"

"Were Mabuhay funds used to monitor and operate against the anti-Marcos opposition, used to pay for informants, and used to conduct acts of violence?"

I reminded the jury that they could hold these refusals to answer against him.

After summarizing the evidence of liability, I turned to damages. I read the judge's instructions, which directed the jury to consider damages for the nature of the injuries, the loss of earning capacity, medical bills and funeral expenses, pre-death pain and suffering, and, for Silme, the loss of love, companionship, and affection of his two daughters from their father.

We ask you to award Ligaya and Kalayaan Domingo for the love, care, the emotional stability, for the companionship and society that they have lost ... Poets call parenthood the greatest love of all. Ligaya Domingo, age three, Kalayaan, aged ten months. All of a sudden, without warning, that man, that tender man, who cooked the food, the only one that could do it for her birthday, wrapped all the presents, made all the decorations, took care of her when her mommy worked, who read to her and comforted her, Daddy was gone. Where is he? Doesn't he love me?

[T]o have had your father you grow up with is so important, that first day of school, the roughhousing around the house, the joys of childhood, the teenage years, what am I supposed to do about these boys, the support and the steady

hand in studies, the college years ... That's what Ligaya and Kalayaan lost.

I tried to show that the idea of awarding damages was a way of "lifting a burden." I asked what society would value as an hourly wage for a father. Five dollars an hour, ten dollars an hour, twenty? I said that if they were to say five dollars an hour was adequate compensation to lift that burden, then the award for the next fifty years would amount to $2 million per child. Ten dollars per hour, for just the twelve hours a day one is awake and parenting, the award would be the same amount – $2 million per child.

I sat down, pleased at the presentation. But then my doubts flooded in, and I was certain I made a mistake. I had asked for too much. Federal court jurors were known to be conservative in awarding damages, and I was concerned that a jury would being willing to award millions of dollars in any case.

The closing argument by Richard Hibey was spirited and strong. He started with the "gang of thugs," as he called them, who took Gene and Silme's lives by vicious violence. He argued that I was just pandering to the prejudices of the jury by talking about Marcos. He hammered on the inescapable fact that the Seattle Police Department had gained three convictions on the theory of a dispute over dispatch, and that our clients' claims just didn't add up. He talked about the extensive FBI investigation which yielded no additional charges. He argued that there was no probable cause to suspect the Marcoses, and that there was no evidence that Marcos ever ordered any physical violence against his opponents.

Then Hibey changed tacks by pointing out what didn't happen but would have if our theory was correct. He challenged the notion that Gene Viernes had even met with the NPA or the KMU in the Philippines, arguing that if he had, he would have been stopped or arrested. If Baruso had really been at the Pulong-Pulong, there would have been some record of it. If Baruso had ever met Malabed, there would have been some record of it. Where was it?

Hibey said if there were clandestine meetings in the US between Marcos agents, Malabed, and Tony Baruso, there would have been evidence of those meetings, but none had been introduced into evidence. Finally, he argued that the official with the most knowledge of the Seattle consulate was the man who worked there, Mauro Domingo, who knew nothing about Silme, Gene, or even the KDP.

It was a strong effort to challenge and exploit some of the holes that we knew were there. But it was also predictable, and I took my time on my rebuttal argument to dispatch each and every argument.

I pointed out that Mauro Domingo was replaced at the consulate by Lt. Col. Dionisio Santiago in the middle of 1980, and that Santiago attached newspaper clippings that mentioned Gene and Silme to his monthly reports to Manila. There was no record of clandestine meetings because the word itself means they are in secret. I pointed out that Wayne Alba had no reason to lie about Baruso's movements and contacts. I reminded the jury that, under the court's instructions, we only had to prove that the Philippine Infiltration Plan was a "proximate" cause, not the only cause, of the murders.

I ended my rebuttal with a plea about the historical importance of this case tried in Seattle and an appeal to the Old Testament's call for justice:

Ladies and gentlemen of the jury, when the next millennium in ten years arrives, and history finally writes about this period of time and perhaps we can all hope that the end of repression is here and the era of human rights and democracy will be established. When we look around the world, profound changes, ladies and gentlemen, profound changes, and the rule of absolute power and tyrants is ending, I hope, and it's a good thing.

And perhaps, when that history of the Marcos regime is written, there will be a small footnote, maybe a paragraph about a case tried in Seattle, and as the decade and hopefully an era drew to a close the paragraph will say that justice was done, that even the powerful dictators in this world were required to compensate the families of those that they victimized.

And your verdict will say in the words of the Old Testament: "May justice flow like water and righteousness come down like a mighty stream." I ask you to write that history with your verdict. I ask you for a verdict for the plaintiffs against each defendant in this case. Thank you very much.

When I turned from the jury, I saw the smiles and tears of our supporters, who had filled the courtroom every day.

And with that, the trial was over. The two alternate jurors were dismissed and told not to discuss the case. The lawyers' briefcases were packed, the clients and witnesses left the courtroom, and the judge left the bench. Hibey "broke camp," as he put it, and headed back to DC. Kate Alfieri flew home to San Francisco. Perhaps they both anticipated a lengthy deliberation process. But our legal team, along with Terri and Cindy, settled into the attorneys' side room outside the courtroom and waited. When the jury was dismissed for home at 4:30 p.m., we all left, but we came back the next morning and waited again.

Sweating a jury is one of the least favorite parts of a trial lawyer's job. Anxiety and second thoughts are served for lunch. Doubts flood in like a tsunami. Vultures circle above.

I couldn't work on anything else. I could only wait and hope I had done a good job. I knew Jeff did. Jim had served the team incredibly well. *But was it enough?* In the last analysis, it was all about Gene and Silme.

We sweated the entire morning, took a lunch break, and then started sweating again.

On the afternoon of December 15, a knock on the door dragged us back from the abyss. "Counsel, the court wants to see you in chambers!" the judge's bailiff shouted through the door.

"Is there a verdict?" I yelled.

"I don't think so. She wants you in chambers as soon as you can."

As we entered chambers, I detected a slight smile on Judge Rothstein's face.

"Counsel, we have a question from the jury," she intoned solemnly, looking at a piece of paper in front of her. "I want to hear you on what, if anything, I should say."

I hate questions from jurors after closing argument. As plaintiffs, we had the burden of proof, and if the jury had a question, it meant I didn't anticipate something, I didn't cover something, or I didn't explain something well. Shit.

"The question is this: Can the jury award more in damages than plaintiffs' counsel asked for in his argument?" Judge Rothstein, again smiling slightly, looked at me. "Mr. Withey?"

In all of my trials, I had never had a jury want to award *more* than I asked for.

"Your Honor, the instruction is clear. The jury is the sole arbiter of the amount of damages to award. I would ask the court to answer it simply *yes*." I was shaking.

Hibey's co-counsel, Sam Coffee, had been left to take the verdict. Coffee was adamant. "Your Honor should not answer that question in any way. Your prior instructions covered that situation, and you should just inform them of one thing: read the instructions."

He had a point. But I took what he gave us and ran with it. "Mr. Coffee is correct. Your damages instructions covered this question. But it would be better for the court to re-read the damages instruction, rather than merely telling them to do it themselves. Inform the jury that they are the sole arbiters of the amount of damages to award by reading the same instruction."

"I think that makes sense, Mr. Withey. Mr. Coffee, I am going to re-read the instruction."

Coffee was apoplectic. "No, Your Honor, to re-read an instruction already given attaches too much attention to that one instruction."

But Judge Rothstein ruled. "The jury has asked a question, and this judge is going to give them the guidance they are requesting. To tell them to re-read all the instructions isn't very helpful."

With that, the judge asked us to return to the courtroom, where she re-read her damages instruction to the jury. I noticed Linda Barber, aka Juror 6 – the juror whose jaw dropped when Hibey rested – had a piece of paper in her hand. She was the foreperson. The jury listened to the judge's final instruction and retired. We went back into our room and tied ourselves in knots trying to figure out what it could mean.

The jury's verdict would apply only to Ferdinand and Imelda Marcos. Dr. Malabed and Tony Baruso were both tried by Judge Rothstein, and we would have to wait for her written decision after the jury verdict came back.

Half an hour later, there was another knock on our door. The jury had returned with a verdict. The courtroom filled with our supporters. The press crowded into the remaining seats. Terri and Barbara joined us at counsel table.

Again, Linda Barber had a piece of paper in her hand.

"Ladies and gentlemen of the jury, have you reached a verdict?" Judge Rothstein seemed upbeat.

Barber stood and answered, "We have, Your Honor."

"Could you hand the verdict to the clerk, please?" Judge Rothstein took the verdict from the clerk, read both pages, and handed the verdict form back to the clerk, who read it out loud.

Question number 1: Was any Defendant a member of the conspiracy alleged by the Plaintiffs?

Answer: Ferdinand Marcos, Yes; Imelda Marcos, Yes.

A roar rose from the benches behind us, followed by dead quiet.

Question number 2: Were the murders of Plaintiffs an overt act of the conspiracy alleged by Plaintiffs?

Gene Viernes, Yes; Silme Domingo, Yes.

The room filled with restlessness, eagerness, and murmurs of assent.

Question number 3: Were any of the Defendants negligent?

Ferdinand Marcos, Yes; Imelda Marcos, Yes.

Question number 4: Was the negligence of any Defendant a proximate cause of injury to either Plaintiff?

For Silme Domingo: Ferdinand Marcos, Yes; Imelda Marcos, Yes.

For Gene Viernes: Ferdinand Marcos, Yes;. Imelda Marcos, Yes.

If you have answered Yes to either Question 1 or Question 3 and 4, please answer Question 5: What were the damages as to each Plaintiff?

	SILME DOMINGO	**GENE VIERNES**
Injury:	$1,000,000	$1,000,000
Pain and Suffering	$1,000,000	$500,000

Medical and Funeral	$44,000	$4,000
Loss of economic capacity	$750,000	$750,000
Loss to children	$10,000,0000	
TOTAL	$12,794,000.00	$2,254,000.00

When the clerk was finished reading the amounts of damages, the audience erupted in cheers and shouts of approval. The judge did nothing to stop the celebration. Years of pent-up emotion, anticipation, and excitement flowed from our supporters like river rapids of righteousness.

Jim Douglas put his head down on the counsel's table and started bawling. Jeff and I hugged, and Ligaya ran up to Terri, asking her what it all meant. "We won," her mother told her simply. "We won."

As the pandemonium waned, Judge Rothstein rose from the bench, smiled broadly at the crowd, and said simply, "Congratulations to the Plaintiffs. You can expect my decision on Dr. Malabed and Tony Baruso at the start of the new year. Have a great holiday. The court stands in recess."

I caught Linda Barber's eye as she turned to go back to the jury room. I smiled and waved, gesturing to see if she wanted to discuss the verdict, which we're free to do once jurors were released. She did.

After the other jurors had left and the courtroom was almost empty, Ms. Barber came out to explain the jury's question. "The jurors thought that the numbers you gave were fine for an average father, but you proved that Silme Domingo was an extraordinary dad. We wanted to give him more than you asked for."

I thanked her. And then I cried.

On January 12, 1990, Judge Barbara Rothstein issued a Memorandum Decision finding Dr. Malabed and Tony

Baruso to be part of the Marcos conspiracy to operate against their US-based opposition and held them each liable to the plaintiffs for an additional $8.3 million in damages, beyond what the jury had ordered against the estate of Ferdinand Marcos. Her ruling validated every element of our case.

She found:

- "Plaintiffs have provided clear, cogent and convincing evidence that the Marcoses initiated, directed, and funded an intelligence operation against their political opposition in the US." These methods included monitoring and surveillance, the commission of numerous acts of harassment, intimidation, and violence against the opposition. She found the operation targeted members of the KDP and MFP and was particularly concerned with the actions of labor organization, given the political and economic situation in the Philippines.

- "Domingo and Viernes posed a substantial threat to the Marcoses. They were rising young labor leaders with ties to powerful labor organization in the US, and they were active and effective members of the anti-Marcos opposition."

- Regarding Exhibit 138, the Mabuhay Statement of Expenses, Malabed's account of the corporation's activities were "chimerical at best." Malabed alternated between a "total lack of recall and outright falsification." She found Malabed's defense "utterly implausible."

- Contrary to Baruso's and Malabed's repeated denials, "[T]he Court finds that Malabed and Baruso did in fact know each other." She credited Wayne Alba's testimony.

Judge Rothstein concluded: "Marcos created and controlled an intelligence operation which plotted the murders of Domingo and Viernes and that Mabuhay funds were paid to Baruso and used to perpetuate the murders."

Case closed.

CHAPTER THIRTY-SEVEN:

VICTORY!

December 19, 1989
Seattle

The word of the jury verdict spread through our community quickly. Soon after, the CJDV held a pre-Christmas victory celebration at the Queen Anne Community Center, and the foreperson of the jury, Linda Barber, attended.

Linda congratulated us all on a tremendous accomplishment, stating that the jurors were very moved by everyone's description of Gene and Silme. "I only wish I had gotten to know these fine young men," she said. "They were your inspiration, and they would have been so proud of you, and grateful." The audience wept and cheered widely.

Terri spoke to the group, thanking us for the many years of sacrifice and struggle it took to gain this important victory. She talked about how her daughters were raised by the movement and, as much as they missed their father, they had grown up aware of his sacrifice. She dedicated herself to the ongoing effort to still have Baruso charged with the murders, saying the next step would be to call on Norm Maleng again as the new year dawned. She thanked her comrades in the Rank and File who stepped up to carry on the work and the struggle. She thanked the legal team for its tireless efforts.

Barbara Viernes and Gene's friend Andy Pascua came from Wapato for the celebration and extended their thanks to the CJDV for keeping Gene's name alive, for honoring his sacrifice with our own, and for proving that those who cut him down in the prime of his life paid a heavy price for their actions.

"We did it!" Barbara yelled. "We did it for Gene, and we did it for Silme."

Ever the fighter, Cindy told the assembly she would not rest until everyone responsible for these murders were held accountable, especially Tony Baruso. She expressed the gratitude of her entire family, and especially Ade, Nemesio Sr., and Nemesio Jr. She paid special tribute to Bruce, Geline, Rene, Dale and Cathy, and the KDP leadership, who had moved on to other endeavors but who had given so much in the early years to provide direction.

When it was my turn to say a few words, I repeated the first words of my closing argument: "It was made to look like a dispute over dispatch." Then I said simply, "We did this because they killed our friends. For those who did not know Gene and Silme," I looked to Linda Barber, "you know them now. We have kept their memories alive and their example deep in our hearts."

I told the gathering that there was one party who got off the hook – the US intelligence community. But I also said we would not rest until even their role is exposed.

"It may take a long time, but that time has come. *Es hora!*"

AFTERWORD

The civil trial of Ferdinand Marcos was not the end of the story.

- The jury verdict against the Marcoses was the largest personal injury verdict in the state of Washington at its time, and it still stands as the only time a head of state of a foreign government has been held liable for the murders of American citizens on US soil.

- After the defendants all filed appeals, the Plaintiffs elected to settle with the Marcoses and Malabed for a total of $3 million. The Plaintiffs received $2 million from Imelda (who was said to have borrowed the money from her friend Doris Duke) and $1 million from Dr. Malabed. A trust fund was set up for Ligaya and Kalayaan to take care of them for life. We never did it for the money.

- The CJDV returned to the King County prosecuting attorney's office to press for Tony Baruso's indictment. By 1990, Joanne Maida had gone on to work in the US Attorney's office, and a new team of prosecutors, headed by Rebecca Roe and Kathy Goater, was assembled. They agreed to charge Tony Baruso. The new prosecution relied on the same successful theory, and many of the same witnesses, that we used in our civil trial. Cindy, Terri, and I testified, along with Raul Manglapus, Boni Gillego, and many others. It was the first time I had testified about the murders. In a bizarre twist, this jury voted

11-1 to convict Tony Baruso of the murders, but a criminal case required unanimity. The hold-out juror only relented when the rest of the jury agreed to convict Baruso of the murder of Gene Viernes but not Silme Domingo. Baruso was finally convicted in November 1991, and sentenced to life imprisonment without the possibility of parole. He died in prison on November 14, 2008.

- In 2011, thirty years after the murders, the names of Silme Domingo and Gene Viernes were inscribed on the Wall of Martyrs in Quezon City near Manila, commemorating those who gave their lives fighting the Marcos regime. They are the only Filipino-Americans so honored. Terri and Cindy attended the ceremony, along with other members of the Domingo family and the KDP.

- Stories of Marcos' wrongdoing, Gene and Silme's deaths, and our case have been featured in a number of fine literary works, including Thomas Churchill's *Triumph Over Marcos*, and Ron Chew's *Remembering Silme Domingo and Gene Viernes: The Legacy of Filipino-American Labor Activist*s. Judge William Dwyer mentions our case in a chapter of his book, *In the Hands of the People*. It was gratifying to all of us that important writers took an interest in this story and helped us keep the memories of Gene and Silme alive.

- In 2014, the Seattle Channel aired a documentary called "One Generation's Time: The Legacy of Silme Domingo and Gene Viernes," which was produced, written, and directed by Shannon Gee and Ron Chew. This wonderful depiction of Gene and Silme's work in union reform and in bringing race discrimination lawsuits against the seafood industry is a lasting testament to the struggle for union justice.

- I received the Washington State Trial Lawyers Association's Trial Lawyer of the Year Award in 1992, was a finalist in the Trial Lawyers for Public Justice's Trial Lawyer of the Year Award in 1992, was awarded the Public Justice Foundation's Champion of Justice Award in 2006, and was given the American Bar Association's Pursuit of Justice Award in 2011 by Federal Judge John Coughenour. These awards were all given in part to recognize the work I did on the *Domingo v. Marcos* case. I didn't do it for the awards.

- In 2016, a crusading Filipina investigative journalist Raissa Robles wrote "Marcos Martial Law: Never Again" (Filipinos for a Better Philippines, 2016), a masterful collection of news, photos and analysis of the human rights abuses of the Marcos regime, including the murders of Gene and Silme (p. 183). Robles drew parallells to the use of "summary executions" by the repressive regimes of both Marcos and the present president of the Phiippines Rodrigo Duterte, who has publicly justified killing suspected drug users and dealers rather than bringing them to justice. Raissa informed me that Duterte's National Security Advisor Hermogeneo Esperon admitted being a NISA agent keeping track of the Marcos opposition in the US from 1977 to 1982.

- In 2017, Cindy Domingo, Bruce Occena and Rene Cruz co-edited a book entitled *A Time To Rise* (University of Washington Press, 2017) which contains the personal memories of many KDP members and their supporters from the days of struggle. These poingent passages describe the foundation of the KDP, the years of struggle against the Marcos dictatorship and for socialism in the US, the KDP's response to the murders of Silme and Gene and a section on "looking back—was it all worth it?" As a KDP member Edwin Batongbacal states in the last chapter "No Regrets": " I sense that what remains true is to be found, not merely in debatable truths in political philosophy, economy and strategy, but also in the subjective and personal realms of what truly constitutes a life worth living."

As a public interest lawyer seeking justice, I learned many valuable lessons. Three are worth mentioning here.

Don't turn over the pursuit of justice in political cases to the government. Retain as much control as you can over the flow of information, pressure them constantly to do the right thing, and define justice not merely as convictions won or verdicts rendered, but as movements being built and leadership trained.

Learn to use the legal system as an instrument of social change, a vehicle to build mass movements and a method of holding wrongdoers accountable. Don't fall for the tired and defeatist notion of "the powerful always win, so what's the use?" We proved that the powerful can lose if you "set the best conditions," as Bruce Occena used to say. The legal system and the rule of law are not infallible—they are tools for the wealthy and powerful to perpetuate their rule, but they can also be used for social change. Exposing the cover-ups of human rights violations can be a function of the civil justice system if used properly.

Never give up.

While justice was served from the Marcoses all the way down to the hitmen, there still remains one party complicit in the murders of Gene Viernes and Silme Domingo which has, so far, gotten off scot-free: US intelligence.

In 2015, and again in 2016, I filed renewed FOIA requests to the FBI, NSA and the NIS.

The FOIA request to the NSA sought any interceptions of communications between Marcos intelligence operatives in Manila and/or San Francisco or Seattle in May of 1981 related to the murders of Gene and Silme, the travels of any Philippine military officer to either city during that time, and any background information on Gene and Silme's travel and activities. The NSA said they could neither confirm nor deny that there were or were not any documents responsive to our request.

The "Forsythe Saga" continues to this day. In June of 2015 independent filmmaker Sharon Maeda and I brought a FOIA request for all documents in the FBI's possession which refer to LeVane Forsythe, the FBI informant who was present at the scene of the murders. The FOIA request, available at **www.michaelwithey.com**, spelled out Forsythe's lengthy history of involvement in shadowy FBI projects and his association with Robert Maheu (the right-hand man of reclusive billionaire Howard Hughes) as described in Chapter 28.

The FBI originally indicated it had 1,500 pages responsive to our request and it would take 7 to 10 months to process. In January 2016, we complained about the slow pace and the FBI then said it had only 1,100 pages and it would take 22 months to comply. Concerned of the suspicious changes, we talked to the FBI's FOIA agent, who stated that the 1,246 pages of documents the FBI had related to Forsythe consisted of a single investigation in Seattle in a loan shark investigation of the FBI from 1980 to 1987.

This was the first time Forsythe was ever connected to the seattle FBI office and it means that his control agent in the FBI in seattle must have known of Forsythe's perjured testimony and did nothing to alert prosecuting atuhorities of this obstruction of justice.

The FBI stated it had no documents related to Forsythe's work as an FBI informant for the DEA/FBI/IRS task force in Southern California. It claimed those documents had been destroyed. Concerned about the possibility that the FBI was not being fully forthcoming in our requests, we contacted our Congresswoman Pramila Jayapal (WA-7), who promptly sent an inquiry to the FBI about the status of the FBI's response to our requests. As of the date of publication of this book, the FBI has yet to provide a single page of Forsythe's FBI file. We supplied to the FBI the names of the 42 FBI agents identified as having participated in its investigation of the murders and asked if it could merely confirm that at least one of those agents was referred to in the 1,246 pages in the Seattle file. It refused to do so. Another obstruction of our justice efforts.

We still don't know who put Forsythe at the scene of the murders and encouraged him to perjure himself to exonerate the hitmen.

Stay tuned.

TO THE READERS:

Though I have told this story from the first-person narrative, the struggle for justice for Silme Domingo and Gene Viernes was a collective effort involving the incredible bravery, sacrifice, and dedication of hundreds of people, many of them not even named in this book.

My role was no more important than that of Terri, Cindy, Nemesio, and Bruce. As Terri has stated on numerous occasions, one of the biggest miscalculations the members of the murder conspiracy made was in thinking that by killing Gene and Silme, all of the problems posed by their work would be resolved. Wrong.

Why? Because the two of the them, and the leadership of the KDP, had trained its cadre to take up the fight after they fell, to carry on as they would have wanted, and to make the personal changes and sacrifices needed to see this through and land the final blow. *They would have wanted it to be that way*, as the "Martyr's Song" said. Going on without them.

I pay special tribute to my incredible legal team. Jim Douglas, who passed away in 2017, was the unsung hero who edited our briefs, tempered my over-zealousness and was the glue who held the team together. John Caughlan passed away in 1999 and was an indispensable senior advisor to our team of young lawyers. His role in influencing the Aquino government to name the Domingo and Viernes case as one of the three top human rights cases was an outstanding piece of legal and political work. Liz Schott also played a vital role in researching and briefing the liability of the Republic of the Philippines in the first lawsuit and in keeping the legal team on task. Jeff Robinson was an unbelievably talented advocate for our case and deserves major credit for the result at trial. Thanks also to all of the great law clerks, investigators and legal workers who contributed so much to our efforts, including our law clerks Howard Goodfriend, Sharon Sakamoto, Andrea Brenneke, Yvonne Ward, Linda Scher, Gary Huie, and Rebecca Cate. Our investigators were terrific, including Christopher Hershey, Father Bill Davis, George Barron, and "Bill." Thank you all. A special and heartfelt thanks also goes to filmmaker and publicist Sharon Maeda, whose press work before, during and after the Marcos trial was unbelievably helpful in getting the word out. Sharon also joined me in filing the recent FOIA requests to the FBI and NSA. Thanks so much, Sharon.

I also want to thank and acknowledge the dedicated contributions of so many who have made the publication of book possible. I hired researchers, law students, college students and my own daughter Lisa to summarize the trial transcripts and depositions, create indexes of the over 20 boxes of legal files and reports, proofread my writing, edit manuscripts, locate documents, find videos from the internet and contribute so much to my determination to honor the legacy of my friends, Gene and Silme. Thanks to Blair Edwards, who created a CD of all the relevant documents; Andrea Gudger, who summarized many transcripts; Brittany Harris, who spent part of law school at UW finding legal citations and creating summaries; and my daughter Lisa Withey Michaud, who created an index and summary of the Dictado trial. I also thank my literary agent Chip MacGregor for finding my wonderful publishers at Wild Blue Press and who introduced me to my fabulous editors, Jenn Waterman and Beth Jusino, and Beth for also providing powerful advice on how to market this book. For sure I would have been lost in the minutiae of the moment had I not had my first editor, the fabulous author Ellie Stephens, take my manuscript and add life, detail and description to each scene. Thanks Ellie! My website designer and all around inspirational supporter Carolyn Anderson and my publicist Sue Evans deserve major credit for getting this book out.

No written thanks could possibly do justice to recognize the precious contribution that my wife Stella McClure Withey has made to the completion of this book. From the first day we met on the tennis courts in Seattle to the day I completed all of our work on this book, Stella has been an amazing source of emotional support, inspiration, and "One Love" for me. Thank you, Stella.

I have often wondered how differently my life might have turned out had Gene and Silme not been murdered. It became the defining political, personal, and emotional moment of my life. But if it ever seems in this book that I put myself above others in our movement, benefited beyond my contribution, or reaped the awards and honors that so many others also deserve for our justice efforts, I am truly sorry.

To me, Terri Mast and Cindy Domingo are the true heroes of this story. Had it not been for their courage, dedication, and leadership, we would never have prevailed. It is to Terri and Cindy that I dedicate this book. In the words of the song I wrote and performed for them, and for Gene and Silme, at the 2011 memorial: "They are deep in my heart. They will always be there."

Despite precedent-setting victories, the CJDV continues its work because our justice efforts are not over. *La lucha continua.* The struggle continues. The fight for justice never ends.

PICTURES

All Photos Credit: Alaskero Foundation

*For additional photos and documents,
visit wbp.bz/segallery*

Silme Domingo

Gene Viernes

Tony Baruso and Ferdinand Marcos

*Pallbearers for Gene Viernes' casket
outside Local 37 Union Hall*

Turn Anguish to Anger March, led by
David Della and Mac Callueng

Emma Catague, Elaine Ko, Terri Mast, Leni Marin
and Cindy Domingo and Silme Domingo's funeral

Ade Domingo, Bob Santos, Terri Mast, Mike Withey and Elaine Ko announcing formation of Committee for Justice for Domingo and Viernes

Elaine Ko describes the interlocking circles of murder conspiracy

Prosecuting Attorney Joanne Maida and Terri Mast
after Guilty verdicts in Ramil and Guloy trial

(S-NOFORN) A new Philippine defense attache tam, headed by the first flag officer in that post since July 1966, has arrived in Washington. The team will help manage President Marcos' forthcoming visit to the US, try to expand ties between the Philippine Embassy and the US Department of Defense, and monitor anti-Marcos Philippine activists residing in the US.

(C-NOFORN) Philippine Army Brig Gen Angel Kanapi, defense attache-designate to the US, arrived on station on 1 July. He will soon succeed CAPT Ernesto Arzaga as Manila's principal military representative in Washington. Kanapi, 50, served with the Philippine Civic Action Group in Vietnam in 1966, graduated from the US Army Command and General Staff College in 1971, and was Superintendent of the Philippine Military Academy (PMA) from 1978 until recently. While at the PMA, Kanapi's leadership came under some criticism as a result of a hazing incident in which the cadet son of another general officer died.

(C-NOFORN) A new team of subordinates will assist Kanapi in his duties in the US. They include CDR Domingo Tucay, 39, as assistant defense and naval attache; Constabulary LTC Roman Maddela, 35, as ground forces attache; Lt Col Melchor Rosales, 37, as air attache; and LTC Narciso Abaya, 32, as assistant ground forces attache. Maddela has been in the US since November, and Rosales and Tucay 2 months or less. Abaya is expected to arrive soon.

(C-NOFORN) The new attache team was selected by Benjamin Romualdez, Ambassador-designate and brother of First Lady Imelda Marcos, and confirmed by Armed Forces Chief of Staff Gen Fabian Ver. The attaches appear to be well-qualified; four are PMA graduates and the fifth, Abaya, is a West Pointer. Maddela is a highly decorated combat of-

**BRIG GEN KANAPI
DEFENSE ATTACHE**

**LTC MADDELA
GROUND FORCES ATTACHE**

ficer. More striking than their professional credentials are their ties to President and Mrs. Marcos and Gen Ver. All have served in the Presidential Security Command, a military organization that is responsible for the security of the First Family and until recently was commanded by Gen Ver. In that capac-

*Deposition Exhibit 4/53 for Id.
JMW 10/14/89*

EXHIBIT

*Berlin L
DK 8/11/89*

Document: New Philippine Defense team

Nemesio Domingo, Jim Douglas, Terri Mast,
Mike Withey and Cindy Domingo outside
federal courthouse after jury verdict

Legal team members Liz Schott, Jeff Robinson,
Mike Withey, John Caughlan and CIndy
Domingo at Victory Party 1989

Cindy Domingo, Terri Mast and Mike Withey
celebrating victory over Marcos

For additional photos and documents,
visit wbp.bz/segallery

APPENDIX A: CHARACTERS

1. **Ablang, Esteban** – A Filipino who was charged with the murder of Boy Pilay in 1983 but escaped prosecution by fleeing to the Philippines.

2. **Agrava, Corazon** – A justice of the Supreme Court of the Philippines who was appointed to head the Commission to investigate the murder of Sen. Benigno Aquino in 1983 and whose report implicated top military officials in the Marcos regime.

3. **Alba, Wayne** – A Filipino American who testified at the trial of Marcos that Dr. Malabed and Tony Baruso knew each other.

4. **Alcaraz, Bart** – Pro-Marcos ILWU Local 142 member in Hawaii who was very close to the Philippine consulate.

5. **Alconcel, Trinidad** – General Consul for Republic of the Philippines in Hawaii during the Marcos regime.

6. **Alfieri, Kate** – Counsel for Dr. and Yvonne Malabed in the civil trial of *Domingo v. Marcos*.

7. **Aquino, Benigno** – Former senator of Philippines and an exiled opponent of Marcos. Murdered in Manila in 1983.

8. **Aquino, Corazon** – Widow of Senator Benigno Aquino and leader of the People's Power Revolution, which in February of 1986 successfully overthrew the Marcos dictatorship. President of the Philippines.

9. **Armacost, Michael** – Former U.S. Ambassador to the Philippines (1982-1984) who helped turn the US against Marcos. My college mentor.

10. **Arrellano, Ernesto** – Secretary General of the KMU.

11. **Avila, Geline** – KDP leader and head of the Coalition against the Marcos Dictatorship and Martial Law Alliance.

12. **Balmeceda, Arturo "Tex"** – Military official attached to Hawaiian Philippine consulate.

13. **Barber, Linda** – Foreperson of the six-person federal court jury in the case of *Domingo vs. Marcos*.

14. **Barber, Valentino** – A Filipino American charged and convicted of the murder of Boy Pilay in 1983.

15. **Barron, George** – An investigator in San Francisco who followed the leads provided by the Mabuhay Corporation Itemization of Expenditures.

16. **Baruso, Constantine "Tony"** – Union president of Local 37 and Marcos loyalist who was the mastermind of the murders of Domingo and Viernes.

17. **Ben-Veniste, Richard** – A former Watergate prosecutor who acted as the Trial Lawyers for Public Justice cooperating counsel to take depositions of US agencies in discovery in the civil lawsuit.

18. **Bever, Judge Lloyd** – The jurist who was the trial judge for the trial of *State v. Ramil and Guloy* in 1981.

19. **Boatman, Detective John** – SPD detective who investigated the murders of Domingo and Viernes.

20. **Bomse, Steve** – An attorney for the Republic of the Philippines in the civil suit after Marcos was overthrown.

21. **Borgeson, Dale** – KDP leader responsible for day-to-day operations, based in Oakland.

22. **Bronstein, Phil** – A Pulitzer Prize winning investigative journalist who wrote articles about the Marcos regime for the *San Francisco Chronicle*.

23. **Callueng, Mac** – A Local 37 member.

24. **Campo, Boyse** – Tulisan gang member

25. **Carroll, Judge Terrence** – The trial judge in the trial of *State v. Dictado* in 1982.

26. **Cate, Rev. Bill** – Head of the Church Council of Greater Seattle.

27. **Caughlan, John** – Part of the CJDV legal team.

28. **Cruz, Abe** – A Local 37 member who was convicted of election fraud with Tony Baruso.

29. **Chavez, Cesar** – President of the United Farmworkers Union who praised Marcos.

30. **Cruz, Rene** – National KDP leader and editor of KDP's newspaper *Nag Katipunan*.

31. **Damaso, Carl** – President of ILWU Local 142 in Hawaii.

32. **Davis, Father Bill** – A former Jesuit Priest who worked as an investigator for the CJDV legal team.

33. **De La Cruz, Lourdes** – A former Philippine consular official close to Baruso.

34. **DeGuzman, Mila** – A Filipino-American activists in the KDP.

35. **Della, Dave** – Key KDP activist who became part of the Local 37 dispatch committee after the murders of Domingo and Viernes.

36. **Dictado, Tony** – Head of the Tulisan gang who drove the getaway car for the murders of Domingo and Viernes.

37. **Diokno, Senator Jose** – Head of the Human Rights Commission of the Philippine Government after Marcos' overthrow in 1986.

38. **Domingo, Silme** – Local 37 Secretary Treasurer, part of the Rank and File Movement, co-sponsor of the landmark ILWU resolution, and father of Ligaya and Kalayaan.

39. **Domingo, Ade** – Silme Domingo's mother.

40. **Domingo, Cindy** – Silme Domingo's sister and KDP activist who became the head of the CJDV.

41. **Domingo, Evangeline "Vangie"** – Silme Domingo's sister, active in the CJDV.

42. **Domingo, Kalayaan** – Terri Mast and Silme Domingo's younger daughter.

43. **Domingo, Ligaya** – Terri Mast and Silme Domingo's older daughter.

44. **Domingo, Lynn** – Silme Domingo's sister, active in Local 37 and CJDV and part of the Rank and File Committee

45. **Domingo, Nemesio Jr.** – Silme Domingo's brother. Co-Chair of the CJDV and co-founder of the Alaska Cannery Workers Association (ACWA), which brought race discrimination cases against the Alaska seafood industry employers in the 1970s.

46. **Domingo, Nemesio Sr.** – Silme's father, Vice President of Local 37.

47. **Dominguez, Teodorico "Boy Pilay"** – Tulisan gang member and part of the hit team that killed Silme Domingo and Gene Viernes. Murdered in 1983.

48. **Doniego, Angel** – KDP activist and former gang member.

49. **Donnelly, J. F.** – Naval Investigative Service officer and NIS special agent who wrote a report authorizing penetration of KDP.

50. **Douglas, James "Jim"** – Co-counsel in *Domingo v. Marcos* and an original member of the CJDV Legal Team.

51. **Draculan, Perceval** – A Local 37 member who was terminated at the Peter Pan Seafood cannery in Red Salmon, Alaska.

52. **Enrile, Juan Ponce** – Secretary of Defense under Marcos. Resigned in 1986 in response to a failed military coup.

53. **Esclamado, Alex** – The anti-Marcos publisher of *Philippine News*.

54. **Falk, Richard** – Professor of International Law who was expert witness in trial of Ferdinand Marcos.

55. **Fernandez, John** – Gene's alias for when he visited the Philippines in March/April 1981.

56. **Fisher, George** – Head of the Seattle Office of the FBI during the murder investigation of Gene Viernes and Silme Domingo.

57. **Fleggerman, Denny** – Worked under Norman Van Vactor at Dillingham cannery of Peter Pan Seafood Inc.

58. **Fong, Judge Harold** – The judge in the US District Court in Hawaii who allowed Marcos' deposition to go forward.

59. **Forsythe, LeVane** – The FBI informant who was at the scene of the murders and testified for the hitmen in the trial of *State v. Ramil and Guloy*.

60. **Fox, Michael** – Civil rights attorney who represented the Alaska Cannery Workers Association (ACWA).

61. **Foz, John** – Member of KDP and Gene Viernes' roommate. He became part of Local 37 dispatch team after murders.

62. **Galman, Rolando** – The "lone gunman" who was falsely implicated in the murder of Benigno Aquino in 1983.

63. **Gillego, Bonifacio** – Retired Philippine Military Intelligence official who testified for the estates in *Domingo vs. Marcos*.

64. **Glennon, Michael** – Chief Counsel for Senate Foreign Relations Committee who published a secret report on the presence of foreign spy agencies in the US.

65. **Goeter, Kathy** – Prosecuting Attorney of King County who tried and convicted Tony Baruso for the murder of Domingo and Viernes.

66. **Goodfriend, Howard** – CJDV summer law clerk who worked on *Domingo v. Marcos* civil lawsuit.

67. **Gorospe, Lito** – Press Secretary for Ferdinand Marcos.

68. **Greer, George** – An attorney for the Republic of the Philippines in the civil suit after Marcos was overthrown.

69. **Grubb, James** – Defense attorney for Jimmy Ramil.

70. **Gruber, Henry** – SPD detective involved in investigating the Domingo and Viernes murders.

71. **Guloy, Ben** –Tulisan gang member and hitman in the murders of Domingo and Viernes.

72. **Nach, James** – US State Department official assigned to the US Embassy in the Philippines who testified in the trial of Marcos.

73. **Hallinan, Patrick** – Counsel who defended Dr. and Yvonne Malabed in *Domingo v. Marcos*.

74. **Halperin, Morton** – National Security expert who worked for the ACLU in the early 1980s.

75. **Herman, James** – President of the ILWU.

76. **Hershey, Christopher** – CJDV member who investigated the murders and wrote and performed the "Martyr's Song."

77. **Hibey, Richard** – Lead counsel for Ferdinand and Imelda Marcos in *Domingo v. Marcos* who defended the case in federal court.

78. **Huckins, James** – Firefighter who was one of the first on the scene when Silme Domingo was shot.

79. **Kashiwahara, Ken** – Producer for ABC News nationally who filmed the last moments in the life of Benigno Aquino.

80. **Kanapi, General Angel** – Marcos military officer identified in the DIA circular as being part of intelligence unit in the US.

81. **Ko, Elaine** – Co-Chair for Committee for Justice for Domingo and Viernes, and KDP activist.

82. **Kozu, Mike** – KDP activist.

83. **Laxalt, Senator Paul** – Former Senator from Nevada who FBI informant LeVane Forsythe worked for and who advised Marcos to flee to the US in 1986.

84. **Lopez, Eddie** – Tulisan gang member.

85. **Madella, Colonel Roman** – A Marcos military man who was identified in the DIA circular as part of the intelligence unit in the US.

86. **Maheu, Robert** – An ex-CIA officer and former top aide to billionaire recluse Howard Hughes who FBI informant LeVane Forsythe testified could vouch for him.

87. **Maida, Joanne** – Prosecuting Attorney of King County who tried Ramil, Guloy, and Dictado for the murders of Domingo and Viernes.

88. **McGehee, Ralph** – Former CIA agent who testified on behalf of the estates against the Marcos regime in *Domingo v. Marcos.*

89. **Malabo, Jaime** – An eyewitnesses who testified against Ramil and Guloy in their criminal trial.

90. **Malabed, Dr. Leonilo** – A staunch ally of Marcos who ran the Mabuhay Corporation from San Francisco. Found liable for murders of Domingo and Viernes.

91. **Maleng, Norm** – Lead prosecuting attorney for King County in the 1980s.

92. **Manglapus, Raul** – Former Foreign secretary of the Republic of the Philippines, also an exiled opponent of Marcos who testified for the estate in *Domingo v. Marcos.*

93. **Marcos, Ferdinand** – President of Philippines from 1965-1986. Found liable for the murders of Domingo and Viernes by a federal court jury in 1989.

94. **Marin, Leni** – Filipino-American activist in Seattle, active in CJDV.

95. **Martinez, Marcelino "Monty"** – Confirmed Navy informant, recruited by the NIS to inform on KDP.

96. **Mast, Terri** – Silme's common-law wife and union organizer. Lead Plaintiff in the *Domingo v. Marcos* lawsuit.

97. **Mendigo, Lieutenant Colonel Edmundo** – Pro-Marcos military intelligence officer for the Republic of the Philippines, stationed in San Francisco.

98. **Meyers, Antony "Tony"** – Ben Guloy's defense attorney.

99. **Mijares, Primitivo** – Former press secretary for Marcos who defected to the US but was "disappeared" after threatening to testify in Congress against Marcos.

100. **Nach, James** – US State Department official assigned to the embassy in Manila, and who testified at the *Domingo v. Marcos* trial.

101. **Occena, Bruce** – National Head of KDP (Union of Democratic Filipinos) and early leader of the Committee for Justice for Domingo and Viernes.

102. **Olalia, Felixberto** – President of *Kilusan Mayo Uno* (KMU) in Philippines who met with Gene Viernes in April 1981.

103. **Olivo, General Prospero** – Head of Metro-Com in Manila implicated in assassination of Sen. Benigno Aquino.

104. **Oreskovich, Dr. Michael** – Harborview Medical Center surgeon for Silme Domingo.

105. **Pablo, Robert San** – Company foreman at the Peter Pan Cannery in Dillingham, Alaska, who testified against Ramil, Guloy, Dictado, and Baruso.

106. **Pascua, Andy** – Gene Viernes' closest friend from Wapato.

107. **Penor, Charlie** – Owner of the 609 gambling club in Seattle who testified for Ramil and Guloy in their trial.

108. **Psinakis, Steve** – Anti-Marcos leader of the Movement for a Free Philippines.

109. **Querubim, Ernesto** – Philippine Consul General in Seattle.

110. **Quitives, Benny** – Pro-Marcos loyalist in Hawaii's Local 142.

111. **Ramil, Jimmy** – Tulisan gang member and gunman who killed Silme Domingo and Gene Viernes.

112. **Reay, Dr. Donald** – King County Medical Examiner who performed autopsy on Gene Viernes.

113. **Rebar, Gary** – ABC TV reporter in San Francisco.

114. **Robinson, Jeffrey** – Criminal defense lawyer who was part of Plaintiff's counsel in *Domingo v. Marcos.*

115. **Roe, Rebecca** – King County Prosecuting Attorney who tried and convicted Tony Baruso for the murders of Domingo and Viernes.

116. **Rothstein, Judge Barbara** – Judge for the US District Court, Western District of Washington who was the trial judge in the trial of Ferdinand Marcos.

117. **Sakamoto, Sharon** – CJDV summer law clerk who worked on *Domingo v. Marcos.*

118. **Santos, Bob** – Activist and co-chair of the Committee for Justice for Domingo and Viernes, and "unofficial mayor" of International District

119. **Scholfield, Judge Jack** –King County Superior Court judge who signed search and arrest warrants against Ramil and Guloy.

120. **Schroeter, Len** – Founder of Schroeter, Goldmark and Bender.

121. **Suson, Glenn** – Member of KDP in Seattle who lived with Gene Viernes. He became part of the Local 37 dispatch team after Gene's murder. He later changed his name to Alonzo Suson.

122. **Swift, Robert** – US lawyer who sued Marcos on behalf of torture victims.

123. **Tactaquin, Cathy** – A national leader of KDP in Oakland who helped run day-to-day responsibilities and who was active in the national leadership of the CJDV.

124. **Tando, Mike** – SPD detective involved in investigating the murders of Domingo and Viernes.

125. **Tangen, Eddie** – Chair of the ILWU Resolutions Committee at the 1981 Convention.

126. **Urpman, Frank** – Seattle firefighter who was a first responder after Silme Domingo was shot.

127. **Van Bronkhurst, Emily** – Leading member of the Local 37 Rank and File Committee and CJDV.

128. **Van Vactor, Norman** – Peter Pan Company operations manager at the Dillingham cannery.

129. **Ver, General Fabian** – Chief of Staff over military and intelligence services during the Marcos regime.

130. **Viernes, Barbara** – Sister of Gene Viernes and Plaintiff in lawsuit against Marco**s.**

131. **Viernes, Gene** –Local 37 Dispatcher, part of the Rank and File Movement, and co-sponsor of the ILWU resolution R-34. Murdered June 1, 1981, at the age of 29.

132. **Viernes, Mariano** – Gene Viernes' uncle, whom Gene visited in the Philippines

133. **Voorhees, Judge Donald S.** – Judge of the US District Court for Western District of Washington who presided over early stages of civil lawsuit.

134. **Viernes, Stan** – Brother of Gene Viernes from Wapato.

135. **Viernes, Steve** – Brother of Gene Viernes from Wapato.

136. **Ward, Yvonne** – CJDV summer law clerk who worked on *Domingo v. Marcos.*

137. **Wicker, Tom** –Contributing Editor of the *New York Times* who wrote an Op-Ed about the murders.

138. **Wilson, Patricia** – Eyewitness to Silme Domingo's appearance on the street after he was shot.

139. **Woo, Shari** – KDP activist and close friend of Domingo family.

APPENDIX B: KEY ACRONYMS

1. **CBCP – Catholic Bishops' Conference of the Philippines:** The organization of the Roman Catholic Church in the Philippines.

2. **CIA – Central Intelligence Agency:** The Central Intelligence Agency is a foreign intelligence service of the US government, tasked with gathering, processing, and analyzing national security information from around the world, primarily through the use of human intelligence.

3. **CJDV – Committee for Justice for Domingo and Viernes:** This organization led the justice efforts to get to the bottom of the murders and hold all who were involved accountable.

4. **COMELEC – Commission on Elections:** The election commission of the Philippine government which oversaw the snap election of Marcos in early 1986.

5. **CPP – Communist Party of the Philippines:** Organization that pursued a classic Maoist strategy, adapted to the "objective conditions" of Philippine society, which included an economy dominated by Marcos and his ruling crony capitalist oligarchs but backed to the hilt by the US.

6. **DIA – Defense Intelligence Agency:** The Defense Intelligence Agency is an external intelligence service of the United States specializing in defense and military intelligence.

7. **ILWU – International Longshore and Warehouse Union:** Labor union founded in 1934 as part of the Pacific Coast District of the International Longshoreman's Association. The ILWU disassociated in 1937 to break away from conservative politics and a focus on skilled craft workers. The ILWU today primarily represents dockworkers on the West Coast of the United States and Canada, including Hawaii and Alaska.

8. **ISAFP – Intelligence Service, Armed Forces of the Philippines:** The Armed Forces of the Philippines (AFP) is composed of the Philippine Army, Philippine Navy, and Philippine Air Force. Under Marcos' martial law, the military was headed by General Fabian Ver.

9. **KDP – The Union of Democratic Filipinos:** The Union of Democratic Filipinos embraced the dual goals of establishing socialism in the US, as well as supporting the National Democratic Movement led by the Communist Party of the Philippines.

10. **KMU – Kilusang Mayo Uno (May First Movement):** Independent labor center in the Philippines promoting militant unionism. It was created on May 1, 1980, to represent progressive workers' organizations that advocated the National Democratic struggle, especially the end of what was seen as US imperialism.

11. **MFP – Movement for a Free Philippines:** The "moderate" or "elite" anti-Marcos organization in the US, including Senator Benigno Aquino, Raul Manglapus, Steve Psinakis, and Bonifacio Gillego, amongst many others.

12. **NAMFREL – National Movement for Free Elections:** The independent election monitoring organization that called into question the COMELEC results of the February 1986 snap election.

13. **NDF – National Democratic Front:** A coalition of progressive social and economic justice organizations, agricultural unions, trade unions, indigenous rights groups, leftist political parties, and other related groups in the Philippines.

14. **NIS – Naval Investigative Service:** United States Naval Investigative Service/US Naval Intelligence

15. **NISA – National Intelligence Security Agency:** The major military intelligence unit in the Republic of the Philippines during the Marcos government.

16. **NPA – New People's Army:** An armed guerrilla wing of NDF and CCP in the Philippines.

17. **PNB – Philippine National Bank:** A financial institution established by Ferdinand Marcos to fund Philippine intelligence operations in the US.

NOTES

INTRODUCTION: THE MURDERS

1. Seattle Firefighters Jim Huckins and Frank Urpman both testified to this interchange in *the State v. Jimmy Ramil and Benito Guloy*, King County Superior Court, Cause No. 81-1-01924-9 Trial transcript, pg. 45 (2465:1-2466:8 and 2466:8-2468:12

2. The Alaska Cannery Workers' Association (ACWA) was founded in 1974 by Filipino activists Nemesio Domingo Jr., Silme Domingo, Terri Mast, Gene Viernes, Asian-American activist Michael Woo, civil rights attorneys Michael Fox and Romy Arditi, and paralegal Emily van Bronkhorst. The ACWA, working with the Labor and Employment Law Office (LELO), conducted an extensive investigation of employment practices in the Alaska Cannery Industry in the mid-1970s. The targets included Peter Pan Seafood, New England Fish Company (NEFCO), Aleutian Dragon Fisheries, Icicle Seafood, Ocean Beauty Seafood, Wards Cove Packing Company, Trident Seafood, North Coast Seafood Processors, and North Pacific Processors. The offenses of these companies included segregated housing and other forms of racial discrimination, most blatantly obvious in the division of labor: supervisory roles were given to Caucasian workers, while "wet" jobs – including direct contact with the fish, and dangerously close and often maiming contact with the machines – were given to non-white and Filipino workers. The ACWA's

counsel, Fox and Arditi, had considerable experience bringing successful race discrimination suits against the Seattle construction industry as well as on behalf of the United Farmworkers' Union in the Yakima Valley. Fox and Arditi brought hard-fought Title VII employment discrimination lawsuits against NEFCO and Wards Cove, which led to attempts to blacklist ACWA union members, including the Domingo brothers. (http://www.socialism.com/drupal-6.8/articles/justice-stalled-alaska-cannery-workers) In the mid- to late 1970s, the ACWA sued Alaskan fish canneries on three different accounts. They charged these isolated and distant canneries with multiple accounts of discrimination and exploitation of immigrant and American-born Filipinos. They challenged union elites, who they claimed were complicit with the unequal standards of living and unacceptable working conditions in the canneries. See Drogin, Bob. "Seattle Case Focuses on Agents of Marcos: Relatives of 2 Slain Unionists Contend U.S. Knew of Covert Operations." *Los Angeles Times*. April 20, 1986. Retrieved online: 9/22/15; and see Griffey, Trevor. "History of the United Construction Workers Association." Seattle Civil Rights and History Project. http://depts.washington.edu/civilr/ucwa_history.htm. 2004. Retrieved on: 9/23/15.

3. The *Katipunan Pg Mga Democratikong Filipin* (KDP or Union of Democratic Filipinos) was a democratic socialist and anti-Marcos organization in the US. It was founded in 1973 following the declaration of martial law in the Philippines, and was active in organizing the Filipino community around issues of housing, immigration reform, job security, and the dictatorial regime of Ferdinand Marcos in the Philippines. It was headquartered in the Bay Area, with strong chapters in Seattle, Los Angeles, Chicago, New York, and

Washington, DC. Leaders included Bruce Occena, Rene Cruz, Geline Avila, Dale Borgeson, and Cathy Tactaquin. Silme Domingo was on its national executive committee, and he and Gene Viernes headed the KDP's national labor sector work. KDP members founded and were active in the Anti-Martial Law Alliance/Coalition (AMLA and AMLC), which lobbied against US support for the Marcos regime and against the US Bases Agreement. Rene Cruz was the editor of its newspaper, *Ang Katipunan*, and Geline Avila headed the Coalition against the Marcos Dictatorship and Anti Martial Law Coalition (CAMD/AMLC), the broad groups built by the KDP. Day-to-day responsibility for the KDP was vested with Cathy Tactaquin and Dale Borgeson. Borgeson had been deported from the Philippines when he was a member of the Pacific Counseling Service, which advised servicemen and sailors about their rights to oppose the war in Vietnam. A number of KDP members including Leni Marin, Mila DeGuzman, and Ia Rodriguez in Seattle were refugees from the Philippines, and they joined the ranks of the International Association of Filipino Patriots (IAFP), which was also opposed to the Marcos regime.

CHAPTER ONE: THE VIGIL

1. The KDP Headquarters and *El Centro de la Raza*. The KDP headquarters was on College Avenue on Beacon Hill, mere blocks from where Chicanos, led by activist leaders Roberto Maestas and Juan Bocanegra, broke into and forcibly occupied an abandoned elementary school on October 11, 1972. They established their own community center and named it *El Centro de la Raza*. The school was occupied by hundreds of supporters for months, including myself and many in the KDP.

El Centro was the unofficial headquarters of the entire movement for minority rights in Seattle. See http://www.elcentrodelaraza.org/about-us/history-evolution/

2. Political junky. My involvement in political activism in Seattle began with helping organize the Seattle chapter of the National Lawyers Guild, a progressive public interest association of lawyers, law students, paralegals, jailhouse lawyers, and other activist legal workers in the United States. The group was founded in 1937 as an alternative to the American Bar Association (ABA) in protest of that organization's exclusionary membership practices and conservative political orientation. It was the first US bar association to allow the admission of minorities. The group declares itself to be dedicated to the need for basic and progressive change in political and economic systems, to the end that human rights should be regarded as more sacred than property interests.

3. Tyree Scott and the UCWA. In August and September of 1969, Scott and the Central Contractors Association (CCA) shut down federal construction sites throughout Seattle and demanded jobs for black contractors and laborers through the utilization of federal civil rights laws (Griffey, 2004). This initiated a chain reaction among other contractors in West Coast cities. Early in 1970, Tyree left the CCA to create the United Construction Workers Association (UCWA). Instead of only working for the rights of contractors, he worked for all black laborers and other minority workers. In this, he fused activism, social work, and political advocacy. The UCWA also played a major role in the founding of the Alaska Cannery Workers Association (ACWA) in 1973 (Griffey, 2004), providing seed money and an organizational model, and training radical Filipino youth. During this pivotal time in Seattle's labor history, Tyree Scott became deeply involved with the Third World

Marxist movement. The "third world" term was utilized to build solidarity amongst people who suffered racial and economic injustices worldwide. He was a founding member of the Third World Coalition, as well as the Seattle Workers Group. His ideological shift became apparent in the UCWA's publication of a newspaper between 1975-1978 "for the third world" called *No Separate Peace* (Griffey, 2004). All *No Separate Peace* newspapers can be read in their entirety in the University of Washington archives at: http://depts.washington.edu/ civilr/NSP.htm.Griffey, Trevor. "History of the United Construction Workers Association." Seattle Civil Rights and History Project. http://depts.washington.edu/civilr/ ucwa_history.htm. 2004. Retrieved on: 9/23/15.

4. "Problems with the local judiciary" My legal career had been founded on the radical, anti-war and anti-racism politics that I espoused. However, the local judiciary had not taken kindly to my activism. In the early 1970s I had been representing a French professor, Frank Giese, who ran a Leftist book store in Portland, of engaging in a "conspiracy to disrupt the war effort in Vietnam." Frank was acquitted of the charge of bombing two Portland Army recruiting stations but was convicted of the nebulous conspiracy charge. At his sentencing, I told the judge that if Frank were guilty of such a vague charge, most of the people in the courtroom who had come to support him were similarly guilty. He was sentenced to the maximum five years in a federal penitentiary. On appeal, I informed the Ninth Circuit Court of Appeals that another lawyer would be handling the appeal and I would remain as counsel of record only to facilitate the transmission of the record of the trial. When Prof. Giese's appellate counsel failed to file the Opening Brief on time, a three judge court of the Ninth Circuit summarily ordered me into a packed courtroom.

They questioned me and then announced that I would be disbarred from practicing before that court. I was devastated, believing my law career was over. I hired counsel and he induced wiser heads on the court to prevail and the disbarment was reduced to a suspension from practice which lasted less than a year.

In the early to mid-1970s, I represented many of the protestors who were objecting to the blatant discrimination in the construction trades in Seattle. See Note 2 above. Hundreds of protestors jammed the construction sites where there were no people of color working. Hundreds were arrested for trespass. During the court proceedings, Tyree Scott, the leader of the United Construction Workers Association (UCWA), told Seattle Municipal Court Judge Patrick Corbett that the police and courts were mere tools of the construction industry and that he did not recognize the legitimacy of the courts. He was promptly marched off to jail. One of my clients, Doug Chin, had a bench warrant issued for him when he failed to show up for an arraignment. The defendants met with me and we all decided to go to court the next day and turn Doug in so he would not be arrested on the streets. As the 50-some protestors filed into the courtroom, Judge Corbett stopped proceedings and accused me of leading a demonstration. I explained I was there with my client Doug Chin to turn himself in. Corbett was visibly angry at me, shouted to the two courtroom deputies to arrest me and all of the other people who came to court and take them to jail. I turned to the crowd, asked if anyone wanted to go to jail. My clients started chanting "The People United Will Never be Defeated" and we all walked out. The judge referred me to the Bar Association which declined to bring disciplinary charges. I was not welcome in Judge Corbett's courtroom ever again.

5. The Red Squad – In the late 1970s, the SPD's Intelligence Unit (Red Squad) was exposed for spying on peaceful movement groups and creating dossiers on everyone from the Left to Santa Claus ("the red"). I had been one of the leaders in the Coalition on Government Spying, which successfully lobbied to have an anti-police spying ordinance passed by the Seattle City Council in 1978.

CHAPTER TWO: THE SEATTLE POLICE INVESTIGATE

1. References to the events in this chapter are supported by the documents of the Seattle Police Department's investigation of the murders.

CHAPTER THREE: FAMILY AND FRIENDS CARRY ON

1. The Anguish to Anger banner - 'Committee for Justice for Domingo and Viernes Newsletter, July 21, 1981'. (1981): 1. Pacific Northwest Historical Documents Collection: University of Washington Libraries, Special Collections. Web. 6 Nov. 2015.

2. Rank and File Committee. This group, led by KDP members, was created in 1980 in order to organize Local 37 union members to support reforms, including aggressive collective bargaining with the industry, a fair and democratic dispatch, Shop Steward training sessions, and enforced contracts. It published a newsletter and had organizing sessions for members. In 1980, R.F.C. candidates won eleven of seventeen seats on the Local 37 Executive Board, Gene Viernes and was elected Dispatcher, and Silme Domingo Secretary-Treasurer.

CHAPTER FOUR: THE CJDV ON THE MARCH

1. Statements by the Union of Democratic Filipinos (KDP) at the Memorial for Gene Viernes and the Memorial for Kasama Silme Domingo. KDP memorial statements can be accessed at www.**michaelwithey**.com. There is also a collection of historic documents detailing the case, the community's loss of Silme Domingo and Gene Viernes, and the continued quest for justice. http://www.**michaelwithey**.com/resources.

2. Committee for Justice's Appeal for Justice to the Community. A copy of this Appeal for Justice can be found on the website www.**michaelwithey**.com/resources.

See Committee for Justice for Domingo and Viernes Newsletter, July 21, 1981'. (1981):

3. Pacific Northwest Historical Documents Collection: University of Washington Libraries, Special Collections. Web. 6 Nov. 2015. http://digitalcollections.lib.washington.edu/cdm/ref/collection/pioneerlife/id/18180

4. Local 37: The salmon canning industry had developed over the decades by hiring the cheapest, most vulnerable, and downtrodden workers they could find. The seasonal work force was largely Filipino, because they were willing to work the worst jobs in the most deplorable conditions. There was another union, the Alaska Fisherman's Union (AFU), which dispatched cannery workers out of Anchorage, there were not enough readily available cannery workers in Alaska to fulfill the needs of the industry. The bulk of the workforce, therefore, was sent out of Local 37 in Seattle, which recruited members from Washington, Oregon, and California. The difficult struggle to unionize this workforce had been fought earlier, but the "Red Scare" of the 1950s

and black-listing of communist organizers led to some of the more opportunist elements, like Tony Baruso and his predecessors, taking over Local 37 and developing pro-industry positions. In 1980, the Rank and File Committee, formed and led by Gene, Silme, and Terri, opposed this form of sell-out unionism.

5. International Longshore and Warehouseman's Union (ILWU). Harry Bridges founded the ILWU in 1937. As president, his Marxist views and support of the USSR led to his red-baiting by the US government, which accused him of being a communist. Despite their efforts, he successfully avoided deportation and went on to battle corruption and garner higher wages for the maritime labor force. The ILWU and the Communist Party of the USA was instrumental in building the Local 37 Alaska Cannery Workers Union in the 1950s with Chris Mensalves, a radical union organizer, as president. In many respects the work of Gene and Silme drew upon the experiences of Mensalves and his fellow trade unionists in fighting the industry for better wages and working conditions and organizing the union. Eventually, Mensalves faced the same anti-communist attacks as Harry Bridges. The Labor Studies Program of the University of Washington is now named The Harry Bridges Center for Labor Studies, of which Terri Mast is a board member. See "Bridges, Harry." *Grolier Multimedia Encyclopedia.* Grolier Online, 2014. Web. 17 Nov. 2014.

CHAPTER FIVE: THE FBI INTERVENES

1. COINTELPRO. See Mike Cassidy and Will Miller's *A Short History of FBI COINTELPRO* at http://www. monitor.net/monitor/9905a/jbcointelpro.html. See also Brian Glick's *War At Home: Covert Action against*

U.S. Activists and What We Can Do about It (South End Press; Boston, 1989), a source for detailed and documented information on the history of domestic covert action against movements for social change. And see Rosenfeld, Seth. *Subversives.* New York: Farrar, Straus and Giroux, 2012. At pp. 213, 712.

2. Hobbs Act - The Hobbs Act, 18 United States Code Section 1951 et seq. "[P]rohibits actual or attempted robbery or extortion affecting interstate or foreign commerce." Section 1951 also proscribes conspiracy to commit robbery or extortion without reference to the conspiracy statute at 18 U.S.C. § 371. Although the Hobbs Act was enacted as a statute to combat racketeering in labor-management disputes, the statute is frequently used in connection with cases involving public corruption, commercial disputes, and corruption directed at members of labor unions. US Department of Justice, "9-1310 - The Hobbs Act - 18 U.S.C. § 1951" 2011. Web. 29 Oct. 2015. <http://www.justice.gov/usam/usam-9-131000-hobbs-act-18-usc-1951>.

3. U.S. Attorney Gene Anderson - Gene Anderson (August 12, 1937 - March 27, 2011) received his law degree from the University of Illinois in 1962 and joined the National Labor Relations Board in Washington, DC, for a few years before being drafted into the army. He served three years in the Judge Advocate General's Corps at Fort Leavenworth, Kansas, and worked in the US Justice Department until he was chosen to lead the newly created fraud division in King County, WA. He was selected to fill the US Attorney post in 1981, and led until 1989. He had a notable career as a prosecutor, continued to private practice, and then taught as an environmental law professor at the University of Washington until his retirement. See Miletich, Steve. 'Gene S. Anderson: Memorial to Honor Trailblazing

Prosecutor'. *The Seattle Times* (2011). Web. 5 Nov. 2015. <http://old.seattletimes.com/text/2015360729.html>.

CHAPTER SEVEN: BARUSO FEELS THE HEAT

1. Tony Baruso. The Committee for Justice for Domingo and Viernes hired an investigator, Christopher Hershey, to produce an extensive file on the background of Tony Baruso. It disclosed that although Baruso was not a town mate of Marcos and Ver, he was a fellow Ilocano. During World War II, he was a sergeant in the field artillery. After the war, Baruso was in the *Sakdal* ("the broom"), an operation on behalf of the US Army to find and punish pro-Japanese Filipinos in the Ilocos Sur and Ilocos Norte regions. So much criminal violence and repression were associated with the Sakdal that Baruso was afraid to return to his hometown for fear of retaliation by those who were mistreated. Instead, Baruso immigrated to Hawaii in 1951, where he was naturalized in a "hand raising" induction that granted citizenship to those who worked with the US military in the Philippines under General MacArthur. Soon after, Baruso started work in the sugar plantations at Kaiwiki Sugar Company. He was active in the sugar workers' union, and later told others he worked with future ILWU Vice President George Martin. He was invited by a union official he met in Hawaii, Benita Mangaoang, to the mainland later in the 1950s to help organize the Seattle-based cannery workers union (ILWU Local 37). He also worked at the Boeing Aircraft Company with stress break machines and received a national security clearance. In 1975, when Local 37 President Anthony Navarro died, Baruso assumed the presidency. He met and married Adelaide Carlos in Hawaii, with whom he had five children. After a messy divorce in 1977, he married Mely Bautista, who he met at Boeing.

CHAPTER NINE: THE EXECUTION PIECE

1. The questioning of Baruso: This narrative is from SPD's Follow-Up Reports on the murder investigation.

2. RPB Industries MAC-10 - The RPB Industries (R. Roby, C. Pitts, & R.W. Brueggemann) MAC-10 was a MAC (Military Armament Corporation) firearm with a two-stage suppressor, designed to both abate noise and make it easier for the shooter to maneuver (Walker 210). The MAC-10 was visually similar to an Uzi, but had a "very different safety and fire selector arrangement" (McNabb 70). The MAC-10 was a 9mm weapon that "incorporate[d] the magazine directly into the pistol grip", with a 32-shot magazine, cyclical fire rate of 1,090rpm, and weighed 2.84kg with one-handed firing abilities (McNabb 69). Walker, Robert. *Cartridges and Firearm Identification*. Boca Raton: CRC Press, 2013. Print.Mac-11.info, Web. 7 Nov. 2015. <http://www.mac-11.info>.

CHAPTER TEN: GENE AND SILME'S LAST MONTHS

1. CJDV Composition. This committee was headed by Bob Santos and Elaine Ko, then Cindy Domingo. It was staffed with labor activists like Velma Veloria, Emma Catague, Paul and Mindy Blaski; minority community leaders like Larry Gossett and Frank Kiuchi; gay and lesbian leaders like Kris Melroe and Ellen Earth; the inter-faith community and progressive church leaders

like Rev. Bill Cate; the Seattle cultural movement, including singers/songwriters Christopher Hershey and Andrea Harrington; family friends like Jackie Agtuca; the legal team; and the international solidarity movements, many of which had cut their teeth in the struggle for justice in Chile, South Africa, Central America, and the Philippines. It was a truly diverse and inclusive body.

2. Journal of Gene's Trip to Philippines. This journal was a great source of information about where Gene traveled, who he met with, and the impressions he was gathering. It is in the custody of the author.

3. The differences with the CPP and the KDP included the role of Maoism and the NPA's strategy of surrounding the cities from the countryside. The KDP had broken with and was openly critical of the basic theoretical doctrines of Maoism, which guided the CPP and the NPA. As a result, mutual suspicions between the two organizations had heightened in recent years. The KDP felt that Maoism, along with the Soviet brand of Communism, were flawed theories for a variety of reasons.

4. Marcos' Rule: The New Society – The so-called "New Society," known as Bagong Lipunan, was Ferdinand Marcos' implementation of his social and political views, utilizing martial law. His self-serving book *Notes on the New Society* (1971) stated that the aim of his 'New Society" was the self-actualization of the Philippine people through nationalistic theories of development. There were seven pillars to the New Society: moral regeneration, nationalism, internationalism, freedom of belief, self-reliance, social justice, Barangay democracy, unity, and identity. However, critics demonstrated this was more a plan of self-aggrandizement than reforms for the public good. "Martial Law pure and simple has been a facade masking the exploitation of our people and

their natural resources by Marcos, his family, and close friends. Any benefits, and there have been few, that have reached the people have been accidental and not the result of deliberate Martial Law policies." (Manglapus, 1981). Marcos was not so much the new answer to old problems, but rather the apotheosis of a broken system, an oligarchy built on the backs of a society marred by colonialism, neo-colonialism, and feudalism. He arrived at the precipice of power with the confluence of the South Asian trend towards authoritarianism and US special interests in military bases to fight the war in Vietnam. He utilized this power to hand positions of authority and economic influence to his friends, thwart his enemies, and do less for the common man than was promised in New Society. H. Monte Hill, "Philippine Martial Law: A Case Study in the Management of Political Participation," paper delivered at the annual conference of the Southeastern United States Region, Association of Asian Scholars, Raleigh, North Carolina, 16 January 1986, p. 3.; Ferdinand E. Marcos, Notes on the New Society of the Philippines (Manila: published by Marcos, 1971), p. 53. Raul Manglapus, interview, 16 March 1981, DeKalb, Illinois. Cited in Monte Hill.

5. Senator Benigno Aquino. "The Aquinos of Tarlac in the Philippines." Munting Nayon. Retrieved October 14, 2013. Psinakis, Steve. *Two Terrorists Meet*. At p. 19. Alchemy Books, 681 Market Street, San Francisco, California. 1981.

6. Senator Raul Manglapus – Former Senator Raul Manglapus was born on October 20, 1918, in Manila, to Congressman Valentin Manglapus of Ilocos Sur, and Justina Sevilla of Malabon, Rizal. He distinguished himself as a student, soldier, statesman, and a civic leader. He co-founded the reformist Progressive Party of the Philippines and the Christian Democratic Socialist

movement in 1968, later renamed the National Union of Christian Democrats (NUCD). His political career began in 1957, when he was appointed as Foreign Minister, and in 1961 he won a seat in the senate, where he served from 1961-1967. He ran for president in 1965 but lost to Ferdinand Marcos. Senator Manglapus evaded capture when martial law was declared; he was in Tokyo, en route to California for a speaking engagement, when the soldiers arrived at his house in Manila to arrest him. He spoke from the United States about the evils of martial law and remained in exile for fourteen years. See http://www.senate.gov.ph/senators/former_senators/raul_manglapus.htm A Pen for Democracy. Raúl S. Manglapus and Lilia Ramos-de León. 1983. MPF. Washington, DC.

7. Light a Fire Movement – The so-called "Light a Fire Movement" was a self-proclaimed revolutionary organization that took responsibility for a series of bombings of governmental and commercial buildings in Manila during the summer of 1979. The avowed purpose was to overthrow the Marcos dictatorship by targeting the regime's repression, extravagant spending, and illegitimate sources of income streaming in from the bombed businesses, especially the "floating casino" (the Sulo Hotel). See Psinakis, Steve. *Two Terrorists Meet.* Alchemy Books, 681 Market Street, San Francisco, California. 1981. "Military Tightening Watch on Incoming Tourists." OW240543. Hong Kong AFP in English 0519 GMT. October 24, 1980.

8. April 6th Liberation Movement – The April 6th Liberation Movement (A6LM) began with the Light a Fire Movement, whose leaders had been arrested in 1980. Marcos claimed that these arrests had put an end to "amateur terrorist attacks on the country." However, several urban guerilla groups, including the A6LM,

trained and organized for the "BIG BANG" on August 22, 1980. The idealist group launched a "destabilization plan" of bombings, assassinations, and kidnappings of public officials and military officers. On August 22, 1980, bombs went off in nine different buildings. Psinakis, Steve. *Two Terrorists Meet.* At p. 19. Alchemy Books, 681 Market Street, San Francisco, California. 1981. Feria, Monica. "AFP Analyzes Various Philippine Opposition Groups." OW240608 Hong Kong AFP in English 0552 GMT. November 24, 1980.

9. Lifting of Martial Law – On January 17, 1981, Ferdinand Marcos announced the lifting of martial law. This was more of a cosmetic gesture and a public relations move than a change in actual policy, brought about by the imminent visit of the Pope. In reality, little changed. Marcos retained all of his powers and then some. Presidential Decree 1737 decreed that Marcos could issue orders for "preventative detention," stipulating that "a person can be arrested at any time, without having committed a crime or even being suspected of having committed a crime." That person could be arrested if, "in the judgment of the President, he is capable of committing a crime in the future." The Filipino people were more at risk after the lifting of martial law than they were previously. Ronald Reagan, as president-elect, tried to discourage the scheduled lifting of martial law in the Philippines to keep US investment interests safe. Psinakis, Steve. *Two Terrorists Meet.* At p. 19. Alchemy Books, 681 Market Street, San Francisco, California. 1981.

10. Local exploitation of peasants in the countryside – Commanders in Marcos' army were frequently rewarded for their service with the opportunity to exploit the local economies where they were stationed. They forced locals to build barracks and

other structures. Profits from monopolistic sugar and coconut industries were siphoned off into the hands of Marcos's friends and followers. This gave military personnel an economic stake to quell peasant dissidents using any methods available. As such, death-squad murders, summary executions, extra-judicial punishments, and kidnappings became commonplace, and the ruthlessness of the military and these practices quickly denuded the middle class of their prosperity and livelihood. Overshot. 1986. *The Rise and Fall of Ferdinand Marcos.* University of California Press. Asian Survey, Vol. 26, No. 11 (Nov., 1986), pp. 1137-1163. Accessed from: http://asia.isp.msu.edu/wbwoa/southeast_asia/philippines/history.htm

11. The KMU and peaceful picketing – The KMU had hoped for a law allowing "peaceful picketing," but instead the regime presented them with Batasang Pambansa 227 on June 22, 1982. This made it unlawful to block entrances and exits of buildings, or for export industries to strike. This angered the KMU, and they fought for the repeal of these anti-labor laws (West, 1997). In January of 1982, Marcos summoned top KMU leaders to ask them to stop the strikes of workers. This proved ineffective, and under Presidential Commitment Order 136 Philippine authorities arrested Flexiberto Olalia for "conspiracy to commit rebellion and inciting to sedition and insurrection," (West, 1997). On April 19, 1982, Ernesto Arrellano, Crispin Beltran, Meldardo Roda, and members of the Philippine Alliance of Nationalist Labor Organizations (PANALO) were also arrested, "based on the belief of the military authorities that KMU and PMP are allied organizations of the Communist Party of the Philippines," (West, 1997). They all pled not guilty and were released on December 12, 1982. However, Olalia had become ill in prison and died shortly following his release. West, Lois A. *Militant Labor in the Philippines*. Temple University Press. Print. 1997. at pg. 101-102.

12. History of Local 142, ILWU – See "What's at Stake is ILWU's Commitment to Labor Solidarity." http://www.transportworkers.org/node/1943. Retrieved: September 1, 2015. (Hereafter "Solidarity, 2015").

13. The ILWU Debate and Resolution R-34 – All quotes are from the Official Minutes of ILWU 24nd Bi-annual Honolulu Hawaii Convention. April 22-May 7, 1981. (Hereafter "ILWU Convention Transcript"). Resolution R-34 stated:

WHEREAS: On September 22, 1972 President Marcos declared Martial Law in the Philippines: and WHEREAS: Under Martial Law the condition of trade unionists and all workers were seriously affected in the following was: (1) Strikes in all vital industries (which has objectively been expanded to include all industries) have been banned through the declaration of Presidential Decree 823: "(2) Wages and benefits continue to be depressed so that workers and their families can barely subsist. In March 1981 the minimum daily wage was set at P20.85 ($4.08) for workers in Metro-Manila, P25.20 ($3.94) for non-agricultural workers outside Manila and P25.20 ($3.36) for plantation workers (Bulletin Today, March 27, 1981). Yet, in January 1981 the government estimated the average cost of daily food and other basic necessities for family of six to be P49.96 ($6.41) for non-agricultural workers and P47.08 ($6.08) for agricultural workers (Natural Census and Statistics Office. Food and Nutrition Research Institute. Bureau of Agricultural Economics). "(3) Due to the inflation rate in the Philippines, second highest in Asia and one of the highest in the world, the real wages of *the workers has decreased by 39 percent from 1972 to 1979 (Central Bank): (4) Even the government-influenced Trade Union Congress of the Philippines admitted that 65.5 percent of the firms were found to be in violation of labor standards (mostly for non-payment of wages, summary dismissal, or preventative suspension of workers) while 36.4 percent of the firms violated health and safety standards; and WHEREAS: On September 2 and 3, 1980 the government arrested 17 labor leaders including Ernesto Arrellano (General Secretary of the Kilusan Mayo Uno Labor Center), Leto Vilear (General Manager of the Cubano Driver's Cooperative), Alejandro Magtoto (President of Wyeth Suceo Employees Union), Rosario Zapanta and Eleurio Tuazon (officers of the Philippine Textile Mills) Zapanta and Eleurio Tuazon (officers of the Philippine Textile Mills Employees Union), and according to the Task Force on Detainees of the Philippines, 27 labor organizers have disappeared or have been 'salvaged' since the beginning of Martial Law, while hundreds more have been detained in prison; and WHEREAS: On January 19, 1981 President Marcos announced the lifting of Martial Law, but all the presidential decrees, including Presidential Decree 823 and the restrictive labor codes remain in effect; and WHEREAS: The ILWU has traditionally supported the effects of trade unionists and workers throughout the world in their struggles to improve wages, working and living conditions and their lives through industrial unions and free expression and RESOLVED: The ILWU objects to the continuation of the restrictive decrees and polices of the Marcos government initiated under Martial Law and which continue to this day: and BE IT FUTHER RESOLVED: That the ILWU continue to promote active interest in the general developments in the Philippines and their effect on the welfare of working people by increased coverage in The Dispatcher, conducting educational programs, and fostering relations with groups which work for industrial democracy and freedom for the Filipino people: and BE IT FINALLY RESOLVED: That the ILWU international officers consider the Philippines as a destination for the next foreign delegation program as a means by which up-to-date information can be obtained on the state of trade unions, working conditions, and civil liberties of Filipino workers.*

14. Benny Quitives's presentation at the Convention, which the KDP team believed was based on information obtained from the local Consul General, included these statistics:

"As far as the rate of inflation, it says here in the resolution that the Philippines has the second highest rate of inflation. The research I have done shows that the Philippines' inflation rate is 15.4 percent. Indonesia, by the way, is 21.7 percent. Anyway, talking about rice. In 1977 alone, 241 million metric tons of rice was exported to the neighboring countries. Total crop production, rice, corn, and other foodstuffs increased from 12.2 million metric tons in 1965 to 15.2 million metric tons in 1972. Reaching 24.4 million metric tons in 1977. The daily minimum wage now exceeds 40 pesos a day, it is now as written here, 30 dollars."

15. Local Consul General in Hawaii: Trinidad Alconcel – Alconcel was born in Caoayan, Ilocos Sur. He graduated cum laude and salutation from the University of Manila and quickly rose in the ranks of Philippine government. In the 1940s he served in the Foreign Service and spent 1947-1956 with the Department of Foreign Affairs. In 1966, his assignment was in Honolulu with the title rank of career minister and consul general (Embassy

Index). He was promoted to chief of mission in 1972 and then transferred to San Francisco in 1973. When Marcos declared martial law, he headed the Philippine consular corps for the Bay Area, while Imelda's brother Kiki Romualdez was the Ambassador in Washington DC. Alconcel was involved in the transfer of money for bribes in the United States (Anderson, 1975). When his wife, Soledad, was diagnosed with cancer in 1976, he returned to Hawaii and was elected dean of the consular corps of Honolulu in 1971 and 1980. As part of Marcos group of close supporters, he introduced, "innovative measures that benefited and gained recognition for the foreign consuls in Hawaii." Philippine Embassy Index. http://www.philippinessanfrancisco.org/philippines-sf/embassy-sf/about-the-office-sf/ Retrieved 9/25/15. Anderson, Jack. "Marcos Bribe Offered cited by Witness." *The Washington Post.* July 2, 1975.

16. *Karen Silkwood* - Kohn, Howard. *Who Killed Karen Silkwood?* New York: Summit Books, 1981. Print. And see: Rashke, Richard. *The Killing of Karen Silkwood.* New York: Houghton Mifflin Co., 1981."

17. *Assassination on Embassy Road* - Dinges, John, and Saul Landau. New York: McGraw-Hill, 1981. Print.

18. Charles Horman - His story is featured in a book and a Criterion Collection film. Hauser, Thomas. *Missing.* New York: Simon & Schuster, 1978. Print. *Missing.* Universal Pictures: Costa-Garvas, 1982. DVD. See: Charles Horman Truth Foundation Website: http://www.Hormantruth.org

CHAPTER ELEVEN: PRESSING THE PROSECUTION

1. Norm Maleng. Maleng was born in Acme, Washington, and grew up on a dairy farm. Known as "Kim" to

those close to him, he graduated from the University of Washington in 1960, then served as an officer in the military. He obtained his law degree in 1966 from the UW Law School, was elected as Prosecutor in 1978, and was re-elected seven times. Maleng was involved in a number of other high-profile cases, most notably the 1983 Wah Mee Massacre, the 2006 Seattle Jewish Federation assault, and the serial murders of Gary Ridgway, known as the Green River Killer. He ran for the Republican nomination for governor of Washington in 1988 and 1996. In 1992, he lost an election for Attorney General to Christine Gregoire. Maleng is credited with bringing several large-scale policy reforms to Washington State's Criminal Justice system, including passage of the 1984 Sentencing Reform Act, tougher penalties for car thefts in 2007, and rethinking the prosecution of low-level drug offenses by placing emphasis on treatment options after a first or second offense, rather than lengthy prison sentences.

2. Hearsay – Hearsay is a declaration by a person who is testifying about what someone else, not in court, stated to that person or in the person's presence. There are many exceptions to the hearsay rule, which normally excludes testimony about what someone out of court said to a witness. A "dying declaration" by someone aware of impending death is such an exception, as is an "admission against interest." See Washington State Evidence Code Section 801 et seq.

CHAPTER THIRTEEN: THE TRIAL OF JIMMY RAMIL AND BEN GULOY

1. Citations to the court record in the trial of *State of Washington v. Ramil and Guloy*, King County Superior Court, Cause No. 81-1-01924-9). The trial was presided

over by the Hon. Lloyd Bever, between August 14 and September 23, 1981. This transcript is hereafter referred to as "Ramil and Guloy Trial Transcript" by volume and page number.

2. Quotes from James Huckins testimony - Ramil and Guloy Trial Transcript. Vol. XX. Pg. 2858-2859.

3. Patricia Wilson – her testimony is found at the Ramil and Guloy Trial Transcript, Vol. VII., Pg. 884-912.

4. King County Medical Examiner Donald Reay - Donald Reay received his medical degree from the University of Utah and served in the King County Medical Examiner's Office for over twenty-five years, twenty-three of which he was the Chief, before retiring in 1999. Before coming to Seattle, he was the lead pathologist for the Armed Forces Institute of Pathology and for the Air Force Academy Hospital. His work in King County gained national attention, and he is held in high regard by his colleagues for influencing notable advances in his field. Because of his reputation and impact, he received the highly prestigious Milton Helpern Laureate Award in October, 2015.Associated Press. 'Retired King County Medical Examiner to Be Honored'. *The Washington Times*. 2015. Web. 6 Nov. 2015. See <http://www.washingtontimes.com/news/2015/aug/15/retired-king-county-medical-examiner-to-be-honored/>.Barker, Kim. ''A Witness for the Dead' – Medical Examiner Retiring After 25 Years'. *The Seattle Times*. 1999. Web. 6 Nov. 2015. <http://community.seattletimes.nwsource.com/archive/?date=19990617&slug=2966973#_ga=1.2 53861832.1779972631.1435337488>.

5. Reay's testimony about Viernes' fatal wounds is found in the Ramil and Guloy Trial Transcript, at pp. 2121-2134.

6. Quotes from Forsythe's testimony - Ramil and Guloy Trial Testimony at p. 2720 (start of testimony) pp. 2821-22. (Court allowing cross examination of Forsythe on his prior testimony) p. 2819 (Melvin Dummar); p. 2823 (Forsythe's denial that he was ever in a trial)

7. Forsythe's prior testimony in the legal battle over the Howard Hughes Empire – Although Joanne did not question him about this testimony, Forsythe was the "star witness" who appeared in the legal battle over control of the Howard Hughes Empire. This fight was between Maheu and what was known as the "Gay-Davis" faction, top Hughes aides who Maheu accused of kidnapping Howard Hughes from his recluse at the Desert Inn in Las Vegas on Thanksgiving, 1971, and moving him to the Bahamas, outside the reach of US authorities or subpoena power. Maheu brought a lawsuit against Gay and Davis, accusing them of fraud and corruption, but he required proof that Hughes was taken against his will. In that trial, Forsythe was called as a witness and testified that he was asked to stand as a guard outside the Desert Inn. While performing this responsibility, he saw security forces bringing a man out of the hotel. Forsythe recognized Howard Hughes from his work on the Corrigan Ranch and other encounters. Forsythe claimed that as Hughes was being placed in a security van, he turned around a said in a clear voice "Get me Bob Maheu." The testimony was used by Maheu's counsel to state that Hughes was trying to get Maheu, who he trusted as his loyal assistant, to stop the kidnapping. The presiding Judge in that trial declared Forsythe as not credible. (Barlett and Steele 603-605). Barlett, Donald L, and James B Steele. *Howard Hughes His Life and Madness*. New York: W.W. Norton, 2004. Print.

8. Descriptions and quotes from Joanne Maida's Closing Argument at Ramil and Guloy Trial Testimony, Vol. XXVI at pp. 3254, 3299

CHAPTER FOURTEEN: THE PATH TO MARCOS

1. Civil Rights Act. The "Civil Rights Act of 1864" 42 U.S.C. Section 1981-1985 contain the Civil Rights Acts passed after the Civil War, which guarantee due process and equal protection of the laws to former slaves and outlaw discrimination based upon a suspect classification, including race, national origin, and religion. The Act created a cause of action for those discriminated against was held applicable to the states and municipalities by subsequent U.S. Supreme Court decisions. 42 United States Code Sections 1983 and 1985 is the primary civil rights act in U.S. jurisprudence. It was written to protect the rights of freed slaves who were the victims of conspiracies to violate their newly-granted freedoms and constitutional rights. Section 1983 authorizes a citizen to bring a lawsuit to vindicate a state's violation of the constitutional rights. Section 1985 allows such a lawsuit to be brought against members of any conspiracy, including private actors. Attorney's fees and costs are recoverable if the plaintiffs prevail. The Act was directed at state, county, and municipal governments, not the federal government.

2. Bivens v. Six Unknown Named Agents, 403 U.S. 388 (1971) ruled that an implied cause of action exists for an individual whose rights are violated, despite the lack of any federal statute authorizing such a suit. The case was subsequently interpreted to create a cause of action against the federal government similar to the one that 42 U.S.C. Section 1983 created against the states.

3. The case and trial of *Silkwood v. Kerr-McGee* are detailed in numerous books, articles, court opinions, and a movie. See Kohn, Howard, *Who Killed Karen Silkwood?* New York: Summit Press (1981). Rashke, Richard. *The Killing of Karen Silkwood.* New York: Houghton Mifflin Co., 1981."*Silkwood* Settlement." *Science News,* August 8, 1986, p. 134.Spence, Gerry. With Justice for None. New York: Times Books, 1989. Stein, J. "The Deepening Mystery." *Progressive,* January 1981, pp. 14-19; Silkwood. 20th Century Fox (1983) (Michael Nichols, director; starring Meryl Streep as Silkwood). *Silkwood v. Kerr-McGee,* 464 U.S. 238 (1984) (U.S. Supreme Court opinion).

4. Liberation Theology. Although liberation theology has grown into an international and inter-denominational movement, it began as a movement within the Catholic Church in Latin America in the 1950s and 1960s, principally as a moral reaction to the poverty and social injustice in the region. The term was coined in 1971 by the Peruvian priest Gustavo Gutierrez, who wrote one of the movement's defining books, *A Theology of Liberation.* Later, the Vatican, under Pope Benedict, launched an effort to distance the Church from this theology, although Pope Francis has recently re-introduced some of its central tenets to combat social and economic injustice and inequality on a daily basis.

5. "Bill's" Preliminary Investigative Report is found at www.**michaelwithey**.com/resources.

CHAPTER FIFTEEN: NEW PRIORITIES

1. The CJDV Newsletters and the Rank and File Committee's *Alaskero News* are available at www. michaelwithey.com.

CHAPTER SEVENTEEN: THE DICTADO TRIAL

1. The official court transcript of the trial of *State of Washington v. Fortunado Dictado,* in the King County Superior Court No. 81-1-02795-1, (Hon. Terrence Carroll, presiding), along with a summary of the trial, is in the possession of the author.

2. Dictado's counsel John Henry Browne wanted the case dismissed because the State had not charged Dictado with conspiracy and had failed to detail what the conspiracy consisted of (who were co-conspirators, what was the goal of the conspiracy, etc.). Maida convinced the judge that the State did not have to charge a conspiracy to take advantage of the exceptions to the hearsay rule that allows into evidence statements made by one conspirator to another in the course of the conspiracy. Browne also attacked the State's use of Dictado's testimony during the Ramil and Guloy trial on the grounds that, at the time of such testimony, he was represented by James Grubb, who was also Ramil's counsel, and that Grubb had a conflict of interest and could not represent both alleged co-conspirators. Judge Carroll denied that motion, finding that Dictado had testified freely and voluntarily without coercion.

3. Ade Domingo, Terri Mast, David Della, Glenn Suson, Lynn Domingo, Angel Doniego, and Ricardo DeLeon testified, as did other witnesses first identified and brought forward by the CJDV, including Jaime Malabo, Rachel Kennedy (Gene's friend), and Janis Johnson.

4. The statements that Dictado gave to the police that concerned Browne were contradicted by other witnesses and Dictado's testimony in the Ramil and Guloy trial, and were summarized by the police as follows:

"Was asked if he knew Tony Baruso and he stated that "they were good friends." Was asked if he had a conversation with Baruso on Saturday 5-30-81. He stated he had not. Asked if he talked with Robert San Pablo and Gene Viernes before Viernes' death. He stated he did not. Asked if he had recently argued with either Domingo or Viernes. He stated he had never argued with either and described both as friends. Afterwards he remembered that he may have spoken with Viernes concerning the Dillingham dispatch and indicated that San Pablo may have been there during the discussion." Dictado Trial Transcript, Vol. IV at p. 470.

5. Quoted testimony of Norm Van Vactor from Dictado Trial Transcript, Vol. IV at p. 578.

6. Quoted testimony from Tony Dictado from Dictado Trial Transcript. Vol. IV at p. 738 et seq.

CHAPTER NINETEEN: THE PHILIPPINE INFILTRATION PLAN

1. The Naval Investigative Service and FBI reports are contained in numerous documents obtained from the NIS and FBI as a result of the FOIA requests brought by the estates in the summer of 1981.

2. Center for Constitutional Rights. A vitally important nonprofit public interest law firm founded in 1966 in New York City, which has brought many precedent-setting public interest lawsuits to vindicate constitutional and civil rights for over fifty years. The Center was counsel of record on the first complaint filed by the Estates of Domingo and Viernes. I knew many of the leading attorneys at the CCR in my work as an Executive Committee member of the National Lawyers' Guild and

its Puerto Rico Legal Project, including CCR's former Executive Director Michael Ratner, Peter Weiss, Liz Schneider, and Franklin Siegel. CCR lawyers discussed the case with us at length and were willing to be listed as representing the estates on the original complaint. In addition, William Bender, a Seattleattorney who worked closely with the CCR, offered valuable strategic advice on how to unfold the case against Marcos and asked Michael Ratner to have CCR sign the original lawsuit as counsel of record.

3. Alien Tort Claims Act, 28 U.S. C. Section 1350 is a section of the United States Code that reads: "The district courts shall have original jurisdiction of any civil action by an alien for a tort only, committed in violation of the law of nations or a treaty of the United States." Since 1980, courts have interpreted this statute to allow foreign citizens to seek remedies in US courts for human rights violations for conduct committed outside the United States. We could not use this statute, because both Gene and Silme were born in the US.

4. Thomas Grey ("Tom") Wicker (June 18, 1926 – November 25, 2011) was best known as a political reporter and columnist for the *New York Times*.

5. Jack and Elsie Withey. My parents. I grew up in the DC suburb of Vienna, Virginia, while my father Jack worked in the Office of National Estimate (ONE), the think tank of the CIA. Fluent in German, he reviewed both overt and covert sources of information to formulate "estimates" of the political and economic trends in West and East Germany after World War II. Before that, our family had lived in Frankfurt for four years in the 1950 and early 1960s. In other words, my dad was a spy. He was a Stevenson Democrat and Irish Catholic who didn't fit into the Cold War mentality and WASP culture that gripped the CIA under Director Allen Dulles. He

left the CIA after the Bay of Pigs and he was responsible in part for me turning against the war in Vietnam. "You can't believe everything the US government is telling you about the Gulf of Tonkin," I remember him saying in 1964, two years before he died of a brain tumor. Much later, we'd learn that the CIA engineered an effort to draw the North Vietnamese Navy into firing on US Naval vessels in that Gulf, setting off a clamor for war authorization in Congress. My mom Elsie had also worked for the CIA, as a secretary in Frankfurt, Germany, in 1953-1954 and 1958-1960. It took her a while to get her security clearance exam, because she had to explain how she got swept up to support the Abraham Lincoln Brigade, which sent volunteers to Spain in the 1930s to fight against the fascist Generalissimo Franco. The Brigade ended upon on the US Attorney General's list of banned subversive organizations, suspected of being communist or communist-influenced. Elsie was always adamant, as was my father, as to where her loyalties were.

6. DC Meetings. In DC, I also met with KDP members Walden Bello, Odette and Rick Polintan, and Jon Melegrito. They were part of Congress Watch, active in exposing the Marcos regime to lawmakers, in particular drawing attention to the human rights violations that Amnesty International and the World Peace through Law representatives had exposed in recent reports. The main effort at Congress Watch at that time was opposing the re-negotiation of the US Bases Agreement, which would extend the life of Subic Bay and Clark Air Force Base for decades.

7. Morton Halperin (born June 13, 1938) is an American expert on foreign policy and civil liberties. He served in the Johnson, Nixon, and Clinton Administrations. He is associated with a number of think tanks and universities,

including the ACLU, Council on Foreign Relations, and Harvard University.

8. Dale Van Atta (born 1951) is a speaker, novelist, and an investigative journalist. He was a personal friend of and co-author with fellow journalist Jack Anderson. In 2008, his book *With Honor* was released about Melvin Laird, the Secretary of Defense under Richard Nixon between 1969 and 1973.

CHAPTER TWENTY: THE ANNIVERSARY

1. The CJDV's newsletters, including the Seattle *Update* and national *Call to Justice* are available at **www.michaelwithey.com**.

2. News articles referred to in this chapter, including the *New York Times* editorial by Tom Wicker, the *S.F. Chronicle* articles, and other news accounts are available at **www.michaelwithey.com**.

3. Copies of the *Philippine News* referred to in this chapter are available at **www.michaelwithey.com**.

4. The CJDV Teach-In on the Letelier murders generated documents and materials, including the speech of Saul Landau, which are available at **www.michaelwithey. com**. The Institute for Policy Studies (IPS) had reached out to the international human rights communities and a number of Congressional subcommittees, including the House Select Subcommittee on Latin American Affairs, headed by New York Congressman Stephen Solarz. Isabel was a wonderful guest, whose personal losses were enormous but who showed the kind of persistence and steely determination to seek justice that we aspired to. Landau was an insightful analyst whose

broad experience at IPS and in the media world brought an historical perspective to our supporters.

5. The national CJDV team was centered in the Bay Area under the leadership of Bruce and Dale, along with Cathy Tactaquin, Rene Cruz, and Leni Marin. Bruce and Cathy headed the investigative work with the legal team in Seattle; and Dale, with Cindy in Seattle, coordinated the national communications. Rene coordinated the link between the CJDV and the Philippine solidarity work. Therese Rodriguez, a longtime KDP activist from New York, heeded the DC component of our work, working with Congress Watch and the national press as well as assisting Seattle-based Elaine and Cindy with fundraising work. Elaine wrote most of the CJDV *Update*, which was used by the national newsletter as well.

CHAPTER TWENTY-ONE: MARCOS SERVED

1. The KDP activists involved included Walden Bello, Rene Cruz, Geline Avila, Odette Polintan, Jon Melegrito and Therese Rodriguez.

2. The BBC Film drew strong criticism from Marcos. See http://www.nytimes.com/1982/08/20/world/marcos-irked-by-bbc-film-showing-critics-of-his-rule.html

3. Quotes from the White House dinner are found at http://www.presidency.ucsb.edu/ws/?pid=42990. In a speech he delivered that evening, Reagan said:

The United States remains the Philippines' leading trading partner, and American firms are the largest foreign investors in your country, reflecting their confidence in your progress and prospects for economic growth...We have welcomed the growing two-way trade between our nations and have been pleased that we've been able to keep our markets for the products of your growing manufacturing and industrial sector the most open of any country in the industrialized world.

Marcos, in response, was no less grandiose.

I did not come to burden you further with additional problems, Mr. President, for I know that, as I have said in many a speech before my own people and before the world, fate and destiny has decreed that the United States of America be the trustee of modern civilization against the threat of a possible second Dark Ages. And America cannot fail. And therefore, we, the Filipino people, come and bring to you a prayer that God, in His divine providence, may grant you guidance, strengthen both your heart and hand, so that that hand may be strong on the lever of power and save our humanity...If America fails, then the world is lost. And thus, Mr. President, I can assure you that throughout all of Asia, there is nothing but a reservoir of good will for you, the American people, and the United States of America.

4. The Philippine government's criminal complaint against Felixberto Olalia and others, filed in August of 1982, and the related criminal investigation were provided to Plaintiffs in discovery in the *Estates of Domingo and Viernes vs. Republic of the Philippines.*

5. The famous *"J'Accuse" letter* from Emile Zola can be found at http://www.history.com/this-day-in-history/zolas-jaccuse-letter-is-printed Zola accused the anti-Semitic upper echelons of the French Officer Corps of a cover-up by attempting to frame Colonel Dreyfuss, a Jewish officer, for passing military secrets to the Germans. It triggered a huge scandal and the

eventual exoneration of Dreyfuss and his return from imprisonment at Devil's Island.

CHAPTER TWENTY-TWO: BOY PILAY

1. Summary of evidence. This detailed discussion outlined all of the evidence of Baruso's involvement in the murder. It started with the fact that his weapon was used to kill Gene and Silme, and his alibi for the firearm stating it was stolen was blown. It described his ties to the Tulisan gang, his dispatch of Pilay to shake down San Pablo, San Pablo's testimony that Pilay told him Baruso paid $5,000 for the hit, his strange conduct at the ER at the hospital, his demeanor when initially questioned by the FBI, testimony that he went to the 609 Club to warn Dictado that they were involved, his conflict with Dictado after the murders, and his motives, including his penchant for taking bribes, kickbacks, gambling proceeds.

2. The history of the Bush Hotel can be found in http://www.seattletimes.com/pacific-nw-magazine/seattles-bush-hotel-ca-1922/

CHAPTER TWENTY-THREE: THE COVER-UP WINS AGAIN

1. Pilay's death was reported in the *Seattle Post-Intelligencer, Seattle Times*, and the CJDV's *Update* (see http://www.**michaelwithey**.com/wp-content/uploads/2015/09/CJDV-update-Justice-has-been-cast-in-deadly-chokehold.pdf) and the *Washington Post.* www.washingtonpost.com/archive/politics/1983/08/24/filipino-suit-links-us-philippine-officials-to-seattle-murders/51b3c4d3-d679-4b9f-a0f6-a9c833604b9e/)

2. Val Barber's conviction was upheld by the Washington State Court of Appeals. See http://courts.mrsc.org/ mc/courts/zappellate/038wnapp/038wnapp0758. htm. Ablang was never found or tried. We received unconfirmed information that Ablang was a confidential informant for a Manila Metro Command intelligence unit used to gather information on various anti-Marcos groups in Manila.

3. Cindy Domingo's comments to the press were reported in the CJDV's *Update* newsletter. http://www.**michaelwithey**.com/wp-content/uploads/2015/09/CJDV-update-Justice-has-been-cast-in-deadly-chokehold.pdf)

CHAPTER TWENTY-FOUR: IMMUNITY

1. The US State Department's Suggestion of Immunity is in the court file in US District Court for the Western District of Washington, in the case of *Estates of Domingo, et al v. Republic of the Philippines et al.* Cause number 82-1055V.

2. The US Defendants Motion to Dismiss is in the court file in US District Court for the Western District of Washington, in the case of *Estates of Domingo, et al v. Republic of the Philippines et al.* Cause number 82-1055V.

3. Plaintiffs' Opposition to the US Motion to Dismiss is in the court file in US District Court for the Western District of Washington, in the case of *Estates of Domingo, et al v. Republic of the Philippines et al.* Cause number 82-1055V.

4. A description of this National Security seminar and summaries of the speeches by Falk, Sarjeant, and Cruz are contained in the CJDV *Update* Newsletter,

available at www.**michaelwithey**.com. The seminar also featured representatives of numerous national and local organizations, including the American Friends Service Committee, the ACLU, the Seattle Mayor's Office, the National Committee against Repressive Legislation (NCARL), and the Lawyers Alliance for Nuclear Arms Control.

CHAPTER TWENTY-FIVE: DISCOVERY

1. Summaries of Baruso's depositions are available at www.**michaelwithey**.com under "Resources."

CHAPTER TWENTY-SIX: THE DIA CIRCULAR

1. The DIA Circular was authenticated by a DIA witness in deposition and can be found at www.**michaelwithey**.com.

2. Judge Voorhees' Order granting the US defendants' Motion to Dismiss is in the official court file in the *Estates of Domingo et al v. Republic of the Philippines,* Civ. 82-1055V (U.S. District Court for the Western District of Washington).

CHAPTER TWENTY-SEVEN: SENATOR AQUINO

1. Sen. Aquino and Ken Kashiwahara are captured on a video taken by Ken during the flight to Manila, which includes his abduction by gendarmes after the plane landed and the shots fired when Aquino touched Philippine soil. That video can be seen at www.**michaelwithey**.com.

CHAPTER TWENTY-EIGHT: THE FORSYTHE DEPOSITION

1. The transcript of Forsythe's deposition. A summary of the deposition is found at www.**michaelwithey**.com.

2. Hal Rhoden was a famous Los Angeles attorney who also represented one of Rock Hudson's gay lovers in a suit against the movie star who gave him AIDS, and Bianca Jagger in her divorce trial against Rolling Stones vocalist Mick Jagger. He was killed in a plane crash in 1989 at aged sixty-six. I met with him in the three-car garage his home in the San Fernando Valley near Los Angeles, amidst boxes and file cabinets full of material from the Forsythe case, and Rhoden graciously gave me access to all of it, because something about Forsythe bothered him. There were boxes full of pleadings, reports, and materials from both the Mormon Will case and the Gay/Davis case. Rhoden said he remained convinced that the 1968 Mormon Will was the only valid will Howard Hughes left, but he didn't appeal the case because there was no error in the trial court proceedings to complain about, and it would have taken hundreds of thousands of dollars to appeal.

3. Forsythe's saga. Something that struck me about Forsythe from my review of the files in Rhoden's garage was that his testimony in both cases was based upon his self-proclaimed respect for his employer, Howard Hughes, but also benefitted Robert Maheu. I was not convinced that Forsythe's testimony was fabricated in either case.

4. The memo is cited in US Congress, Senate, Interim Report of the Select Committee to Study Governmental Operations with Respect to Intelligence Activities, Alleged Assassination Plots Involving Foreign Leaders, 94th Cong. 1st Session, p. 74-77. It is also described

in the book: *Howard Hughes: His Life and Madness,* by Donald L. Barlett and James B. Steele (Norton and Company 1979) at pp.283-284. It states that the CIA advised the FBI that "any prosecution in the matter would endanger sensitive sources and methods used in a duly authorized intelligence project and would not be in the national interest."

5. Laxalt's involvement with Howard Hughes is described in detail in *Howard Hughes: His Life and Madness* at pp. 291-292; 305-314; 322-339; 442-451; and 487. In 1967, when Hughes and Robert Maheu were involved in purchasing Las Vegas casinos, Laxalt was the Governor of Nevada and supported Hughes' purchase of the Desert Inn with the Nevada Gaming Commission, after Hughes promised to fund the University of Nevada Medical School to the tune of $6 million. Laxalt also published a book entitled *My Conversations with Marcos.*

6. Rebecca Forsythe's deposition in the *Estates of Domingo v. Republic of the Philippines* case and the transcript are available from the author.

7. Ralph Hernandez's deposition in the *Estates of Domingo v. Republic of the Philippines* case and the transcript are available from the author.

CHAPTER TWENTY-NINE: THE QUIET YEARS

1. The *Update* can be found at www.**michaelwithey**.com under "Resources."

2. The Reagan Administration's "turn" against Marcos is described in a book by the *New York Times* reporter Raymond Bonner entitled *Waltzing with a Dictator.* "The Marcoses and the Making of American Policy"

in Chapter 15: In Search of a Policy, pp. 355-384. This shift took years, but included State Department officials, former Ambassador to the Philippines Michael Armacost, and his underling James Nach. Bonner describe the fact that in 1985 Marcos, increasingly aware that the State Department was no longer his ally, bypassed then Ambassador Steven Bosworth by creating a "back channel" to the White House through Senator Paul Laxalt. See Bonner at p. 383. Laxalt's further involvement in ushering Marcos off the stage of history, as detailed in this chapter, is described by numerous sources, including in Bonner's book at pp. 383-388; 401-402 and see Bonner, Chapter 16: "A Blunder Leads to an Election."

3. *The People's Power Revolution* is also described in many publications. The descriptions in this chapter, including the strength and resiliency of the opposition, the events leading to Marcos' ouster, the role of the Catholic Church, the defections of pro-Marcos loyalists, and the roles of Michael Armacost and Sen. Paul Laxalt are based principally on Raymond Bonner's book. See Bonner, Chapters 16-17.

4. *Michael Armacost.* The advice of my former college professor and faculty advisor was a significant reason I chose to go to law school after college. As my professor, Armacost assigned a paper on the legality of the US intervention in Vietnam. I read the State Department position detailing that the US was justified in defending an attack of North Vietnam against the South, and that of leading human rights and international law professors, such as Prof. Richard Falk, who claimed that international law forbid a foreign government from intervening in what was essentially a civil war. My paper argued for Falk's position, and Armacost not only gave me the highest possible score, but urged me to pursue

a career as a public interest lawyer. Finding out that Armacost probably had a hand in Marcos' ouster was gratifying on a personal level.

5. The CJDV's Fifth Anniversary Memorial in June of 1986 is described in the CJDV newsletters which can be found at www.**michaelwithey**.com under "Resources." Saul Landau's speech, quoted in the text, can be found at www.**michaelwithey**.com.

CHAPTER THIRTY: THE SMOKING GUN

1. The "World Peace Through Law Conference" is sponsored by the American Society of International Law, an international organization of international law practitioners and law professors, human rights activists, civil society organizations, and bar associations adherents which convenes at various times and in different locations around the world. It publishes the highly respected American Journal of International Law.

2. *The New York Times* and *San Francisco Chronicle* articles on Malabed can be found at **www.michaelwithey.com**.

3. *"The Spy Network of the Marcos Dictatorship in the US"* authored by Bonifacio Gillego can be found at **www.michaelwithey.com**.

4. The entire transcripts of the Marcos Depositions are available from the author and a summary can be found at www.**michaelwithey**.com.

5. The role of Michael Armacost in the ouster of Marcos is detailed in numerous books or articles, including Raymond Bonner's *Waltzing with a Dictator*. The Marcoses and the Making of American Policy" in Chapter 15: In Search of a Policy, pp. 355 et seq.

CHAPTER THIRTY-ONE: THE AFTERMATH

CHAPTER THIRTY-TWO: THE COCKROACH OF TRUTH

1. Marcos depositions. The quotes and descriptions of these depositions of Ferdinand and Imelda Marcos are based upon the author's recollection, and the entire transcripts are available. Summaries can be found at **www.michaelwithey.com**.

2. The Order of Magistrate Phillip Sweigert is found in the court file and pleadings in the *Estates of Domingo and Viernes v. Ferdinand and Imelda Marcos.*

CHAPTER THIRTY-THREE: A NIGHT IN CAMELOT

CHAPTER THIRTY-FOUR: SETTING THE BEST CONDITIONS

1. The pre-trial legal proceedings described in this chapter are referred to in the pleadings found in the court file in the *Estates of Domingo and Viernes v. Ferdinand and Imelda Marcos.*

2. The Trial Lawyers for Public Justice, (TLPJ) now the Public Justice Foundation, is a national public interest law firm organized by trial lawyers who believe it is important to bring cases against wrongdoers in a just cause even where the private bar cannot afford or is unwilling to bring such cases. Its mission is to protect the civil justice system, bring cutting edge and precedent setting litigation on behalf of the poor, oppressed, and

downtrodden. See www.publicjustice.org. I was the president of TLPJ in 1995-96 and have sat on its Board of Directors since 1992. TLPJ took on the *Domingo v Marcos* litigation in a limited role, assisting with our discovery against the US intelligence agencies. Our cooperating counsel, Richard Ben-Veniste, distinguished himself as a tireless and dedicated counsel for the Senate Select Committee investigating the Watergate break-in and cover-up in 1972.

3. Judge Rothstein's Order reinstating the Marcos defendants is found in the pleadings found in the court file in the *Estates of Domingo and Viernes v. Ferdinand and Imelda Marcos.*

4. The documents obtained from the Republic of the Philippines in discovery are in the possession of the author, and indices and summaries are found at **www. michaelwithey.com/resources**.

CHAPTER THIRTY-FIVE: THE TRIAL OF THE ESTATE OF FERDINAND MARCOS

1. Trial proceedings. The quotations, descriptions and summaries of the trial proceedings and testimony are found in the official transcript of the trial. For portions of the trial not transcribed, these descriptions are based upon the author's recollections and notes.

CHAPTER THIRTY-SIX: THE HEART OF THE CASE

1. The jury verdict reached is found in the court file in the *Estates of Domingo and Viernes v. Ferdinand and Imelda Marcos* and available at **www.michaelwithey. com/resources**.

2. The Memorandum Decision of Judge Rothstein holding Dr. Leonilo and Yvonne Malabed and Tony Baruso liable and awarding the sum of $8.3 million in damages against them is found in the court file in the *Estates of Domingo and Viernes v. Ferdinand and Imelda Marcos* and can be found at **www.michaelwithey.com.**

For More News About Michael Withey
Signup For Our Newsletter:

http://wbp.bz/newsletter

Word-of-mouth is critical to an author's long-term success. If you appreciated this book please leave a review on the Amazon sales page:

http://wbp.bz/sea

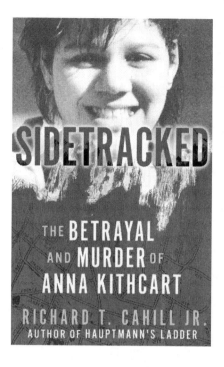

ALSO AVAILABLE FROM WILDBLUE PRESS!

BETTER OFF DEAD by MICHAEL FLEEMAN

A frustrated, unhappy wife. Her much younger, attentive lover. A husband who degrades and ignores her. The stage is set for a love-triangle murder that shatters family illusions and lays bare a quite family community's seedy secret world of sex, sin and swinging.

http://wbp.bz/bod

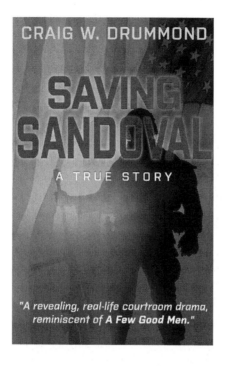

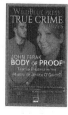